The Decision Loom

A Design for Interactive Decision-Making in Organizations

Vincent Barabba

Published by:
Triarchy Press
Station Offices
Axminster
Devon. EX13 5PF
United Kingdom

+44 (0)1297 631456
info@triarchypress.com
www.triarchypress.com

Cover design and image by Heather Fallows ~

ISBN: 978-1-908009-44-9

This book is dedicated to the memory of Russell Ackoff and Peter Drucker.

Although I never had the opportunity to attend any of their formal classes, I was, in so many ways, the beneficiary of their friendship, interest, and advice during the Journey that is described in this book. Without their counsel, there would have been far fewer successes and I would have learned less from my mistakes.

Acknowledgements

It would be nearly impossible to acknowledge everyone who has
in some way contributed to what I have learned over the last 50
years. Although I have not mentioned by name everyone who
participated in the stories, I hope those who did participate will
recall with pride what we were able to accomplish.

I want to thank my wife Sheryl and our children Heather Buff
and Jason Barabba for their understanding and patience during
the years in which these stories were being developed.

I also want to acknowledge the efforts of Andrew Carey of
Triarchy Press – a true partner in the writing of this book.
Although I take credit for the accomplishments identified in
this book, his effort to clarify how the story was told was beyond
measure.

Contents

Foreword

During his fifty year career, Vince Barabba not only worked in a wide range of enterprises, he also documented what he learned from both his successes and his failures. In fact, a great deal of this book is about his reflections on the unique experience he has gained from his journey working in both government and private enterprises.

I met Vince when I was asked by the late Russell Ackoff to assist him with the work he was doing for GM in the mid-1990s. At that time, Vince was the general manager of Corporate Strategy and Knowledge Development. Ackoff's relationship with Vince was an old and special one. Ackoff was on the American Statistical Association Advisory Committee to the Census Bureau when Vince was nominated to become the director. Based on what he knew about him at the time, Ackoff did not support his appointment, which was an act that he always regretted: he referred fondly to Vince as his greatest mistake.

During his career, like many executives in Fortune 25 companies, Vince had the opportunity to work with number of prominent management consultants – among them, Peter Drucker, Russ Ackoff, Adrian Slywotsky, C.K. Prahalad and Ian Mitroff. Not only did he benefit from his interactions with these individuals, he has also provided them and many others the opportunity to try out their new theories in the real world of decision-making in government and business.

This book is evidence of Vince's "integrative mind." His remarkable ability to synthesize seemingly conflicting ideas into a feasible, workable framework is noteworthy. In keeping with his "systems thinking" mindset, he has here created a generalized design approach that takes into account various ideas and constructs in a workable structure that allows others to develop their own specific applications.

Reflecting on his broad experiences, he recognizes that in today's complex and unpredictable world the only sustainable competitive advantage is the speed with which organizations can learn and adapt. He recognizes that "learning" is not a natural act for organizations and, therefore, organizations need to incorporate systems that provide them with the ability to learn and adapt rapidly. Influenced by Ackoff's teachings and the wisdom of West Churchman and other luminaries including Peter Drucker, he develops an innovative approach for designing a Decision Loom, a function that would provide decision makers with the right information at the right time and at a cost they would see as offering good value, taking into account the decision context. In particular, he approaches the hierarchy of the content of learning - data, information, knowledge, understanding and wisdom – not as ladder for organizations to climb, but as a system of interacting parts. His approach to knowledge management is premised on the work of West Churchman who said that "the value of knowledge is in its use, not in its collection." The critical point is the role that a Decision Loom can play in the business model that Vince calls "anticipate-and-lead".

The other important contribution is the recognition that learning from past decisions is only the start of the learning process: the true value is achieved when possible future mistakes are avoided. With that belief in mind, the framework developed in this book not only allows decision-makers to learn from their past mistakes, but also to learn what could go wrong and cause a future decision to fail (pre-mortem).

In this book, systems thinking is offered as the mindset to get decision-makers to see enterprises differently and to help them address "messy" problems at the speed demanded today. Additionally, his approach to design is presented as a methodology to assist with overcoming current challenges. In this respect, many real-world examples and experiences are shared as a means to demonstrate practical aspects of the theoretical underpinnings of the approaches discussed in the book. Additionally, many established approaches to problem-solving and decision-making are elaborated upon as examples of alternative approaches, and innovative ways of using them are presented, all within the context of dramatically improving executive decision-making and enterprise performance.

John Pourdehnad

Associate Director
Ackoff Collaboratory for Advancement of the Systems Approach (ACASA)
University of Pennsylvania

Introduction

In 1941 Edna St. Vincent Millay lamented that, although there were many ills facing society at that time, there was no way to use our collective knowledge and wisdom to address them.

> *Upon this gifted age, in its dark hour*
> *Falls from the sky a meteoric shower*
> *Of facts... they lie unquestioned, uncombined.*
> *Wisdom enough to leech us of our ill*
> *Is daily spun; but there exists no loom*
> *To weave it into fabric...*
>
> 'Huntsman, What Quarry?' – Edna St. Vincent Millay

Today, society is still faced with many ills, lots of data, and is, in the judgment of many, even more in need of a Decision Loom to weave what is known into meaningful fabric – as she so eloquently called for seventy years ago.

Designing an experienced-based Decision Loom

Upon reflection, the early part of my career was spent contributing to the "meteoric shower of facts." Eventually, I came to learn that in many ways the facts that were collected sometimes lay "unquestioned, uncombined." Later, others taught me to understand the importance of focusing on the use of information: "Wisdom enough to leech us of our ill is daily spun." Finally, I saw the need to develop approaches that encouraged an interactive dialogue between providers and users of information (particularly the creative and imaginative users) through the construction and use of a decision "loom to weave it into fabric."

As described in *Part 1: The Journey*, in my career I have had both the satisfaction of contributing insights that led to important new products and services; and regret at having equally valid insights acknowledged but not implemented – to the detriment of the enterprise and its stakeholders. While reflecting on this journey and its lessons, my thinking about the need for a Decision Loom has evolved – based on what worked and what did not. Drawing on those experiences, in *Part*

2 of this book, I propose that the leadership of an enterprise, whether private or public, should design and implement the equivalent of a Decision Loom that encourages a more interactive decision process. It should be a design that augments the existing intellectual power of decision-makers as they seek to make the right decisions in the complex and often uncertain conditions we face today.

When designing a Decision Loom for a complex and uncertain future, think first... then analyze

One of the most rewarding experiences of my career was the opportunity to work with and learn from Peter Drucker and Russell Ackoff. Since my interaction with them was on separate projects I was not aware of the extent to which they knew each other -- that changed in March of 1999 when, during a meeting with Peter Drucker, he asked me what else I was working on. I told him that, in addition to my work at GM, I was working on a presentation to be made at a dinner honoring Russ Ackoff on his 80th birthday. Peter smiled and said that he had great respect for Russ Ackoff and asked if I would be willing to carry a message from him to Russ on his birthday.

His letter appears as he actually wrote it on his typewriter. From previous correspondence with him, I knew that when he really wanted to emphasize a point he would type the words in all capital letters. Peter's message also reflects something that I learned from both of them and that forms a key part of this book.

> Dear Russ;
>
> Happy birthday - and many more healthy, productive, achieving years!
>
> AND THANKS - MY WARMEST THANKS - for your ENORMOUS contributions, and especially for the wonderful contribution you made to ME, all of FIFTY years ago. I was then, as you may recall, one of the early ones who applied Operations Research and the new methods of Quantitative Analysis to specific BUSINESS PROBLEMS - rather than, as they had been originally developed for, to military or scientific problems. I had led teams applying the new methodology in two of the

world's largest companies – GE and AT&T. We had
successfully solved several major production
and technical problems for these companies –
and my clients were highly satisfied. But I was
not – we had solved TECHNICAL problems but our
work had no impact on the organizations and on
their mindsets. On the contrary: we had all
but convinced the managements of these two big
companies that QUANTITATIVE MANIPULATION was a
substitute for THINKING. And then your work and
your example showed us – or at least, it showed
me – that the QUANTITATIVE ANALYSIS comes AFTER
the THINKING – it validates the thinking; it
shows up intellectual sloppiness and uncritical
reliance on precedent, on untested assumptions
and on the seemingly "obvious". But it does not
substitute for hard, rigorous, intellectually
challenging THINKING. It demands it, though – but
does not replace it. This is, of course, what YOU
mean BY system. And your work in those far-away
days thus saved me – as it saved countless others
– from either descending into mindless "model
building" – the disease that all but destroyed so
many of the Business Schools in the last decades
– or from sloppiness parading as "insight."

And thus I owe you profound thanks for a
decisive breakthrough at a critical state in my
development – and so do countless others. And
so again: A MOST HAPPY BIRTHDAY AND MANY MORE
JOYOUS, HEALTHY AND PRODUCTIVE YEARS.

In reflecting on the note I was reminded that whenever I approached either Peter or Russ for help with a problem, their first comment usually started out with "WHY was I working on the problem?" After a while, I came to appreciate the fact that our meetings were more productive when I spent time THINKING before I asked for their help.

As the stories told in *Part 1* will demonstrate, the need for the decision loom that Edna St. Vincent Millay called for still exists. The passage of time has simply made the need even more compelling.

Weaving together the threads of imagination and knowledge – the constructive interaction of which is required to resolve, in a more holistic manner, many of today's problems

A common dilemma occurs when creative and imaginative people and organizations with interesting and exciting ideas face a torrent of information that sometimes undermines – rather than supports – what they want to accomplish. The dilemma and its possible solution can be better understood by examining apparently conflicting statements made by two very accomplished individuals:

> *Imagination is more important than knowledge* – Albert Einstein

> *Knowledge is power* – Sir Francis Bacon

Let us look at these statements in the context in which they were originally presented:

"Imagination is more important than knowledge"

Einstein's words come from a 1929 in-depth interview by George Sylvester Viereck in the *Saturday Evening Post*.[1] After an interesting discussion of the problem of excessive analysis, Viereck asked two questions: "If we owe so little to the experience of others, how do you account for sudden leaps forward in the sphere of science? Do you ascribe your own discoveries to intuition or inspiration?" Einstein replied, "I believe in intuition and inspirations. I sometimes feel that I am right. I do not know that I am. When two expeditions of scientists, financed by the Royal Academy, went forth to test my theory of relativity, I was convinced that their conclusions would tally with my hypothesis. I was not surprised when the eclipse of May 29, 1919 confirmed my intuitions. I would have been surprised if I had been wrong."

Viereck then asked: "Then you trust more to your imagination than to your knowledge?" Einstein replied: "I am enough of the artist to draw freely upon my imagination. Imagination is more important than knowledge."

Often left out of the quote is the basis on which Einstein made his judgment. "Knowledge is limited, imagination encircles the world." In this context Einstein recognizes that knowledge still has value, but,

---

1   Viereck, 1929

particularly at the time of his comment, is limited in its scope. Whereas imagination is about the ability to conceive of ideas, especially of things never seen or experienced directly.

"Knowledge is power"

Bacon's words are normally used in the sense that, by controlling knowledge, one gains power. That is not what Bacon had in mind. The phrase was used in relation to a view that Bacon had developed on the relationship of knowledge of God to God's power. In fact, what he actually said was, "For knowledge itself is power," which, in the context of 16th Century England, was more likely to imply that knowledge is the power through which humankind could create a better life here on earth. For Bacon and his contemporaries, knowledge was a resource that helped individuals (perhaps imaginative ones) to cause good things to happen.

The power of AND versus the limitations of OR

By putting both quotations in their original contexts, we see that these two men were not in deep disagreement. For example, if further questioned on the *relationship* of knowledge and imagination, it is not a stretch to imagine Einstein weaving together both concepts and saying:

> *Although not as broad as imagination in its scope, knowledge is an important resource to be used by imaginative people to cause good things to happen.*

A statement with which Bacon would likely have agreed!

In this book I provide many examples of the benefits of effectively using information in the decision-making process. I am also aware that imaginative people have come up with new products and services and have successfully introduced them without the support of market information evaluations or public opinion surveys. There are, however, many instances when that approach did not work and would have benefited from an evaluation prior to introduction. It is not about one approach *or* the other... it is about one approach *and* the other and choosing which, or what combination, is more likely to be successful in different situations.

Whether in a public or private enterprise be sure your enterprise's decision process is capable of interacting with, and adapting to, changing conditions

Because my experiences were gained across diverse activities like political campaigns, government, and business engagements, the idealized design for the Decision Loom that I suggest in *Part 2* fully recognizes that what works in one place at one time does not necessarily work in all other places at other times. Based on my experiences, I recommend that the elements of the interactive decision process described in *Part 2* be considered by any enterprise as ideas and concepts that can be adapted or "reinvented"[2] to better fit the particular style and needs of the enterprise.

This adaptive approach is based on the belief that enterprises choosing to act on the suggestions made in *Part 2* will, thereby, be better positioned to see interactions with the systems within their enterprise and the containing systems in which their enterprise operates.

Drawing from my own experiences and from the many people who contributed to those experiences, this book identifies the strengths and limitations of an array of enterprise capabilities and the importance of understanding their interdependencies.

Based on fifty years of experience, it is my strong belief that if an enterprise does not learn to manage these interdependencies, including the interaction of their enterprise with the communities and countries in which they operate, they will not be around for much longer.

This book does not provide the answers to your questions… it provides several ways to think about possibilities and then encourages you to select the right combination of approaches that provide the best answer for your enterprise.

The journey described in *Part 1* of this book leads in *Part 2* to a 'sketch' of a Decision Loom – an idealized design for interactive decision-making that uses available technology and knowledge to augment the concepts found in systems thinking, design thinking, decision analysis, Dynamic Modeling and a whole host of other approaches. They are

---

2   The term 'reinvented' is explained more fully in Episode 3.

presented to demonstrate that an enterprise does not have to stop using viable aspects of one approach to gain the advantages of another approach. Too often, developers of a new approach believe the only way they can get their idea started is to highlight the limitations of an existing alternative approach. All approaches have their strengths and their limitations. I will attempt to show that in a properly designed Decision Loom there is room for many different and useful combination of threads found in alternative approaches to improve the manner in which decision-makers weave together the interactions of what is known and unknown. The reason I use the term 'sketch' and not 'blueprint', is that the decision-making processes inspired by the suggested idealized design are more likely to be adopted if readers are allowed to apply the inherent principles as they see fit, and are not 'restricted' to a set of rules requiring them to use the tools in a specified way. This leaves the eventual user better positioned to consider how to address the interactions of the components of the decision in the context of:

1. The organization structure in which they operate

2. The environment within which the decision will be made

3. The collection and development of the required information

4. The selection and implementation of the most useful decision processes.

This book identifies the strengths and limitations of an array of, but not all, decision-making methods based on how well they handle the interaction of the parts and how well they contribute to developing a whole that is greater than the sum of the parts.

A learning approach

This approach is based on what I have gleaned from years of experience in the public and private sectors providing information while engaging in dialogues in support of decision-makers (and sometimes making the decision). During this period, I was given the opportunity to administer the expenditure of billions of dollars in the collection and distribution of information for public and private policy development and decision-making – some of which led to positive outcomes and some of which did not.

The relevant experiences that have led to my understanding are described in *Part 1: The Journey* using real-life stories that occurred while working with some pragmatic and some contemplative people (and some who were both).

These stories provide a contextual setting to assess and consider the benefits and risks of implementing a new, more interactive decision process and the capabilities that are required to allow it to work on your behalf in *Part 2*.

The goal is to suggest that a decision process supported by a range of enterprise capabilities will increase the likelihood that reliable and relevant data and information is efficiently turned into valuable knowledge and understanding in order to effectively reach the right decision for a particular problem.

Hopefully the book will also help uncover faster and more affordable ways of acquiring and using relevant and sufficiently accurate societal and market information by providing examples of projects that make effective use of new technologies. The Internet, in particular, has the potential to become a more reliable resource for information collection. So, I'll use some stories to help identify where the Internet has been useful and describe the value of using techniques that develop dynamic simulated environments and calculate the expected value of future information.

Practitioners and academics – benefits of a shared learning experience… in the real world

It would be relatively easy for me to claim that this book is about the real world and not about new theory. But, in fact, many of the concepts set out here represent my own interpretations of valuable theories developed by thoughtful academics who were as interested in seeing their ideas tested as they were in developing them. In some instances the applications discussed will show a very close resemblance to the original theory. In others I will be presenting what I was able to implement in the enterprise in which I was working at the time. Where I was only able to implement some elements of a theory, this does not mean that I thought the other parts were wrong. Inevitably, what was implemented was generally governed by the context of the enterprise's current situation and the willingness of its decision-makers to try something new.

In 2007 MIT Professor Glen Urban and I discussed the value of this approach in a presentation entitled *Stereotypes, prototypes, and keys to success in improving decision-making.*[3]

Our presentation started by offering stereotypical perceptions of one another held by practitioners and academics. To reinforce the stereotype of academics held by practitioners I said:

> *The problem with the lack of implementation of marketing science to improve decision-making lies with the academics – they are irrelevant, interested in theory only; and willing to make any assumption, realistic or not, to allow their models to work. Their goals are (a) publication, not improving practice, (b) working on a long time horizon (assuming past is prologue), and (c) to achieve tenure by specializing in a narrow niche.*

Glen then countered with the stereotypical view of practitioners held by academics:

> *I respectfully disagree. The lack of implementation is caused by business executives who do not use the results of research – particularly if it doesn't fit their mental model of the world. Managers are interested in short-term results and deliverables, they want immediate sales and profit results, seek absolute proof that the methods will work, and want personal promotion and bonuses.*

We then moved to a more balanced view of how Glen, as an academic, and I, as a practitioner, had developed our own cooperative efforts over a 25-year period. We tried to show the need for academics (theorists) and practitioners to work together – if the theories they were working on were to bear fruit and if the practitioners were to benefit from the new ideas.

---

3   The presentation was made at the 2007 Informs Society for Marketing Science (ISMS) Practice Program Conference at the University of Pennsylvania's Wharton Business School.

Upon reflection, I benefitted from encounters with a broad range of academics from whom I learned a lot and who, in turn, gained the opportunity to test their ideas in the real world.[4]

This book's underlying premise

One of the ideas that inspired the thinking about creating a more wholly interactive decision process came from C. West Churchman – the distinguished philosopher of science:

> *...to conceive of knowledge as a collection of information seems to rob the concept of all of its life. Knowledge is a vital force that makes an enormous difference in the world. Simply to say that it is storage of sentences is to ignore all that this difference amounts to...* **knowledge resides in the user and not in the collection. It is how the user reacts to a collection of information that matters** *(emphasis added). Although on a daily basis we see (and are sometimes subject to) examples of unfortunate decisions, where the information used was not relevant or even correct, there are also many instances where relevant and correct information was available and the decision-maker for a variety of reasons did not react constructively to it.*

To benefit from Churchman's sage advice, and avoid situations where compelling information is used wrongly or ignored during the creative process, requires us to develop procedures to ensure that those who collect data and transform it into information interact with those making decisions – including determining that they are indeed working on the right problem. This constructive engagement must also begin early enough in the process to ensure that the plan for design, collection, and analysis meets the requirements of the decision-makers and idea-creators – at the time it is needed, in a form that is relevant to the idea being considered, and at a price that is perceived to be of great value.

---

4   The list of academics includes: Thomas Davenport, John Henderson, Ronald Howard, Ralph Kilmann, Ian Mitroff, John Sterman (through his students Mark Paich and Nick Pudar), John Pourdehnad, C.K. Prahalad, Jack Rockhart, John Little, Everett Rogers, Stephen Toulmin, Glen Urban, and Jerry Zaltman.

The design of this book (How to read it)

What comes first? Reading about *Part 1: The Journey* (which serves as the experience-based foundation of the design of a Decision Loom)? Or, starting with *Part 2: The Decision Loom* itself? As with any complex decision... it depends.

- If you want to make sure there is a reliable basis for the suggested interactive decision process and enterprise capabilities – or just want to read the "stories" – then begin with *The Journey*.

- If you want to get started with the practical suggestions set out in *The Design of a Decision Loom* then *Part 2 is* self-contained and you can begin there.

If you are unsure where to start, there is a summary of the lessons learned at the end of *Part 1* (starting on p.129). It tells you where in *The Journey* the lesson was learned as well as where to find the relevant aspects of the Decision Loom that are required to implement what was learned.

Part 1: The Journey

And now to the stories that will provide the basis for considering the type of thinking and interactive decision-making capabilities that are described in *Part 2*. The stories make clear that we still need the decision loom that Edna St. Vincent Millay wrote about in the 1940s.

I believe that, even by themselves, reviewing each of these individual stories has value. Their true value, however, is revealed when combined with the totality of the lessons learned from the other stories. In the spirit of this book's title, like threads in a tapestry, single threads of information all have value. However, when woven together properly they form a coherent pattern of even greater value. That tapestry, based on these individual threads, is described in *Part 2*.

Episode 1: Planting the Seed

Had I collected and used information based solely on what was being taught in business schools and industry seminars in the early 1960s, many of the experiences upon which this book is based probably would not have occurred. At that time the primary focus of problem-solving was on analysis. We learned how to break a problem down into its components, and then improve the way that each part operated. If we were not able to deal with the complexity or the uncertainty of a particular component, we simply held it constant. By avoiding complexity and uncertainty, we created the illusion that we could accurately predict what was going to happen.

Pretending certainty

In the early part of the 20th Century, the eminent economist Lord Alfred Marshall characterized both the benefits and the limitations of the economist's approach to addressing uncertainty in his discussion of the role of *Ceteris Paribus*, which is Latin for 'all else being equal.'

> *The element of time is a chief cause of those difficulties in economic investigations which make it necessary for man with his limited powers to go step by step; breaking up a complex question, studying one bit at a time, and at last combining his partial solutions into a more or less complete solution of the whole riddle. In breaking it up, he segregates those disturbing causes, whose wanderings happen to be inconvenient, for the time in a pound called Ceteris Paribus. The study of some group of tendencies is isolated by the assumption other things being equal: the existence of other tendencies is not denied, but their disturbing effect is neglected for a time. **The more the issue is thus narrowed, the more exactly can it be handled: but also the less closely does it correspond to real life** (my emphasis).*

Marshall then went on to justify the action by saying:

> *Each exact and firm handling of a narrow issue, however, helps towards treating broader issues, in which that narrow issue is contained, more exactly than would otherwise have been possible. With each step more things can be let out of the pound; exact discussions can be made less*

> *abstract, realistic discussions can be made less inexact than was possible*
> *at an earlier stage.* [5]

What has become clear is that decision-makers no longer have the
benefit of putting a critical variable on hold "...in a pound called *Ceteris*
Paribus." We can longer wait to address certain variables later or act as
if we are operating in a world of certainty. In Capability 4 (in *Part 2*)
there is a partial list of decision approaches that address the issue of
uncertainty in a more transparent manner.

Addressing complexity

We now better understand the downside of fixing one part of a system
at the expense of other parts and, as illustrated in this journey, we have
also learned that we need not just to understand how the components of
issues we are working on interact but also to consider interactions with
the containing system in which the issue exists. Russ Ackoff provides a
succinct description of the role of management in a world of synthesis:

> *Management should be directed at the interactions of the parts and not*
> *the actions of the parts taken separately.*

An introduction to the silo problem

My first encounter with the silo problem occurred in 1962 during my
senior year at California State University at Northridge (then called San
Fernando Valley State College). One of my professors had developed
a computer-based business simulation game in which he divided
students into teams that competed in making and selling a product. The
year I took the class, instead of assigning students to a particular team
at random, he organized the teams according to a student's academic
major. This led to strikingly different team outcomes:

The Marketing majors (my team) spent most of our time and money
on sales and promotion. We acquired an impressive share of the total
market, but at high cost, and were bankrupt before the game ended.

The Accounting majors aimed at maximizing profits by minimizing
investments in products and promotion. With no new products and

---

5   Marshall, 1920

only meager promotion of existing ones, the accountants lost market share and slipped by degrees into bankruptcy.

The Production majors spent all their money on product development and manufacturing processes. They ended up with great products at the right prices, but, with no money to tell customers about them, they, too, went out of business.

To the consternation of all concerned, the Personnel majors won. The Marketing majors ran out of money, the Accountants ran out of products, and the Production majors ran out of customers. The Personnel majors occupied themselves with endless changes to the organization chart. Having spent no money, they simply ran out of time and won the game by default.

The silo problem that was made evident by the business simulation game was partially a result of how business classes were taught, with the curriculum tailored to a particular function. One of the most succinct descriptions of the problem associated with silo thinking was provided by Abraham Maslow:

> *I suppose it is tempting, if the only tool you have is a hammer, to treat everything as if it were a nail.*[6]

This business case simulation of a real-world problem provided context as I came to understand the ramifications of the silo mentality. With a greater appreciation of the importance of looking across functions throughout my career, I kept looking for something besides my functional hammer to improve my capacity to help decision-makers – even if I have to go outside the comfort zone of my own training and experience.

Learning to question what appeared to be true

Also that year, I was taking two other classes: one in market research and the other in the history of philosophy. Both classes were taught by teachers who were tolerant of unusual requests.

Toward the end of the semester, the class assignment in market research was to define and show the relationship between Philosophy, Science, and Market Research. At the same time the Professor in the Philosophy course was telling us about the 5th Century B.C. in Athens

---

6   Maslow, 1962

and about Plato's concern over the rise of Sophism which he used (as we frequently do now) as a term of disparagement.

While preparing to write the paper for the Marketing course, I was reading materials for my Philosophy course when I ran across a passage from the *Dialogues of Plato* in which he expressed his concern about the Sophists by having Socrates point out:

> *... knowledge is the food of the soul; and we must take care... that the Sophist does not deceive us when he praises what he sells, like the dealers wholesale or retail who sell the food of the body.*

After observing the differences between buying food or drink which you take home in some sort of a vessel, he drives home his main point:

> *For there is far greater peril in buying knowledge than in buying meat and drink... you cannot buy the wares of knowledge and carry them away in another vessel; when you have paid for them you must receive them into the soul and go your way, either greatly harmed or greatly benefited; and therefore we should deliberate and take counsel with our elders; for we are still young – too young to determine such a matter.*[7]

The passage caused me to think about what appeared to be a similarity between the behavior of the Sophists and some of the practices involved in marketing goods and services. Since the similarities were observed by no less an authority than Plato, I accepted what I read and began to think about writing one paper for both classes around the possible similarities between Sophism and Marketing.

When I suggested to both professors that it might be interesting to write one paper for both classes, they, to their credit, did not laugh, even though each did crack a thin smile. Although quite skeptical, they were persuaded to let me try when they saw the proposed title of the paper:

SOPHISTS, INC.
The Trivium Building
Madison Avenue
Athens, Greece

---

[7]   Plato, 1952

The introduction to the paper started out this way:

> *If we are to find a common ground between Philosophy, Science, and Marketing Research, I believe it lies in the area of the search for truth. The difference being, the degree of truth that is obtained, or even desired, and the use to which it is put.*

The paper drew primarily on the writings of Plato, who said that the Sophists, rather than searching for truth, "were skilled at making the worse case appear the better." I tied the Marketers to the Sophists using the criticisms of marketing found in *The Hidden Persuaders* by Vance Packard. After 20 pages, I concluded that the Sophists of both the 5th Century BC and 20th Century AD were happy to have information that advanced their arguments in ways that masses of people would believe and that they weren't overly concerned with truth. Both professors accepted the paper. The Philosophy professor gave a passing grade with the side comment, "the title of the paper carried the day."

Although meeting my initial goal of passing two classes with one paper, the paper's conclusion – which limited the role of marketing function to, as Plato suggested "…making the worse appear the better" – left me in a somewhat conflicted state. Given that marketing was to be my chosen profession, could I really be comfortable in a career where my goal was to "make the worse appear the better"?

An opportunity to revisit the question of my chosen profession occurred a year later when I was enrolled in the MBA program at UCLA. One day I discussed my concern over the conclusion to my Sophists Inc. paper with one of my professors. He suggested that I revisit the paper, challenge the facts that I presented and determine whether the conclusion still held.

There is, of course, another side to almost any story

While at UCLA I was employed as an instructor in the marketing department at California State University at Northridge. One day, while discussing my concerns with Mal Sillars who was in the speech department at the University, he said he would look over the original paper and provide his observations. His review was quite direct. He in essence said:

Vince, you have a very shallow understanding of the Sophist movement and what it actually contributed. You've based your understanding on what you have read from the philosophers who were being challenged by the Sophists. They were not historians, they were critics. You've taken Plato's criticism of the Sophist Protagoras' dictum, 'Man is the measure of all things' as meaning the Sophists taught others how to make the worse appear the better through the use of false reasoning.

Mal suggested several books and journal articles that would help me understand the other side of the story. For the next several months, I was ensconced in the UCLA college library and not the graduate business school library. I was both surprised and impressed by the suggested readings. There was overwhelming evidence that the Sophists acquired a reputation for "making the worse appear the better through the use of false reasoning" from the writings of philosophers who were critical of them during that era. In fact, many distinguished historians concluded just the opposite. They documented the extent to which the Sophists excelled in taking information that was known only by a few and providing it to the public at large. As it was summarized by Windleband:

Their work was first directed, with an eye to the people's needs, to imparting to the mass of people the results of science.[8]

The other side of the Sophists' story was compelling. In their endeavors to influence people through rhetoric, they were among the first to look at ideas and the development of those ideas. They were not the shallow purveyors of false reasoning that Plato portrayed.

Insight into the limitations of the critics of marketing was gained by reviewing Raymond Bauer's well-documented challenge to Vance Packard.[9] Bauer provided another perspective that questioned the amount of power I had attributed to the Marketers in their ability to persuade citizens and customers:

One way of reading the history of the development of techniques of persuasion is that the persuaders have been in a race to keep abreast of the developing resistance of the people to be persuaded.

---

8   Windelband, 1901

9   Bauer, 1958

My second paper, a major revision of the first, also noted a similarity between the Sophists and the Marketers. But this time, with the benefit of studying the behavior of both parties with a more open mind, the similarity I identified was in their desire to use what they had learned from their own experience or that of others to present an argument or a product or service in the most efficient and effective manner to those who would approve or benefit from what was being presented. Mal Sillars' advice to review alternative points of view taught me that no matter how esteemed the provider of a point of view, you need to not only check their facts but also their motivations. That is true even for revered philosophers like Plato.

I was starting to think better of my chosen profession. Like many professions, those involved in marketing demonstrated neither all good nor all bad behavior by their actions. At 31 years old, I was ready to embark on a career in marketing. I was also enjoying my paper on Sophism and Marketing, the revision of which had now satisfied the requirements for a third class!

The primary lessons learned during my college education

Lesson	Description	Addressed in Part 2
1	Avoid the Silo Problem. Be careful not to let your area of expertise restrict your willingness and ability to interact with and learn from others who are experienced in fields in which you are not.	Capability 2
2	Avoid starting out with a specific point of view which may cause you to look for and find only information that supports that position. Appreciate the wisdom found in concepts like selective perception, cognitive dissonance, and convergence theory.[10]	The Decision Loom Capability 1 Capability 3

3	When presenting a point of view, make sure that all aspects of the underlying arguments are revealed and understood.	The Decision Loom Capability 4
4	Do not put variables of which you are uncertain in Alfred Marshall's pound called *Ceteris Paribus*. Make uncertainty explicit.	Capability 3 Capability 4

The extent to which I learned from these early lessons (sometimes by making additional mistakes) will be shown in several of the following stories – particularly the lesson of avoiding starting out with a specific point of view which is discussed in Episode 5 when I was faced with the decision of whether or not to adjust the 1980 Census and in Episodes 8 and 9 when developing product and strategic plans at General Motors.

---

10   Barabba & Zaltman, 1991, pp. 41-45

Episode 2: Political Campaigns: The value of knowledge is in its use

Although I did not fully realize it at the time, I was about to enter into a decision-making domain that could use more relevant and dynamic approaches to addressing problems than those I had learned and made use of during my education. I also learned the importance of understanding the surrounding context of the problem I was asked to solve. The extent to which the problems I would be asked to address required new approaches was set out by James Gunn following a presentation I made at the 'Ethics of Controversy: Politics and Protest' symposium at the University of Kansas in 1968:

> We all know…the ultimate difficulty of transferring one thought to one other person. When one multiplies that by the number of persons with whom a candidate must communicate a thought, it becomes an incredibly difficult proposition. So that basically, it seems to me, a person like Mr. Barabba and his firm are trying to help someone communicate. And this we should all understand and appreciate because we do need to have candidates who communicate better and who get communicated with better, who understand more and who will act wisely on that understanding. Presumably if they communicate better we will understand whether they are wise enough to act well upon what it is they understand.[11]

With that as background, let's fast forward to an event which occurred in 1972, six years after I left UCLA's Graduate School of Business with an MBA.

The re-election of Senator John Tower

In January 1972, we conducted an initial survey for the campaign to re-elect John Tower. The survey indicated that he was running ahead of his likely opponent, Harold Barefoot Sanders with 53% of the likely vote and Sanders with 34%. At the time of this survey, Sanders was running in the Democratic Primary against Ralph Yarborough, who had served as a Texas Senator from 1957 until 1970. Yarborough had

---

11   Barabba, 1968

developed a voting record that caused many Texans to consider him a liberal. In 1970, Yarborough was defeated in the Texas Democratic Senatorial Primary election by then-Congressman Lloyd Bentsen, who was perceived as a conservative Democrat.

During the 1972 primary campaign, Sanders positioned himself as being more conservative than Ralph Yarborough, and, on June 3, Sanders defeated Yarborough. Following the primary election, we conducted a survey that indicated a significant shift in voters' preferences. Sanders' support had grown by 11 points to 45%, and Senator Tower's support had dropped 17 points to 36%.

The campaign management team was advised that the initial review of the survey showed that Senator Tower was now behind his challenger. One of the campaign's senior advisors informed me that Senator Tower would reject the results since he believed that, as the incumbent and a known conservative, he would be ahead of the more liberal candidate, Sanders, in a conservative state like Texas. I told the senior advisor that an early survey is not a prediction of eventual results; the survey merely provides current information of public perceptions and possible actions. But the advisor still didn't want to be there when Senator Tower got the news. I offered to present the information to the Senator without the advisor being present.

In preparation for what promised to be a testy meeting, we reviewed the results of a post-election survey conducted in 1970 to find out why Lloyd Bentsen defeated George H. W. Bush in the race for the U.S. Senate. The analysis made it clear that, in a Texas state-wide political campaign where the Democrat candidate was perceived to be as conservative as the Republican candidate, the Democrat candidate was likely to win.

This review of past elections gave credence to the idea that, following the Democrat primary election in which Sanders defeated the perceived liberal Ralph Yarborough; the Texas electorate now saw the Democrat Sanders to be as conservative as Senator Tower.

*Be prepared to present what you found in your analysis as it is...
not the way your client might prefer to hear it*

In June 1972, I met alone with Senator Tower in the St. Anthony Hotel
in San Antonio, Texas. As I entered the room, Senator Tower, who was
already sitting down, said in a stern tone, "Sit down, young man. I
understand that you have some bad news for me – which I am also told
is not correct."

I explained that the information being provided was accurate but was
only a measurement of the preferences at the time the survey was
conducted and not a prediction of the outcome of the race. I also said
the results showed that Sanders was perceived as more conservative
simply because he had defeated a perceived liberal in the primary.
Senator Tower interrupted me and said the survey was not accurate –
it was well known that Sanders was not a conservative. I pointed out
that we weren't measuring reality. We were just measuring perception.
Then I smiled and said, "That's the good news."

Senator Tower gave me a perplexed look and asked me to explain
myself. The explanation was simple. If the actual record showed that
Sanders was indeed more liberal than Senator Tower, all Senator Tower
had to do was show the facts.

"You're right," the Senator said, now smiling and much more
enthusiastic. "That will not be too difficult to do. That is good news!"

*It is not just presenting the information... it is providing a level
of understanding as to what the numbers mean*

He then asked what his campaign staff should do. I suggested
he provide explicit examples of where his positions were more
conservative than those of Sanders. In addition, Tower was to get as
many conservative Democrats as possible to endorse his candidacy or,
at the least, to not publicly endorse Sanders. In the months between the
June survey and a follow-up in August, the following occurred:

- Ed Clarke, a very well-known conservative Democrat, was
  named Chairman of the Tower Campaign Committee. Other
  Democrats joined Texans for Tower and publicly endorsed his
  re-election.

- George McGovern, a liberal, became the Democrat Nominee for President. Sanders had indicated he would support the Democratic ticket.

- Sanders received very little publicity and conducted virtually no press conferences.

- The Tower campaign ran early advertisements on radio and in newspapers, supplemented by a heavy publicity campaign, stressing Tower's voting record and conservative Democrat endorsements.

Our August survey showed:

- John Tower up 9%

- Barefoot Sanders down 16%

- Undecideds up 8%

The manner in which we selected the sample for the study conducted in September played an important role. From a precinct priority list that we had developed and from a voter name list created for canvassing, we drew a random sample of Texas voters for the survey. The information from this survey was used to assign a probability to vote for Tower to a voter list that provided the campaign organization with a list of likely Tower voters for its 'get out the vote' campaign.

In November, John Tower defeated Barefoot Sanders 55% to 45%.

The value of information is in its use… not its collection!

The basic point of this story is that the information from the surveys did not cause John Tower to be re-elected. What caused his re-election was the manner in which Senator Tower and his campaign organization addressed issues that the survey identified. In other words, it was the Senator's willingness to overcome his early reservations about findings that were inconsistent with his perceptions and his acceptance that the survey was not a report card on him personally, that led to *uses* of the information that mattered. And now back to how my career in politics started.

1964: actions which led to my leaving an academic career

In 1964, in between my MBA and getting into the PhD program at UCLA, I became involved in political campaigns as part-time work. The first major campaign I was involved in was the Republican Presidential primary campaign in California between Nelson Rockefeller and Barry Goldwater. Working for the Rockefeller campaign, I was assigned to an area in southern California. I soon realized that campaigns could be significantly improved if people better understood the different political behavior and preferences of smaller geographic areas within the larger area for which the campaign was targeted. That got me interested in small-area data analysis of electoral data. It soon became clear that there was additional value in combining the electoral data with the demographic data. At that point, I formed a company called Communication Associates and got to know electoral and Census data a lot better. That led to more political campaigns in 1965 and 1966. At that point the administrators of the Graduate School of Business, UCLA indicated it was time to return to start the PhD degree. I was in the middle of several Los Angeles City Council campaigns and working on some interesting ideas. Faced with the choice of continuing with what I was enjoying or stopping and enrolling back at UCLA, I made the decision to stay with what I was doing and dropped out of the PhD Program. Although I left an academic career, as some of the following stories will show, part of me lingered in that mental model.

1966: an interesting year

In addition to working on the campaign to elect Ronald Reagan as Governor of California, I was also engaged in the management of a Congressional campaign in Michigan. A friend who was attending Harvard Business School had suggested that I should contact Don Riegle, who was seeking his Doctor of Business Administration degree while also considering running for Congress as a Republican in Flint, Michigan. I contacted Riegle and we met in Flint, in the lobby of the once elegant and storied Durant Hotel, named after William C. Durant, the founder of General Motors.

Flint, located seventy miles north of Detroit, was a blue-collar town that was home to GM's Buick City, at that time their largest manufacturing plant. Given the significant amount of automotive assembly and parts plants, there were more than 100,000 members of the UAW within the Congressional District, which had a Democratic heritage. The incumbent Congressman and his supporters had no reason to expect a Republican challenger to present a serious threat, especially one from Harvard Business School. After meeting with him and sensing his enthusiasm I felt Riegle could be a good candidate to make use of the tools we were developing, and he thought we could help, so he hired us as consultants to his campaign.

Determine whether methods that worked in the past are still working as well under current conditions. If not – try something different!

We quickly found that the incumbent, John Mackie, was identified as their Congressman by a lower percentage of his constituents than we had seen in any previous campaign. We believed that, because Mackie would anticipate little challenge from Riegle, he would not change his style and get more involved in publicizing himself.

Our first surveys in May indicated that Riegle, as might be expected, was trailing Mackie 63% to 26%, with 11% undecided. By September, Riegle was narrowing the gap, though many in the campaign felt the change was not happening fast enough. Among a representative sample of all registered voters, Riegle trailed Mackie 51% to 31%, with 16% undecided.

Design your research collection process so that the results can be used with other information and communication tools

Many people were not aware, however, of some crucial work that was going on. We had combed through Census data and past voting behavior to identify the precincts most likely to contain registered voters who would support Riegle. These areas were contacted by phone, and a determination was made as to their likelihood of voting for Riegle. In areas considered to have more doubtful voters, Riegle went door-to-door. Any voters who appeared likely to vote for him were also added to our list. On Election Day, everyone who was likely to vote for Riegle was contacted and encouraged to vote. Those likely Riegle voters who needed assistance were given help in getting to the polls.

During the party at the Biltmore Hotel in Los Angeles celebrating Ronald Reagan's election as Governor of California, one of the more rewarding phone calls I received came from Don Riegle. He had defeated Congressman Mackie 54% to 46%.

Georgia politics during a transition

In 1970, we were retained to work for Jimmy Bentley in the Georgia Republican Primary for Governor. This was an interesting period in Georgia politics because several Democrats, including Bentley, had joined the Republican Party. The first meeting with Bentley's campaign organization was enlightening. Realizing that many of the voters were more likely to identify with liberal or conservative labels than with party affiliations, I started by discussing how we would ask respondents to use the 7-point Likert Scale, where liberal was on one side and conservative on the other to determine their political position.

A man who identified himself as a farmer from southern Georgia said the Likert approach might be better than "asking a person straight out." He then said, "Let me tell you how I feel about this liberal/conservative thing. First, a person or a government should not buy things on credit – if you don't have the cash in hand, wait until you do. I'm willing to pay very high Federal taxes for the national defense of our country. I am willing to determine how many acres of peanuts I grow based on the level of government subsidies. And last, I do not want my children to be forced to go to an integrated school. OK, what's my number?"

Fortunately we had been using a set of "agree-disagree" questions which measured the extent to which a person was liberal or conservative on economic and social questions. I explained, based on his example, how we would employ those questions in Georgia. He seemed satisfied with my answer.

At that point another person entered the room and everyone, including the candidate, Jimmy Bentley, stood up and said, "Good morning, Mr. Lawyer." The person was Lamar Sizemore, one of Democratic Senator Herman Talmadge's inner circle. After he sat down, the person who had asked me "what's my number?" reported that I had shown them a pretty good way of measuring how people felt on liberal and conservative issues and went ahead and articulated the approach almost to the letter. Lamar paused, looked at me and said, "You're about the first Yankee that's come down here with an appreciation of how complex things can be." At that point, we were retained by the Bentley for Governor Committee. Lamar Sizemore was one of those people that other people go to in an effort to get things done. What I found most interesting was his ability to cross party lines and support a former Democrat running as a Republican without losing favor with the Democratic leadership.

A month later, I went back to Atlanta to deliver the results of our first survey. The survey was not quite complete when I left our offices in California for another meeting in the East, so I arranged to have it forwarded to me in Atlanta. While preparing my presentation, I reviewed the sample's political efficacy rankings based on a set of questions that had been developed at the Center for Political Studies at the University of Michigan. The battery of questions measured a citizen's trust in government and their belief that their involvement can influence political outcomes. As I reviewed the results I was somewhat surprised since these were the lowest political efficacy scores I had ever seen. In fact, the distribution of the scores on each of the questions appeared to be just opposite of what we would normally see. It was clear to me that someone had transposed the numbers in the coding process.

Gain insight in the information you have collected by learning to walk in the respondent's shoes!

I had already scheduled a meeting with Lamar to brief him on the results prior to the meeting. I told him of what I thought was a coding error and said I would have the data re-run. He then, in essence, said:

> Vince, I know this will be difficult, but put yourself in the shoes of a typical Georgia voter for a minute. It will be difficult because you probably would not agree with the positions that these typical voters have taken. But relative to the question you've raised, you'll have to role play a Georgia voter to understand why the responses you received in your survey turned out the way they did. First, as a Georgian, you have voted to maintain a system that existed since 1917, that each of the State's Counties be represented, based on their population, by either 2, 4, or 6 voting units for nominating Governors, Senators and other State-wide office holders. Without your participation, the process was overturned by the courts in favor of a more one-person-one-vote formula. You've also

voted for very strict registration procedures to ensure fair elections, and that was overruled because it was determined to be discriminatory. In 1964, for the first time, your state voted for a Republican for President (Barry Goldwater), and he was overwhelmingly defeated in the electoral count.

He listed several more examples and asked: "Now what do you think the chances are that you would believe it was worth your time and effort to participate in the political process?"

After dinner, with that lesson vividly in my mind, I completed the presentation that I had started before Lamar had me walk in the shoes of a Georgia voter. It showed that, if Jimmy Bentley won the primary, he would be a strong contender in the General Election. As it turned out, a strong minority within the minority Republican Party resented a Democrat "coming in to take over the party," and Bentley lost the primary campaign. The man who beat Bentley in the primary went on to lose the general election to a relatively unknown state legislator from Plains, Georgia, named Jimmy Carter. I would meet Jimmy Carter nine years later in a future career.

An experience-based form of learning had just started

During my seven years in campaign management I gained considerable practical experience to complement (and sometimes challenge) what was learned from my years in college. By 1972, I had been to more than thirty states where our firm had participated in more than sixty political campaigns covering state legislative, mayoralty, Congressional, Senatorial, and Gubernatorial elections and one Presidential election. I had been the beneficiary of the fact that most of my initial efforts were in highly contested political campaigns – where limited resources and uncertainty are two givens. Our clients needed help in bringing to the surface the few highly salient factors that were most important to address a problem – whether it was a voting decision or a public affairs issue.

There is more to getting an innovation adopted than just creating it. Keep in touch with academic research...

The approach we developed may not sound revolutionary today, but relative to how most campaigns were being conducted at that time, it was an innovation. By thinking of what we were doing as an innovation, I was able to use the ideas from a book I had read at UCLA, The Diffusion of Innovations, by Everett Rogers. Rogers identified a typology that listed the attributes of an innovation that would facilitate or inhibit its adoption. This insight was helpful because many potential customers were quite wary of this company from California that used computers to alter the existing rules of a political campaign.

Learning how to use technology to augment existing knowledge

Using Rogers's insight, we demonstrated the value of taking advantage of electronic technologies to bring the wealth of public information becoming available to:

- Identify partisan strongholds

- Communicate in a manner to mobilize the vote in those solid areas

- Identify 'swing' areas, along with the borderline issues that might push a voter to support our candidate over an opponent.

In a world that was increasingly connected – and peopled by interactive casts of thousands – 'chaotic' was certainly a word to describe the campaign environment in which I was learning my trade. We soon learned that we could use technology to augment and make more useful what decision-makers already knew based on their experiences. We accomplished this constructive interaction by designing general purpose tools that allowed us to listen to – and use – what the decision-makers believed was important and then showing them the results of their ideas. In many cases this insight led to reconsidering some strongly held beliefs and the opening of their minds to new ideas.

Practicing Systems/Design Thinking... without knowing what it was

Without realizing its significance at the time, we were beginning to apply a form of 'Systems/Design Thinking' to our work with information and strategic decision-making because all other existing approaches generally fell short.

- The approach we developed required that both information and decision-making processes address the interactions of the totality of what is going on, rather than relying on isolated bits and pieces to predict the future of the whole.

- The approach assumed that the past is not always a good indicator of the future, as components of the system are subject to change because of the high degree of uncertainty at any given time. Similarly, it assumed that there are alternative futures that may be shaped by the decisions we make about a system today.

- The approach required multiple tools for addressing a problem because seldom is a single source of information or guidance adequate to describe the complexity of the whole.

Of course, our approach did not appear – nor was it accepted – overnight; just as problems do not emerge or resolve themselves overnight. Our political campaign work was, in essence, a series of quick and decisive experiments in which we tried new ideas and then measured their effectiveness in causing shifts in attitudes and election outcomes.

The work involved experimental, hands-on exploration of how to help our clients understand the interactions of a campaign's elements. At the same time, others, like Russell Ackoff and Peter Drucker, were working in a similar vein to expand academic theory and applying that theory in enterprises as they attempted to improve organizational behavior and the practice of systems thinking and strategic decision-making. Eventually I would be the beneficiary of our paths crossing, as we found that common principles and pursuits carried over from the political sphere and academia to the arena of government and the corporate world.

It ended up that, following my education, I entered a world of interacting parts, a high degree of complexity, uncertainty, and an accelerating rate of change. All this, plus the increased pressure for timely information, had provided a prime training ground for the next phase of my career.

Unintended consequences… some of today's campaigns are not what we had in mind

In 1994, my friend Richard Wirthlin and I participated in a conference that included most of the then prominent political consultants and survey researchers. With so much talent in the room it was surprising to me how little insight came out of the discussion. There was, however, one statement – made by Richard – that was not only insightful but painfully correct. During that discussion he said the following:

> …one of my great concerns is that the campaign dialogue is becoming more and more negative rather than positive. And I think it's that those of us who provide counsel to politicians are part of the problem in creating the cynicism. And unfortunately, that arises because, in fact, a negative message is more potent in a political campaign than a positive message.

He then addressed one of the other participants, who he had worked against in a campaign 8 years earlier and said,

> If you go back to that campaign, we were playing with soft kid gloves compared to the kinds of negative messages that both of us are seeing these days. But I do believe that – and this is not from a political perspective, but more from a social perspective and it especially holds for Presidential and Gubernatorial races – unless the political process has some connection to the way an individual governs, the people suffer. And that would imply the need for a positive component in the campaign. At some juncture, my feeling is that what people don't have and yearn for are campaigns that speak to the issues; without that… the campaigns face the possibility of being ignored. Speaking to the issues is a good move because sticking to the issues generally has to be done in a positive context. But we surely are not there yet.

Unfortunately, Richard's advice has not been fully appreciated and, if anything the desire to win at any cost has led to even more negative campaigns. That is not what we had envisioned when we started out in the business of supporting decision-making in political campaigns. We developed tools that helped the candidate present his case in the most positive and cost-effective way possible. If something the opposition candidate was saying was not true, the tools helped determine how to respond and how to deliver the message.

What we had in mind was reflected in the following quote attributed to Abraham Lincoln in 1840 when he was a state legislator in Springfield, Illinois:

> Divide the county into small districts and appoint in each a committee. Make a perfect list of the voters and ascertain with certainty for whom they will vote. Keep a constant watch on the doubtful voters and have them talked to by those in whom they have the most confidence. On election day see that every Whig is brought to the polls.[12]

The primary lessons learned during my involvement in political campaigns

Lesson	Description	Addressed in Part 2
5	Communicate effectively the results of the information you collected… even when, for the wrong reasons, they are not likely to be well received.	The Decision Loom Capability 1 Capability 4
6	Continually test and assess the extent to which things that worked in the past still work.	The Decision Loom Capability 1 Capability 2
7	Learn to step back and take a holistic look at the conditions surrounding the activity you are working on.	Capability 2 Capability 4
8	Make sure you go beyond what respondents answered to your survey questions and find out why they answered in the manner they did – walk in the respondent's shoes.	The Decision Loom Capability 4
9	Determine whether there is some technology (old or new) that will help augment, not replace, the application of what is already known.	Capability 4

---

12   Later, after I had time to check the authenticity of the quote, I found out that what had been sent to me was a slightly edited version of a Campaign Circular from a Whig Committee which had been developed at the Whig State Convention.

Episode 3: An Introduction to Public Life

In addition to working on Senator Tower's re-election campaign, our company had conducted several national surveys and a major, county-by-county analysis in support of the re-election of President Richard Nixon in 1972. After the elections, I was contacted by a member of the Republican National Committee and asked if I would be interested in having my name put forward to the President for nomination to be the Census Bureau Director. Based on the very positive impression I had developed of the Bureau and its personnel while a member of the Census Bureau's American Marketing Association's advisory committee, and based on conversations with my family and my partners, I said yes. Little did I know about the events that would soon become public and affect the nomination process.

What I did not know at the time I accepted the offer was that the Nixon Administration was in the midst of an unfortunate argument with the Bureau of Labor Statistics over the interpretation of the monthly employment data. Then, as now, the data were prepared by the professional staff, independent of any review or approval by the political leadership of the Department or White House, released on a pre-agreed schedule, and presented at a public meeting of the Joint Economic Committee, virtually at the same time as seen by the Administration. As a sign of its displeasure with the tone and substance of the analysis, the Administration abruptly removed some of the senior BLS staff and cancelled the monthly hearings before the Committee. Without getting into the merits (or lack thereof) of the Administration's actions, the action certainly did not help my nomination. The statistical, economic, and demographic professional communities were outraged by the actions of the Administration and their suspicions and displeasure were very quickly directed at the President's nominee to be the director of the Census Bureau. In this case, the nominee was not only completely unknown to any of these groups, but, worse yet, was found to be a "political pollster" who had conducted surveys on the President's behalf. Opposing my nomination became a cause célèbre — at least in the professional statistical world.

During the Senate debate on my confirmation, Senator Tower spoke on my behalf, and I was reminded of our meeting the year before in the

St. Anthony Hotel in San Antonio, when his staff had been reluctant to share some information they believed he would not want to hear:

> *I know he is a man who, having gathered data and analyzed it, tells it to you the way it is, and not the way he thinks you would like to hear it.*

On July 24, 1973, the Senate approved my nomination. The vote was Yeas - 73, Nays - 20 and not voting – 7. On July 31, the Secretary of Commerce swore me in as Census Bureau Director. I had been serving as Acting Director for four months.

Meeting Russell Ackoff

Following the nomination process, the next event on the calendar was meeting with the American Statistical Association's Advisory Committee to the Census Bureau, of which Russell Ackoff, who had opposed my nomination, was a member. Based on reviewing his accomplishments and his effectiveness as a speaker, I entered the meeting with some trepidation.

On the agenda was a presentation of the Census Bureau's planning process. When the presentation was finished, Russ asked to be heard and gave one of the clearest, most concise, and most constructive criticisms of planning that I had ever heard. That was followed up by a discussion about idealized design that was even more impressive.

Following the meeting, I asked him to stop by my office where I asked if he would be willing to consult with us on ways to improve our planning process. He thanked me for my interest but said it would be improper for him as an advisory member to be retained to address an issue that he had brought to our attention. He then suggested I contact Ian Mitroff, a former student of Russ's colleague C. West Churchman, who he was quite sure could help us. That meeting with Russ was the beginning of a wonderful experience that lasted for 37 years until his death in 2010. It was a learning journey for which I will always be grateful. He went from being a critic, to a teacher (in a real-world classroom), to a colleague and, most importantly, a trusted friend.

Learn to listen carefully to your adversaries – you may learn from them

The underlying premise of Ackoff's critique was that most planning processes are more reactive than proactive. He suggested trying to shape the future, and, after much discussion, we began planning for the Census in 2000, even though it was still only 1973.[13]

The bureau accepted Ackoff's challenge for a number of reasons. The challenge was provocative and interesting in itself. It came at an opportune time; that is, our executive team already felt the Bureau ought to be engaging in some form of long-range strategic planning.

Make sure those who will approve and implement a strategy are deeply involved in developing it

To ensure the participants did not feel the process was going to be top down, I suggested that the executive staff should not participate in the project's initial activities. I soon began to get feedback that the participants were having a hard time getting out of their current view and were not as enthusiastic as I had anticipated. About that time, the noted futurist Herman Kahn came to the Bureau to provide his vision of what the future might be. He gave a well-thought-out presentation, and after his discussion we took some time to review the Census 2000 project. I mentioned my initial impression about participants' lack of engagement. He asked whether I was actively participating in the project. I said I wanted to minimize management influence in the early stages. His response was direct:

> You are not the first executive who has made this mistake. Although your motivations were good, your employees have probably interpreted your actions to mean that this is not important enough for you and the executive team to participate.

When I met with some participants, they confirmed Kahn's assessment. I reversed my earlier decision and had the executive team join the

---

13 Mitroff, Mason & Barabba, 1982. This report was awarded first prize as the best case study on planning by The Institute of Management Science's College of Planning.

program, and everyone appeared to be more energized. It was an important lesson that I found useful on several subsequent occasions.

In line with Ackoff's initial challenge, the participants were told to think about what the bureau ought to be like in 2000, without regard for the operating constraints in 1973. They were cautioned, however, about applying practices that were beyond what could be expected by 2000 (e.g. 'Beam me up, Scotty'). The outcome was sixteen possible scenarios. Later Ackoff would alter the timing objective of the process of idealized design by stating "...such a redesign is an explicit statement of what the designers would have now if they could have whatever they wanted." [14]

At Ackoff's suggestion we had engaged Ian Mitroff, who was then at the University of Pittsburgh and his former student colleague Dick Mason with whom he studied under C. West Churchman. Based on working with Ian and Dick, I soon became aware that thoughtful academics could also be practical. The connection with Mitroff led to further beneficial collaboration and continues even today. His assignment was: (1) to suggest a schema for evaluating the initial reports, (2) to assist in the evaluation of the reports, and (3) to assist in the formulation of recommendations.

There is a lot more to having people adopt an innovation than just inventing it

In 1976, I asked Everett Rogers the author of *The Diffusion of Innovations*, whose ideas on the adoption of innovations I had found to be very useful in my campaign management experience, to apply his theory to the precursor of the Census Bureau's TIGER geographic tracking system. I believed what we had developed to be a real innovation. As it turned out, that initial concept now serves as the geographic information base for many of today's commercial mapping and direction applications.

This was not an academic exercise. Then, as now, a comprehensive and accurate geographic information system was at the heart of the Census. The Bureau of the Census also believed that the system should be designed to support the use of information for public and private

---

14   Ackoff, 1978

organizations at the local and national level. The reason was this: the more value the public and private agencies saw, the more they would allocate resources to keep the system up to date. We also knew we could learn about the system by determining both where it was, and where it wasn't, fully utilized.

In Rogers's research design he studied what facilitated and what inhibited the diffusion of the geographic information base. He included a 'tracer' technique in his study design that used more qualitative assessments in eight selected regions. He found, to his surprise, that the Census Bureau's geographic information system had been adopted across an extensive range of functions. The reason for the unexpected success, it turned out, was that the Census Bureau, to meet the requirements of the many local jurisdictions, wrote the software so that it could work on any computer. The generic character of the software meant that local jurisdictions could get it up and running quite quickly. The software's generic approach, however, meant that it ran inefficiently on any computer – but jurisdictions were able to 'fix' it rapidly. In Rogers and his colleague's minds, a new model of innovation emerged:

> *Reinvention is the degree to which an innovation is changed by the adopter in the process of adoption and implementation after its original development. Reinvention may involve both the innovation as a tool and in its use. Thus, the same technological innovation may be put to a different use than originally intended; alternatively, a different innovation may be used to solve the same problem. In addition, the intended or potential consequences of an innovation may be changed through reinvention.*

> *The concept of reinvention also recognizes that an innovation is often really a bundle of components; it is possible to adopt some components and change or reject others.*[15]

Once again, it is how the parts interact that really matters.

---

15   Rice & Rogers, 1980

A really important lesson about leadership

When I left Decision Making Information to join the Census Bureau in 1973, it was a firm with around twenty talented employees and revenue of several million dollars. It was my impression (not necessarily a fact) that I could do anything in our company at least as well as anyone else and often found myself attempting to do so. Arriving at the Census Bureau, with its more than 3,000 employees, many of them with distinguished careers in specialized fields, my outlook changed. I could not do anything as well as any of the highly trained and experienced individuals in the Bureau's divisions. What was my role to be?

Fortunately, I had wise career employees at the Bureau. They said the Bureau needed leadership that could provide the right direction, the resources to perform their mandated functions, and a politically free environment. In other words, they provided a government services perspective on a key Russ Ackoff lesson: "The role of management (i.e. The Director) is to manage the interaction of the parts and not the action of the parts taken separately" and in this case to make sure those parts interacted positively in the containing system.

Seeing the benefits of being surrounded by people who were more competent than I was in their area of expertise was to prove extremely beneficial throughout the rest of my career. I also came to understand that there was little difference in the competency of people working in government and those working in the private sector. There were very competent (and some not so competent) people in both sectors.

Time to move on

In 1976, Gerald Ford was up for re-election, and my family and I started thinking it was time to go back to the private sector. I had been recruited by the Xerox Corporation, and I wanted to get back into marketing – this time not working for a small company but working at a large company, with all the potential opportunity to implement what I had learned.

The primary lessons learned during my time in an agency of government

Lesson	Description	Addressed in Part 2
10	Involve the leadership of the organization throughout the entire process when developing strategic concepts that will have to be implemented by them.	Capability 2 Capability 3 Capability 4
11	Learn how to help people (more competent, in their special skills, than yourself) to apply their skills so as to improve the overall capability of the entire organization. In the words of Russ Ackoff, "Manage the interaction of the parts and not the parts taken separately."	The Decision Loom Capability 1
12	Engage practicing academics who are actively seeking opportunities to test out, under real-world conditions, new ideas that address both current and past problems.	Most of the ideas discussed in Part 2 came, in part, from practicing academics
13	There is a lot more to having people adopt an innovation than just inventing it – it helps when you design your invention so that those who you want to adopt it can reinvent it for their purposes.	Why a Sketch? Capability 4

Episode 4: Finally... A Marketing Job in the Private Sector

On May 25, 1978, 20 months after becoming the Xerox Manager of Market Research for copiers and duplicators, I flew down from Rochester, NY where the copier division of Xerox was headquartered to the Corporate Headquarters in Stamford, CT to make a presentation to senior executives. The presentation was based on a recently completed survey that found a big problem in the Xerox forward-planning process. The survey showed that the amount of copies for which Xerox copiers could be used was approximately 35% less than the number used in the current long-range plan.

When I finished the presentation, there were several comments made regarding changes that would have to be made to the long-range plan. There were no questions as to whether the numbers I presented were right or wrong. The CEO, Peter McColough, thanked me for providing valuable information, and I was excused.

I went to Westchester Airport and waited in the company hangar for Don Lennox to arrive for the flight back to Rochester. Don was the senior executive in charge of copier manufacturing and had stayed until the end of the meeting. As we flew home, Don told me he thought the presentation went well. I said I was pleased with the acceptance of what was obviously bad news but was a little surprised that there were so few questions. Don smiled and said, "That was because your group had done a good job in preparing them for what was very bad news, and they were prepared to discuss what to do about it rather than argue about whether the information was right or wrong."

He said it was high time that Xerox made some adjustments. Because of the optimistic long-range plan, several years earlier he had been instructed to increase Xerox's copier manufacturing base in Rochester – and now he was forced to convert one of his two new factories into a warehouse to store unsold copier equipment made in the other.

Why the Xerox senior leadership focused on what to do about the information instead of arguing about whether it was right

When I arrived at Xerox in October 1976, the company held the No.1 position in the copier market and was one of the fastest-growing companies in the United States. I was hired because some of the management team sensed that the competition was getting better (existing customers were replacing large Xerox copiers with several small copiers made in Japan), and certain patents had expired. Additionally it was rumored that both IBM and Kodak were developing large copiers. Management needed to better understand the market.

During my interview, I asked why management had waited so long. I was informed that Xerox felt it had a good sense of the market; all their copiers were leased, with pricing tied to the number of copies made, so they could just look at their records to see what was happening.

Upon arriving in Rochester, I was pleased to find out that the market research staff were very competent and were excited that someone had been hired to make sure the information they were collecting would actually be used.

Make sure the individuals who will allocate resources are involved in the design of the research project – including the development of measures to confirm whether the findings are relevant and realistic

Based on my experience of working with them at the Census Bureau, I asked Ian Mitroff and Ralph Kilmann to help me organize an approach to address the complexity of this problem. After reviewing existing studies and conversing with senior managers, we concluded that it would be necessary to design a knowledge-use system. We started out on two tracks:

- We created the Research Utilization Group to find out what decision-makers really wanted to know and in what form they wanted the information.

- We designed a retrieval system that would give users easy access to the information they required from the same database as their colleagues in different functions.

After several months, the group concluded that the changing market required a comprehensive study, and quickly. Considerable effort was expended because the study was complex, was the first of its kind, and was likely to have important implications. We wanted to be sure that we could explain the results fully and that senior management would accept them. So, we:

- Determined what information we needed by involving relevant managers, with the understanding that senior management would review and approve the work.

- Hired a research firm to help us be rigorous about the survey design. The firm, Westat, had several former distinguished Census Bureau employees and developed a geographic-based area probability sample. The basic design was to identify a representative sample of areas and then have those areas canvassed to develop a list of businesses. From that list, we randomly drew businesses that would be interviewed. Because there was very little existing information available, the study turned out to be one of those accurate, not so fast, and very expensive studies.

Before the results were available, the Research Utilization Group, using existing Xerox administrative records, prepared estimates of the level of Xerox reprographic activity to be compared to the results of the survey.

It was already clear that many assumptions about the size of the total market had been overstated – in some segments by a factor of two. There was concern that the dramatic differences between the study results and the existing planning assumptions would lead to a confrontation over which was correct.

Some members of the Research Utilization Group toyed with understating our findings, so they would show that Xerox had a problem but would hide the full extent of that problem. The notion was to get within the comfort zone of management, but, after some soul searching, the idea was discarded.

Fortunately, because Xerox leased and did not sell its products, we had records showing not only the number of Xerox copiers in the market but also the number of copies each copier was making. The Research Utilization Group compared those records against the results from the Sample Survey and found them to be within a few percent of each other, adding credence to the remainder of the survey's measurements.

Armed with this evidence, the Research Utilization Group arranged meetings with management to provide preliminary results and allow sufficient time for review and questions. The information was formatted and presented carefully, to ensure the results would not be misunderstood or rejected. By the time I made the presentation to senior management at the Corporate Headquarters mentioned at the beginning of this Episode, each of their direct reports had given them the background on the study and the possible implications. Management was almost wholly in agreement with the results. Senior managers were not only prepared to hear the facts but also had sufficient understanding to direct the product and market planning management to alter existing plans.

An introduction to very sophisticated (and useful) market models

One of the things that attracted me to Xerox was the company's research activities in California at the Palo Alto Research Center (PARC). I met with a group that was developing advanced market research, analytics, and forecasting techniques. I wanted to see how the process they were developing could integrate the capabilities of the market research, modeling and planning communities.

I happened to visit PARC when the group was working on a forecasting model for the Xerox 9700 – a computer printer that eliminated the need to strike a typing font against a ribbon to make a mark. The new printer used technology found in the recently introduced Xerox 9200 copier. Aside from the technology, I was most impressed that the group had arranged the project so that their team was joined by the group planning the 9700 program, and by the corporate market research group. I was told the initial meetings had all the hallmarks of the conflicts that arise when silos representing different functions try to do something together.

Fortunately, the team found ways to address their differences. By the time the team was finished finding out what worked and what did not, the resulting forecasting model was owned by all participants.

I was also impressed with their ability to build a separate model of the operations of each of twenty-two companies that served as a sample of all potential customers. They accomplished this by making visits and estimating the copy volume of each company, then asking company operating managers to check the model output against known results. Once they confirmed the reliability of the models, they could forecast their acceptance of the new, non-impact machine not only at the industry level, but how well it would be received by the different types of companies for which they had specific measurements of their operations. This information would prove beneficial to the sales division as they developed plans for selling across the industry. A later study found that they were right about Xerox placements of a new-to-the-market product to within 5%.

During that initial visit, I asked if I could have a copy (Xerox Copy, that is) of a presentation made by Dick Smallwood. He said yes, hit a key on his computer and then walked me into another room to retrieve the copy from a modified Xerox Copier. That was in 1976, and, wow, was I impressed.

The relationship with Dick Smallwood continued throughout the rest of my learning journey. As will be shown throughout the book, what was learned at Xerox PARC was further developed by Dick as I moved on to other assignments where I continued to be the beneficiary of his skills.

A call for help that led me back to the Census Bureau

In 1978, I received a call from Pat Caddell, who had served as President Carter's survey researcher and strategist. Caddell indicated that he was concerned about conditions at the Census Bureau and was looking for suggestions about what the Carter Administration could do to improve things. The conversation soon led to a discussion about the need, based on what I had learned from Russ Ackoff about Systems Thinking, to begin a project to look at the Census Bureau in the context of the broader containing system in which it worked – other federal statistical agencies, the public, legislative bodies, the Administration and the press. Toward the end of the project, it was becoming clear that the Director who succeeded me at the Census Bureau was having some difficulty with the Administration and the Congress. Pat indicated they were going to have to find another director. I indicated that I would be willing to help in the selection. Pat said, "We were thinking that you might want to come back and finish up what you had started before leaving in 1976." I eventually accepted.

The research utilization concept continued to benefit Xerox

When I informed Xerox management that I would not be returning following the completion of the 1980 Census, they selected Vince Vaccarelli to head up what was renamed the Xerox Business Research Group. Under his leadership the group continued to support the decision-making process by providing timely and relevant information to encourage a shared perspective and agreement. This effort by Vince Vaccarelli and his team contributed to Xerox's Total Quality Management initiative which culminated in 1989 when Xerox won the Malcolm Baldrige National Quality Award. As Vince Vaccarelli pointed out to me in a recent correspondence,

> *The critical value of dialogue is not just agreement, but the adaptability to customer requirements that it fosters, facilitating 'outside-in' perspectives and integrating the 'inside-out' advantages of technology. Today, Xerox utilizes Lean Six Sigma processes to continue such dialogues in order to adapt to continually changing customer requirements with state-of-the-art technologies, allowing Xerox today to compete successfully in markets for advanced office products, production printing systems, and the dynamic market for document systems, services and consulting.*

One can only wonder, if the ability to weave together imagination and knowledge in a constructive dialogue had been in place in the 1970's when Xerox PARC was populated with some of the most competent and creative computer scientists, what products and services might have been introduced by Xerox and not Apple, Adobe and others.

The primary lessons learned during my Xerox Corp. experience

Lesson	Description	Addressed in Part 2
14	Engage mid-level management in the process of ensuring the information gathered and analyzed is relevant to the needs of the enterprise. Ensure that they assist in preparing their senior managers for receiving, accepting and acting on the results.	The Decision Loom Capability 1 Capability 2
15	Make sure that understanding and appreciation of business conditions exists throughout the enterprise and reaches deeply into places where specialists, engineers, and scientists formulate and assess ideas.	Capability 2 Capability 4
16	Whenever possible, make sure your market measurements allow information users to see the effects of alternative strategies and how individual customers respond and are not limited to observations based on averages of all customers or segments.	Capability 3 Capability 4

Episode 5: The Conduct of the 1980 Census: Making Decisions in a Highly Uncertain, Political and Litigious Environment

"There are only two itty-bitty things at stake here: Money and Votes"

Atlanta Mayor Maynard C. Jackson
at a Congressional Hearing on the 1980 Census

Anticipating and preparing for the legal battles

The legal problems facing the Census Bureau would prove to be complex and difficult. Although the official resident population count of 226,504,825 was transmitted to the President on December 31, 1980, it took more than seven years before the 1980 Census count was finally clear of all legal challenges.

The importance of being neither arbitrary nor capricious

Because of some issues that had cropped up during the 1970 Census, we knew that some groups might claim an undercount of the population in 1980 and might challenge the Census count and request it be adjusted to account for people missed during the enumeration process. As an example, one 1970 case challenged the use of the mail to conduct the enumeration in metropolitan areas because it decreased the count of poor minority groups. Others claimed that the Census form was difficult for people of Hispanic origin to fill out and would undercount them. The court ruling drew on a principle in administrative law. They decided that the Bureau, based on conditions at the time, had not acted in either an arbitrary or capricious manner and, therefore, upheld the results.

As we began to develop the plan for the release of the 1980 Census results, it was clear that the courts would expect the Bureau to be more cognizant of the changes taking place in society and to demonstrate that all of our actions were neither arbitrary nor capricious. But we would need to answer several important questions. The most worrisome was: how could we tell if an undercount had occurred? Others were: which groups had been affected and by how much, and was there anything we could do to 'adjust' the population counts after the fact?

Studies following the 1970 Census suggested an estimated undercount of the population of about 5.3 million. Assuming that this number had remained relatively stable over the decade, a perfect count in 1980 would include those missed in 1970, resulting in an estimated count of 226 million in 1980.

What makes the undercount an even more important issue is that the total undercount hides a differential rate of under coverage between the majority white population and the minority groups. In 1970, it was estimated that 2.7% of the total population was missed. The assessment indicated that nearly 6.5% of the black population was missed, whereas the under enumeration of the 'non-black' population was only 2.2%. The disparity raised issues about the fairness of the distribution of electoral representation and allocation of government funding and services, given that the black population's under count was nearly three times that of the rest of the population, and led to the question of whether it is appropriate and possible to adjust the count to reflect these disparities.

Preparing to be seen as neither capricious nor arbitrary

Upon returning to the Bureau in 1979, I asked Ian Mitroff and Dick Mason to lead us through a Strategic Assumption Surfacing and Testing (SAST) process similar to the one they conducted at Xerox that helped us understand how many copiers were actually in existence and how many copies were truly being made. The SAST process would, I felt, make maximum use of the richness of the multiple perspectives that were held by the many people and organizations that would be affected by the outcome of the 1980 Census. In this case, the process focused on how to address the undercount issue in a way that would be accepted by those who had a stake in it.

The first workshop was conducted in September 1979. The process required that we develop different teams to represent the different perspectives of individuals within and outside the Census Bureau.[16] Each team was asked to defend its position but, to ensure that everyone felt comfortable in raising critical assumptions without jeopardizing their careers, everyone was expected to role play. They were told to take as strong a position as they could in support of their team, whether or not they believed in that position. To encourage the role playing, each team was asked to give itself a name that emphasized how different it was from the others. The teams described themselves like this:

Convention A: 'The Headcounters from Missouri'

> Under this plan, only the headcount itself would be used, without any adjustment other than the Census Bureau's traditional uses of imputation procedures. Those procedures generated data for unanswered questions by 'imputing' an answer from someone else who had the same other characteristics of the person who left the question unanswered. The crucial issues of this convention were around the credibility of the Census Bureau and the concern that an adjustment could set an unfortunate precedent.

Convention B: 'Triple B Non-adjustment Company'

> Under this plan, the headcount would be adjusted using only the procedures used in the 1970 Census. These procedures included imputation not only about specific households but about classes of households – if we didn't have information about those classes, we would use information from a special survey to generate data about those classes. For example, the proportion of housing units initially reported as vacant might be adjusted based on the survey. This group argued that it was important that state-of-the-art tools be used to ensure the credibility of the bureau and the Census count.

---

16   Mitroff, Mason & Barabba, 1982 provides a more comprehensive discussion of the process.

Convention C: 'The Equalizers'

Under this plan, Census data would be adjusted for undercount by age, race (black/non-black)[17], and sex. Adjustments would be made utilizing a simple synthetic approach. The synthetic approach would take the percentage of African Americans who are uncounted in all of the U.S. population as a whole and distribute that number proportionately to the population of each of the states. Thus each state would get its proportionate share of the uncounted or missed African Americans in the U.S. population as a whole. Although the easiest to apply, one would have to assume that the undercount of African Americans was equally distributed across each state for this approach to be accepted. This approach also implies the preparation and existence of two complete count tabulations, one adjusted and one unadjusted. This group felt that the disparity of the undercount was important and should be corrected for, and that estimates of the relative undercount were available for age, race, and sex. This group argued that, because no other characteristics have known amounts of undercount, adjustments should not be done on the basis of any other characteristics.

Convention D: 'All or Nothing at All'

Under this plan, the headcount and other crucial variables would be modified using as much pertinent information as possible. These crucial variables include age, sex, ethnicity, relationships, income, race, and language. There is the assumption in this instance that evaluations, results, and reliable estimates were available for the uncounted population at the state level. This group argued that, if any adjustment was done to the actual counts, it should correct the undercount as completely as possible. An implicit assumption was that the Census Bureau was the body best qualified to develop such an adjustment procedure and to perform this adjustment.

To get at the underlying assumptions that would have to be true for their convention to prevail, the teams were directed to identify key stakeholders who could affect or be affected by that team's convention.

---

17   At the time of the taking of the 1980 Census the term 'black' had not been replaced by the current term 'African Americans.'

The teams identified stakeholders like Census Bureau Director, White House, Secretary of Commerce, Congress, the GAO, other Federal Statistical Agencies, State and Local Governments, Recipients of Government Programs, the Legal Community, Employers, Labor Unions, etc. With the key stakeholders identified, the teams listed the assumptions that would have to be held by these stakeholders for the team's position to prevail over the other conventions. More than sixty-one assumptions were surfaced. After the teams listed their assumptions, each team then identified the assumptions from the other teams that would be most damaging to their perspective (the Sophists would have been pleased.)

The following are limited examples of assumptions surfaced by a given team, with a comment on how the other teams thought it was most damaging to them. They are presented here to provide an indication of the type of assumptions that were surfaced.

Convention A: 'The Headcounters from Missouri'

The group assumed the Courts would support it as the least arbitrary and capricious. If true, this would be most damaging to Convention C and D; why would you go through such complex solutions only to have the courts say you were being either arbitrary or capricious in your changes?

Convention B: 'Triple B Non-adjustment Company'

This group assumed that, even if the more complex and complete adjustments could be made, they couldn't occur until the end of 1983, well after the apportionment of the members of congress and most state redistricting would have taken place. If this was true, it would be most damaging to Convention D; why would you go through such complex solutions only to have all the decisions for which you made your changes already be decided prior to your ability to deliver the adjusted information?

Convention C: 'The Equalizers'

This group assumed that timely adjusted counts are wanted by major stakeholders for many purposes beyond redistricting. If true, this would be most damaging to Convention B because there were other important decisions to be made when the improved statistics were made available.

Convention D: 'All or Nothing at All'

This group assumed that the White House would support the methodology that had the highest political acceptability and visibility. Convention D, in providing greater detail, would gain the broadest political support, and all others would be damaged. This approach would be most damaging to Convention A because A lacked the political dimension.

A debate was then held in which only the damaging assumptions were considered. The outcome of the debate was a listing of critical issues that needed to be addressed.

Here, we will discuss only one of the seven issues – the one that led to the final decision on the adjustment issue. The basic assumption was that, no matter what the Bureau decided, we would face litigation. This assumption led the Bureau to take two specific actions:

First, the Bureau would maintain complete documentation of the process and procedures that led to the final decision.

Second, based on previous litigation and legal precedent, it was believed that the courts would follow the standard that if the Bureau was neither "arbitrary nor capricious," its decision on adjustment would be upheld.

As important as the other issues were to the final decision, the assumption that the standard of "arbitrary and capricious" would be applied ended up being among the most important and critical. If the standard had been which convention was the most "accurate" or "fair," the courts would have been faced with making a decision based on conflicting and extremely technical assessments from equally qualified experts.

Whenever possible, show those who will be affected by the results of your decision the process by which the decision will be made and allow them the opportunity to comment on your approach

On October 20, 1980, the Census Bureau summarized and made public the work that had been completed in planning for the adjustment decision. As stated in the introduction to our report, we were summarizing a full two years of deliberation on the issues; we were also inviting a final round of comments before we made decisions on whether to adjust – nothing arbitrary or capricious there.

On December 17, 1980, the Census Bureau placed a final notice in the Federal Register, evaluating each of our critical assumptions and explaining our decision, which was not to adjust. We wrote:

> *Based on preliminary data for areas containing almost all of the nation's population, we believe that the 1980 Census count will fall within the range of 225.7 to 226.0 million. The Bureau's preferred demographic analysis estimate of the 'true' population (exclusive of illegal residents) is near 226 million. Taken together, these figures indicate a tiny, or nonexistent measured undercount.*[18]

We acknowledged we likely had undercounted legal residents, to a degree that was roughly offset by the fact that we included undocumented residents, but said we had "no sound statistical basis" for trying to adjust the numbers.

Thanks to Justice Thurgood Marshall the count was finally delivered… and on time!

On December 31, 1980, Commerce Secretary Philip Klutznick and I forwarded the final Census count of 226,504,825 persons to President Jimmy Carter. The count was delivered following a decision the evening before by Supreme Court Justice Thurgood Marshall that stayed the ruling from Judge Henry Werker that had prevented the Bureau from submitting the official count.

Sometimes it takes a long time for the 'truth' to prevail

It was not until December 8, 1987, more than seven years after the start of the 1980 Census, (and after more than fifty lawsuits were filed) that United States District Judge John E. Sprizzo decided that "arbitrary and capricious" action was the appropriate standard for deciding whether the Census Bureau decision against adjusting the 1980 Census should be reversed. Judge Sprizzo went on to say:

---

18   Federal Register, 1980

Episode 5: The Conduct of the 1980 Census:

> *The extensive testimony at trial overwhelmingly demonstrates that the determination as to whether the use of the currently available adjustment techniques will provide a more or less reliable estimate of the population than the unadjusted Census is an extraordinarily technical one, about which reasonable statisticians and demographers can and do disagree. Certainly the Bureau, which has the necessary experience, expertise, and resources to collect and analyze the complex statistical data, is better equipped than the courts to decide whether, in view of this dispute among the experts, the Census should be adjusted.*

In a footnote, the Judge commented:

> *The Court rejects plaintiffs' [City of New York] argument that the Court should not defer to the Bureau's determination because the Bureau's decision not to adjust allegedly 'rested on non-technical, political grounds.' That claim is simply not supported by the evidence. The Court finds as a matter of fact that while non-technical consideration played a minor role in the Bureau's decision not to adjust, the Bureau's decision was primarily based on its determination that it was not feasible to develop and implement an adjustment methodology which would be more accurate than the Census itself, a determination supported and confirmed by the evidence at trial.*

Judge Sprizzo's findings brought to a successful close a tremendous effort on the part of many hardworking and talented Census employees. Their effort resulted in a 1980 Census count for which the eventual under enumeration was estimated at 3.2%, the lowest rate in the 4 Censuses before 1980.

An introduction to Eastman Kodak and Phil Samper

When I was working at Xerox my wife and were invited to a party at the home of a Kodak executive I had met during my first tour at the Census Bureau. At that I party I was introduced to Phil Samper, the head of Global Marketing at Eastman Kodak. Phil expressed an interest in what I was doing at Xerox and had done at the Census Bureau in my first go-round. After receiving approval from my Xerox supervisor, we arranged a meeting at my offices at Xerox. We met for about three hours. Phil asked some very thoughtful questions, learning more about what I was doing than some of my supervisors at Xerox – I was impressed. After that, we met from time to time at social events and started becoming friends.

Another meeting with Phil Samper… this time with a different purpose

In the fall of 1980, as the end was in sight for my second stint at the Census Bureau, I received a call from Phil Samper. He said he was coming to Washington and wanted to visit me. During that visit Phil asked if I was in any way officially tied to Xerox while in the employ of the government. I said no, but that Xerox was still interested in hiring me when my government tenure was over. He smiled and said the lack of formal ties was good, because there was an understanding that Kodak and Xerox, both being located in the relatively small town of Rochester, NY, would be careful about hiring people away from the other company. Given that I was no longer a Xerox employee, Phil wanted to know if I'd be interested in joining Kodak. Phil's request posed an interesting dilemma and opportunity. If I stayed with Xerox and attempted to accomplish the tasks in which I was most interested, I would eventually have to move to the Corporate Headquarters in Stamford, Connecticut. My family had really come to enjoy living in Rochester, and we were not looking forward to another move. With Kodak, I could start working on all the things I wanted to do and still live in Rochester. Additionally, it became clear that Phil wanted me to work on the things we had talked about during his visit to my office at Xerox. I chose to go to work for Phil and Eastman Kodak.

The picture was taken as I was leaving the Census Bureau by my executive assistant Carolee Bush, after she jokingly challenged me to do something exciting for a change. It was a Kodak moment in more ways than one.

The primary lessons learned from my second Census Bureau experience

Lesson	Description	Addressed in Part 2
17	Surface and make explicit the underlying assumptions that would have to be true for your particular problem-solving approach to prevail – even in a court of law.	Capability 4
18	Engage and inform those who will be affected by a decision – about both the process and the basis upon which the decision would be made before the decision is made.	Capability 4

Episode 6: Back to the Private Sector with Eastman Kodak
Some great wins and one big disappointment

Coming into Kodak was in some ways quite similar to my coming to Xerox – and at the same time quite different. It was similar in that that, like Xerox, Kodak was a successful company that was starting to feel the pressure from its competition, specifically Fuji Photo.

It was different in that Xerox was a successful new company where everyone was relatively new and came from another company. Kodak was a successful old company and nearly all of its senior executives had come up through the company ranks. Each of them having a long history of working in a successful enterprise led to an attitude bias that what worked in the past would certainly work in the future. This more insular environment required Phil Samper to do a lot of selling to his colleagues to get approval to bring on board this outsider to improve their understanding of the market.

In particular, people wondered why I was requesting that the function I was to lead be named Market Intelligence and not Market Research. Based on my now 14 years of experience in both the public and private sectors, I responded that market research at Kodak had historically been "ad hoc... mostly reacting to management requests to deal with specific market problems, some of which were not well understood or defined prior to the expenditure of funds for data collection." By renaming the group, I was underscoring that I wanted to "broaden the traditional concept of market research" so that requests for market information would be "explicitly stated" and would "become an integral part of the planning and decision-making process."

Gaining the CEO's confidence – if someone questions your work they may be really interested and answering their questions may be worthwhile

In an effort to improve senior management's use of information, and to address what I perceived to be Walt Fallon's continued skepticism about market research, I arranged to brief him before any large market research study went into the field. This evolved into a very interesting relationship. He found great pleasure in finding something wrong with whatever was brought to him for approval. In my case, that turned into his attempts to find at least one thing wrong with any study brought to him. To my surprise, he could. Twice, he uncovered questionable parts of a proposed study. In response, I found myself spending more time preparing for his reviews. Over time, our relationship became a spirited competition, to see if I could get past him without his finding any flaws.

The byproduct of these reviews was that, since he wanted to see how his suggestions affected the study, he spent more time reviewing the results. Based on my experience at the Census Bureau with Everett Rogers and the adoption of innovations, it became clear that by his active engagement in trying to find something wrong, he was involved in 'reinventing' each of the studies so they became his own – even when the results did not support some of his earlier points of view.

The 'review' that I recall with great fondness occurred when we were working on a study to determine how digital devices might affect Kodak's silver halide film business. Given the importance of the study, I had really prepared so Walt wouldn't find any faults in the design. Just before my review with Walt, I tested the study with about 20 senior technical and planning managers. One asked a simple question: "What about electronic video (motion) cameras?". Incredibly, we had left out this form of electronic imaging. Kodak had gotten out of the amateur motion picture camera business, so we hadn't looked at electronic video cameras as a threat. Yet video cameras really just capture a series of still images. With our bias made visible, we revisited the study as if we were employees of the Sony Corporation. We made several modifications.

In my subsequent meeting with him, Walt asked what I had done to ensure that this study would provide meaningful and relevant information rather than simply reinforce what was already known. I told him about how we spent several days redesigning the study as if we were Sony employees. Walt said he would look forward to seeing the results of the study. The meeting had ended before it even began.

"Wait a minute," I said. "What happened to your normal critique and comments? Our group has spent a lot of time preparing for this meeting, and this study will withstand any questions you can think of."

He said something to this effect: "You've addressed my biggest concern by expanding your thinking outside of a traditional Kodak perspective." He added with a smile, "In our previous discussions you've acted on my concerns. Now, given all we pay you, isn't it about time you started doing these studies on your own!"

Getting behind the 'Silver Curtain'

The heart of Kodak's technological advantage was a group of chemists and scientists who were extremely knowledgeable about what could and could not be done with silver halide chemistry, which was the key element in film's ability to capture light. The people who worked on silver halide technology at Kodak did so under the strictest of confidentiality and privacy rules. Access to them was limited to "an as-needed basis, to be approved by senior management." This intense focus on keeping their knowledge within Kodak led some to refer to their work as "behind the silver curtain."

During one of our studies, we asked customers to compare and express their preference for sets of color prints that were developed using Kodak technology with prints developed using Fuji technology. Although a majority preferred Kodak to Fuji, the percentage that preferred Fuji exceeded its current market share. The chemists and other scientists behind the silver curtain rejected the implication that the results suggested Fuji could gain market share. They cited technical evidence that Kodak prints came closer to 'true color' than Fuji's did, and said we probably did not provide customers with properly developed prints. We agreed to replicate the study and asked them to produce the prints, as well as participate in the study's implementation and analysis.

The results of the new study replicated the findings of the first. This time, when the scientists couldn't simply deny the results, one said he knew how to slightly modify Kodak's existing film so that Kodak's level of preference would match its market share. Importantly, because the scientists had been involved in our study and had seen for themselves what customers wanted, the change was made without going through the very expensive and time-consuming process of first testing a new film across Kodak global markets. The modified film, which used a new emulsion technology, was a breakthrough created by a combination of creativity and market knowledge. We had solved a problem before it became one.

The appropriate use of mathematically based models

After I had been at Kodak for a while and our group's efforts were becoming accepted, I started to be invited to product development meetings.

At the time Kodak had access to some very talented mathematical model builders. These model builders were able to offer very valuable insights into alternative strategies in developing 'scientific' models to optimize photographic film and paper emulsions that could be produced and used in different conditions around the world. The positive experience with these models earned them a high degree of credibility with senior management. When I arrived, it became clear that the credibility of these models was being transferred to models being developed for more complex and uncertain business issues and decisions.

My concern was initially related to how the models were being oversold to our management. At that time, in an effort to get access to scarce resources, some of our model builders were over-promising, either by errors of commission by overstating the model's capabilities, or by errors of omission by not revealing the model's limitations. Too often I was hearing, in response to whether these models could address some of the most complex and difficult of questions, "Of course, the model could answer that question – and it could do so at the push of a button!"

The genesis of Barabba's Law – "Never say, 'the model says...'"

During one of these meetings the proponent of an idea, when asked why the company should accept his idea, simply responded, "The model says it will be successful." Knowing something about the limitations of the model he was referring to, I commented something to the effect, "Never say, 'the model says...'; tell us what you believe, based on your understanding of the model's output – and limitations."

In 1987, after I had left Kodak, Herb Blitzer one of the very talented people that came to the Market Intelligence group from the operations research group, referred to this comment when he opened his commentary on a paper discussing a new mathematical model as follows:

Before getting into a commentary on the substance of the paper, I feel compelled to comment on one specific aspect. Consider Barabba's Law: "Never say, 'the model says...'" Any hint of such behavior could lead to the complete discrediting of the whole effort. Since no model can accurately capture the complexity of a real situation, anyone with an interest in the outcome of an analysis can always find at least one issue to stall even the best analytical work. Managers have a natural need to understand the logic of proposed actions, and logic is what they should be given... This paper frequently states 'the model says...'.[19]

Conducting a strategic assessment of possible changes to customer behavior and market conditions[20]

As a part of my Kodak 'education,' Walt Fallon sent me to visit one of Kodak's largest retail photo finishing customers. On the last day of my visit, I had dinner with the owners. The founder asked me to ask Walt Fallon and Colby Chandler the following question: "What is the time period over which silver halide technology will retain its superiority over digital technologies in capturing images and making prints?"

When I returned from the trip, Walt and Colby scheduled a meeting to discuss the question. By this time, I knew enough to realize this was one of those questions for which the right answer starts out with, "It depends." It depends on who is taking the picture. Do they want a high-quality print? Would they be satisfied looking at an image on a television screen? Do they want a permanent record of the image? How quickly do they want to see the image? *Et cetera.*

At the meeting, Walt Fallon said something like: "Well, since we brought you in because of your reputation as an expert in information and decision-making, how would you suggest we go about answering this question from this very important customer?"

Fortunately, having a clear recollection of the advantages of the Strategic Assumption Surfacing and Testing (SAST) process we used in determining whether or not to adjust the 1980 Census, I had prepared a description of how the process might work. I informed the group

---

19   Blitzer, 1987 and Barabba, 1994

20   Carroll and Mui (2008) provide a more detailed discussion of Eastman Kodak's missed opportunity in digital photography.

that the quality of the effort would reflect the extent to which senior executives participated in the process.[21]

The process began by gathering input from people throughout the company who had diverse backgrounds in imaging technologies – including members of the research and technical functions who were familiar with the capabilities of digital and silver halide technologies. Following the process that was used at the Census Bureau, teams were formed to take strong positions on whether silver halide or electronics would dominate capturing images by 1990. Each team debated their positions with the purpose of uncovering and assessing the most important assumptions that would have to be true for a particular point of view to be accepted. Out of this debate grew a list of critical assumptions upon which Kodak would develop its longer-term strategy. All of this led to a 1981 document, which made the following claim:

> Technological innovation will enhance the growth of personal picture taking, and today's photographic industry participants [Kodak and its business partners using silver-halide technology] will share in that growth in the foreseeable future…
>
> (The foreseeable future was defined as a period ending in 1990.)

In essence we alerted the management team that change in the capturing of images through digital technologies was coming, and that they had a decade to prepare for it.

To ensure that assumptions would stand up to internal and external review, not only the information that supported each assumption, but also the rebuttal for each assumption, was made available.

With this insight as background several key members of Kodak's management team concluded that traditional still photography would continue to grow and remain the predominant form of amateur picture-taking throughout the 1980s. Furthermore it would be at least into the next decade before an acceptable all-electronic still camera would become available to the market. The process used made it clear that an electronic camera would happen, but that such a camera

---

21 I gratefully acknowledge permission received from Eastman Kodak Company to discuss the results of the approach used to reveal underlying assumptions found in this section.

faced significant and formidable obstacles before it would appeal to a mass market. It also made the point that technical capability does not necessarily mean mass market practicability.

As it turned out, as the study determined, silver-halide-based photography held its own throughout the 1980s, and digital cameras and display technologies did not come into their full force until the 1990s.

The good news: what Kodak did right based on the results of the study

1986: Kodak research labs developed the first megapixel sensor, which could record 1.4 million pixels – somewhat greater than the 1 million pixel sensor that the assumption surfacing exercise indicated might be able to produce prints of acceptable quality (in this case limited to 5x7 inch prints). The research also explored algorithms and technology to improve photographic prints and several other promising technologies.

In essence, Kodak initiated a number of activities that led to digital technology that would position them to compete sometime in the future with other manufacturers of digital cameras – while focusing on methods to improve silver halide technology.

The bad news: what Kodak did that was not beneficial

Management did not determine a strategy – as the company founder, George Eastman, had when he replaced existing still profitable old technology with new technology – to replace silver halide with digital. Instead they chose a path of using digital to improve silver halide rather than replace it. This strategy eventually led to others, like Sony and Cannon, to do it to them. In the examples of Senator Tower, Congressman Riegle, Xerox, and the Census Bureau, we pointed to Churchman's wisdom that the value of information is in its use and not its collection. In the case of the information that was provided to Kodak management about digital photography we have a negative example of information that lost considerable value because it was not used to the extent to which it should have been. In this case, it proved to have been a very costly example.

The primary lessons learned during my Kodak Corp. experience

Lesson	Description	Addressed in Part 2
19	Reach out beyond senior managers and actively engage engineers and scientists in the design of market research projects to improve their understanding and acceptance of those projects.	Capability 4
20	Follow Barabba's Law – "Never say, 'the model says…'"	The Decision Loom Capability 4
21	There is more to making a contribution to the enterprise than just pointing out what the future holds. Put in place the tools to ensure that the subsequent decisions of the enterprise take those findings into consideration.	The Decision Loom Capability 4
22	It is far better to build models of individual behavior than to combine individual responses into data for an aggregate respondent. This provides a rich source of data about individual consumers each with their unique set of preferences and biases. (Provided by Dick Smallwood)	Capability 4
23	You cannot sell sophisticated quantitative analysis directly to a client in the first project. You must first gain their trust before moving on to more complex – and valuable – approaches. (Provided by Dick Smallwood)	Capability 4

Episode 7: Getting Started at General Motors

Fast forward from 1985 to 1990… going 70 miles from Flint, Michigan to Detroit – in 24 years

In 1990, I was in the GM boardroom of the former historic GM Building on Grand Avenue in Detroit as a GM employee with my former partner, Richard Wirthlin, by then a noted political and strategic researcher who had helped guide Ronald Reagan's successful Presidential elections. We were there to present the results of a study (which I had asked Richard to conduct) to GM's Market Planning Council about a very complex problem. For years, GM's leadership role in the auto industry had been slipping, yet management had been denying that this trend would persist. Finally emerging from denial, some members of the management team wanted to understand what had happened and what it would take to bring GM back from the brink of financial disaster.

I considered the irony of meeting Don Riegle at the Durant Hotel (named after GM's founder) and the political activity in which we had participated 24 years earlier, in Flint, Michigan, then the home of GM's Buick City. As described more fully in Episode 2, Richard and I had helped 28-year-old Don Riegle upset an incumbent Democratic Congressman and begin a nearly 20-year career in the U.S. House and Senate. The incumbent, confident because of past successes, hadn't worried much about the young Republican with his Harvard Business School background, thinking Riegle was not a good fit for the blue-collar district where the election was being held. Yet auto workers' social values were changing, and with our help, Riegle figured out how to tailor his positions on issues to take advantage of those changes and win the election. Now, GM was in a fix similar to the one that Riegle's opponent had created for himself. GM had counted too much on past successes and hadn't noticed how much the world in which it operated was changing.

Before the meeting in the GM boardroom started, I leaned over to Richard and commented that we had come a long way from the back room of the political campaign in Flint, though just 70 miles away, to the board room of the General Motors Corporation. We both smiled.

GM's market research… getting started and uncovering some startling history – the Buck Weaver Story

In 1985 when I joined GM, the impression I had about the enterprise, which was shared by the many people I talked to, was that it was primarily a manufacturing-based company that had an incredibly powerful position in the market place. The power of the organization structure developed by Alfred Sloan, the dominance of its brands, and its financial resources had contributed to its being a Fortune 100 company. There were, however, doubts being raised over the future of the enterprise.

As I was settling into my new job in the historic GM Building on Grand Avenue in Detroit, several of my new colleagues suggested I review the archived reports in the market research library. I wandered through the stacks and, on the very top shelf, almost out of reach, I found a series of bound annual reports from when the department was under the direction of Henry Grady 'Buck' Weaver. One covered 1934, the year of my birth, so I decided to thumb through it before moving on to the more current documents. It quickly became clear that 'Buck' Weaver had put into place the same sort of approach that I had just been hired to put in place 50 years later.

It is humbling to discover that principles you thought you helped develop were, in fact, well-understood and used by your predecessors. The discovery also made me wonder what caused GM to discontinue the path-breaking process that Weaver developed and what that decision said about the prospects for my plans. Weaver was a pioneer in market research and market-based decision-making. He wrote:

> Successful manufacturing rests upon a knowledge of natural laws on the one hand, and a knowledge of human needs on the other hand.[22]

I found out later, during discussions with Peter Drucker, that he worked closely with Weaver while conducting the research on GM that led to the publication of Drucker's Concept of the Corporation. Drucker

---

22   Weaver, 1931

said Weaver's contributions to GM went beyond market research. He recalled that Alfred Sloan, the early chairman and president of GM, had a very small group of what he referred to as 'Brains,' and Weaver was a member.[23]

The following excerpt from an interview[24] with John Sculley describes the late Steve Jobs's initial approach to product development in terms similar to those of Buck Weaver, but in the context of a much more dynamic and complex societal environment:

> *I didn't know really anything about computers nor did any other people in the world at that time. This was at the beginning of the personal computer revolution, but we both believed in beautiful design and Steve in particular felt that you had to begin design from the vantage point of the experience of the user.*

> *He always looked at things from the perspective of what was the user's experience going to be? But unlike a lot of people in product marketing in those days, who would go out and do consumer testing, asking people, "What did they want?" Steve didn't believe in that.*

> *He said, "How can I possibly ask somebody what a graphics-based computer ought to be when they have no idea what a graphic based computer is? No one has ever seen one before." He believed that showing someone a calculator, for example, would not give them any indication as to where the computer was going to go because it was just too big a leap.*

> *Steve had this perspective that always started with the user's experience; and that industrial design was an incredibly important part of that user impression. And he recruited me to Apple because he believed that the computer was eventually going to become a consumer product. That was an outrageous idea back in the early 1980s because people thought that personal computers were just smaller versions of bigger computers. That's how IBM looked at it.*

The discussion of business designs that are most appropriate to Jobs's approach to product development is discussed in Capability 3 in *Part 2* where the process used to develop OnStar is described.

---

23   Correspondence with Peter Drucker, February 27, 2003.

24   Sculley, 2010

The need to regain Weaver's lost legacy

How did Weaver fall into such obscurity? How did his incredible contribution to market research and GM end up hidden away on the top shelf of a small market research library in the same building where he made his valuable contributions? And why was GM rediscovering what it apparently already knew, 50 years after the original discovery?

Market factors tell much of the story. For the duration of World War II, GM stopped production of personal vehicles. In the period following the war, the American economy and the movement to the suburbs led to unprecedented demand for new vehicles. GM and other manufacturers were able to sell everything they made. This practice – coupled with belief in their success – led to an attitude of "we know what the consumer wants, better than the consumer knows – and we have the sales records to prove it!" This, of course, was the same attitude that existed at Xerox and Kodak. However, as the decades progressed, supply began to exceed demand in the American automobile market. As new competitors from overseas entered the market, customers suddenly had more options, and GM suffered. To get back on the road to recovery, GM once again had to get back to basics – as Weaver put it, "finding out what people like, doing more of it, finding out what people don't like, doing less of it."[25]

Meeting Harvey Bell

Based on my experience with the silver halide chemists at Kodak, I appreciated the importance of allowing people who actually design and make things to listen directly to customers, as a supplement to the information gathered by market research personnel. This approach proved to be important in 1988, as we were conducting a study aimed at understanding customer requirements for the *Pontiac Firebird* and *Chevrolet Camaro*.

An engineer working on the program, Harvey Bell, asked to observe our interviewing, and we took him along. He captured a deep level of understanding. Among other things, we were recording specific answers to questions regarding 'stopping distance' – that is, how long

---

25   Time Magazine, 1938, p. 66

it takes the car to stop after the driver steps on the brakes going 60 mph. As Harvey listened to customers talk about the sporty *Firebird* and *Camaro*, he understood that the ability to control the vehicle while braking was, for this particular type of customer, critical to overall satisfaction and confidence. Customers didn't just want to stop quickly; they wanted to feel that the car was under their control while doing so. With Harvey's insight, we began to understand that the traditional parameter of stopping distance was a necessary, but insufficient, measure for the potential buyers of these vehicles.

Using his knowledge of hydraulics and braking systems, Harvey took the customer's need to feel calm and assured and translated it into appropriate design requirements. In addition, his team created new measures for braking performance that were incorporated into subsequent GM brake testing and evaluation. The value of his efforts was publicly recognized when the newly designed braking systems were introduced. Following a test drive, a reviewer wrote in the Pennsylvania Times Leader on April 26, 1993, "The brakes, which provide terrific road feel and stopped the Z28 like an egg hitting the sidewalk, were helpful in New York's rush hour, but I appreciated them the most when a deer decided to say hello while I was on the interstate heading toward Virginia." The writer closed his story by saying, "See what happens when a car company listens to the people who buy their products."[26] Buck Weaver would have been proud.

Decision-makers (those who allocate resources) – and people who are responsible for innovation and design – need to engage in active listening

Because engineers are like anyone else who has a strong point of view, they also have a tendency to have a built-in bias and are also likely to hear what they want to hear. That is why you don't want people involved in operations doing their own market research. On the other hand, you don't want market research doing things that are not relevant for the people who are seeking to relate customer input into their 'deep' functional knowledge as they seek to satisfy the customer. You have to find the right balance between the insights of the operational groups and of market research.

---

26   Wasser, 1993

When market research is driven by functional interests, it is more likely to focus on confirming existing assumptions based on the long-held biases of those in that function; they want to show that they're right. There is, of course, value in that. The price you pay is that you diminish the chances of hearing something outside of the existing perspective that is also of value. That's where active listening comes in. Both focused and active listening have value, but neither is sufficient by itself.

Laying the groundwork for designing the equivalent of a Decision Loom

After my first encounter with Harvey, we would find reasons to meet often. During one of those subsequent meetings, he told me he was frustrated that:

- GM had spent a considerable amount of money on educating and training him to develop both 'cost' and 'performance' measurements to determine the optimum design of a vehicle or of a particular component of a vehicle.

- But that he could never get anyone to give him a revenue curve that he could relate to his understanding of cost and performance measurements so he could determine what customers would be willing to pay for alternative approaches to improving the vehicle or the component.

I told Harvey that, although what he was asking for was very difficult, we would try. The opportunity occurred in 1992 when Harvey became the chief engineer of the *Camaro Firebird* development team. One of his biggest concerns was that the 3.4-liter engine then being used in the cars didn't provide enough performance or technology. Given the sports car appearance of the vehicles and the aerodynamic design that was being developed, he referred to the vehicles as 'sheep in wolf's clothing.' In his mind, if GM really wanted to satisfy the targeted customers, the cars needed a higher-performance engine.

The rationale for just upgrading the existing 3.4-liter engine with some available new technology was cost savings: GM could use the unused capacity of its current production facilities, with minimum retooling, and would get economies of scale. The marketing divisions felt that, while a more powerful engine was desirable, pricing was so competitive at the time that customers wouldn't pay for the additional cost. The Chevrolet and Pontiac divisions felt that experience and past market research supported their belief.

Harvey sought evidence to support his hypothesis. He put the challenge to our group this way: "Don't tell me which engine to use in my car. Just describe the performance customers want, and let me know their willingness to pay. I'll use my knowledge and experience of engine development to take care of the details." Harvey and Buck Weaver would have really got along with each other.

Given the progress we had made in developing useful analytical tools and by expanding the capabilities of the Customer Decision Model we created what became known as the Marketing Dynamics Model (MDM) to attempt to address Harvey's challenge. The information used in MDM's analytics was collected using conjoint methodology, which breaks the vehicle down into a bundle of independent attributes. Customer responses to a series of trade-off questions generated scores that indicated how much customers would be willing to pay for various attributes and the extent to which the improvements could be priced so the program would return an acceptable profit.

The *Camaro Firebird* engineers used MDM to evaluate how their ideas for changes in performance and fuel economy would affect sales volume and customer satisfaction. In other words, would more customers see the value in the performance of a modified 3.8-liter V6 over the existing 3.4-liter V6? Would that increased customer value perception lead to greater sales and profits?

The synthesis of customer and engine performance data revealed that customers *would* pay more if engineers could provide simultaneous increases in both fuel economy and performance. The basis for this assessment was that many *Firebird* and *Camaro* customers couldn't afford a V8 sports car like the *Chevrolet Corvette* but still aspired to a higher-performance vehicle. The challenge to the engineers was to break the existing mindset that it would be very difficult to increase power and fuel mileage at the same time. Not only would they have to break the paradigm but they would have to do so at a price the customer was willing to pay.

Harvey and his team put their experience and imagination together and found a solution. They improved GM's very successful 3.8-liter V6 engine's 0-to-60 performance from 10 to 8.5 seconds and simultaneously increased composite fuel economy from 25 miles-per-gallon to 26.5 mpg. Following a thorough review with all the interested parties, the decision was made, with reasonable confidence, to introduce the 1996 *Camaro Firebird* with the modified 3.8-liter V6.

The results were clear: knowledge of customer preferences and the engineering team's imagination and creativity developed a successful new product

After the *Camaro Firebird* was launched in 1996, market research compared the satisfaction scores of the 1996 buyers of the cars with the new 3.8-liter engine to that of 1995 buyers of the cars with the existing 3.4-liter powertrain. The data spoke for itself.

Engine Feature	1995 3.4L	1996 3.8L	Points Improvement	% Increase Improvement
Freedom From Engine Noise	69.0	93.0	24.0	35%
Acceleration/Pickup	75.8	98.8	22.0	30%
Fuel Economy	52.7	66.7	14.0	27%
Smoothness of Idle	80.9	94.2	13.3	16%
Transmission Smoothness	81.5	91.8	10.3	13%
Freedom From Transmission Whine	81.7	94.4	7.7	16%

Harvey Bell, in a review of the program's performance, spoke for the launch team regarding the use of market research and decision support models: "The substantial increase in both performance satisfaction and fuel economy satisfaction is confirmation that MDM can be used to establish market-based targets simultaneously for fuel economy and performance, from which a business case can be established."

In this case, deep understanding of customer requirements and their willingness to pay for what they really wanted helped overcome significant differences of opinion between engineering, finance, and marketing functions. The key to the team's success was the manner in which they discussed the issues and the available information *together*, and then came up with a creative solution – with the customer's preferences considered throughout the dialogue – through a decision tool that synthesized consumer behavior with cost and performance knowledge.

Getting behind GM's version of the Kodak 'Silver Curtain'

Wayne Cherry, then Vice President of GM's Design Center, surprised me with a question in 1992. He wanted to know if I would be willing to move the market research group from the corporate headquarters in Detroit to the Design Center in the Detroit suburb of Warren. Wayne and I had a very good relationship, based on some research our group had conducted on his behalf. Still, the request was surprising because, before Wayne was put in charge, as the manager of the market research function, I always had to get special permission to get 'past the door' and into the Design Center studios to review new vehicle programs.

Without hesitation, I accepted his offer and our group became residents of the design center.

The importance of finding out the thinking process of the users of your information – walking in their shoes

After we moved in one floor above his office, Wayne had another request. This time, he asked if I would be willing to transfer Jeff Hartley, one of GM's more creative market researchers, to the design function so he could work on a day-to-day basis with the designers to better understand their information needs.

Jeff accepted the assignment with the objective of uncovering how designers thought about their jobs; how they viewed market research; and what they thought retail customers could tell them – all in the context of what influenced their designs.

He quickly found that, whereas market researchers thought in terms of PowerPoint presentations, designers thought in terms of 20-foot display boards of drawings and illustrations. Their knowledge of customers was based on popular magazines like *Car and Driver*. Designers were more likely to treat these publications as the truth, just as they accepted input from other designers. It was quite common to see a 20-foot board covered with sketches and *Car and Driver* excerpts. To his dismay, market research was nowhere to be found on the 20-foot boards.

He also found that designers only saw market research as 'customer clinics' were their almost finished ideas were shown in concept vehicles and customers were asked for their reaction. When the clinics were conducted and reported during the product development process, the designer felt that at that time there was little to learn and that clinics could only cause pain. Because of this, designers treated research as very fallible, making it easy to ignore research that didn't fit their chosen direction. Designers believed strongly that customers couldn't tell you what they would want in five years and hence were not a good source of input for today's decisions.

Additionally he found that designers had trouble digesting market research because reports tended to be quantitative, and designers think more about images than about numbers. In addition, market research didn't operate at the right level for designers. Research might conclude that exterior styling is important to a certain type of customer, but that wouldn't help a designer answer questions about what personality a car should have. At the time of Jeff's joining the Design Staff, market research did not have a good answer to that type of question.

Based on his experience, and with the trust-based relationship he had developed by becoming a part of the team, he learned that designers were inclined to be 'shooting ahead of the target,' producing cars that might not quite fit with where the market was at the time of their introduction. Jeff characterized such designs as having high reach but perhaps lower current appeal. He described the conflict by pointing out that a designer would be pleased to have achieved a high reach score for the more progressive customers, but because the design went beyond the comfort zone of most customers, the low average score would be interpreted as the design being unappealing. To get out of the 'this or that' dilemma, Andy Norton, now head of GM's Global Market Research, developed 'Reach-Appeal' charts to show how the two elements interacted, leading to a decision based on the right balance of reach *and* appeal.

As he was gaining a deeper appreciation of the designers' needs, the market research function was moving toward working with decision-makers to support decisions, rather than just reporting on their effect after the decisions were made. What we had to overcome was that many market researchers felt their job was to write the perfect research report, statistically sound and methodologically rigorous, elegant and well-presented. Generally, this resulted in having researchers spend two weeks after the completion of a study, fine-tuning the report. But in today's more dynamic world, while the market research group was writing the report, designers had moved on, based on their intuition and direction from their management. The marketing function was also forming its position, based on their viewing of the focus groups that the research group conducted. When the report was released, depending on the manner in which the results were communicated to all the parties, two very different results could occur:

- In the first situation, those involved in the decision would have differing interpretations of what to do about the agreed findings of the study. The resulting dialogue about how the alternative positions addressed the accepted findings of the study tended to be more constructive – helping the decision process because they sharpened ideas of how to address the 'agreed to' problem and often encouraged the use of the intuitive and experiential strengths of the participants.

- In the second situation, those involved would have failed to establish a common set of facts to interpret. Usually power, not merit, dictated the final decision – if a timely decision was made at all. This practice tended to be more destructive and ended up being both time-consuming and potentially costly.

Jeff's experience led to a profound change that would make the second outcome less likely. Researchers were instructed to share results with people in marketing and design prior to the first product review, rather than wait until a 'perfect' report could be prepared – much like the approached developed at Xerox when the information about the actual size of the market was presented and discussed in Episode 4. This approach allowed the data to be evaluated by designers at a time when it was fully relevant. In essence, Jeff had learned that it was market research's job to assist the designer's intuition by working with him –

not see our job as publishing 'report card' research reports. Our job was to help designers (and others) make the thousands of decisions they faced daily. The eventual goal was to get consumer research into the design studios to complement the insights gained from *Car and Driver*, etc. on the 20-foot boards.

Jeff's foray into the world of designers led to the development of new kinds of research that involved direct interaction between customers and designers, engineers, marketers, and planners – early enough in the vehicle-development process to have an impact on their efforts. Later we would find additional ways to gather information to address broader cross-functional needs. The importance of designing inquiry systems that assist decision-makers seeking support for intuitive insights, analytical approaches to help sort out alternatives, and approaches that encourage collaboration across functional groups, is addressed in Capability 4.

But some really bad news was coming. . .

The good news was that GM was getting better at using market information. The bad news was that GM was losing money...fast! Back in 1992, the company lost $4.8 billion, and the pension fund had a deficit of $21 billion. Part of the problem was that GM was locked into a 'make-and-sell' business design that relied on correctly predicting the type and volume of vehicles that would be accepted by consumers. This approach was highly successful following World War II and led to GM's pre-eminent position in the market place. That approach led to a very large manufacturing base that was becoming more costly due to increasing wages and retirement and health care costs. However, because the market requirements were changing rapidly and as there was an increase in the number of competitors, a radical change was required. An approach to considering the advantages of alternative business designs is discussed in Capability 3.

As the beginning of this Episode I drew a comparison between the incumbent Congressman from Michigan's 7th District, who was over confident of his re-election because of his past successes and chose not to worry about the young Republican challenger with his Harvard Business School background. The incumbent believed the challenger was not a good fit for the blue-collar district where the election was being held. In the same way, GM had ignored many of the changes that were occurring and that were having negative effects on the enterprise. As this Episode points out, the decision was made to improve GM's understanding of the market. But, it was also clear that we couldn't just improve our use of market information. We had to do more.

The primary lessons learned during my getting started at GM

Lesson	Description	Addressed in Part 2
[19] modified	Reach out beyond senior managers and actively engage engineers and scientists in the design of market research projects to improve their understanding and acceptance of those projects. Engage individuals who are willing to reach out to other engineers and designers to translate what you are finding into terms that they can not only understand but actually work with and suggest improvements to.	Capability 2 Capability 4
24	Walk in the shoes of an eventual user of information. The value is similar to the benefits of walking in the shoes of the respondent (as I did in Georgia).	Capability 1 Capability 4
25	It is OK to find out that some of your basic ideas are not new, as long as you seek ways to improve on the old ideas by understanding how they were used and employing new technology to further improve on them.	All of Part 2
26	Breaking an organization's habits developed during a successful past period requires direction from the leadership of the enterprise and a lot of hard work.	Capability 2 Capability 3

Episode 8: Learning How to Learn… while making improvements in very difficult times

In 1992 GM was reporting huge losses, and there was little evidence that enough was being done to reverse the problems facing the enterprise. The Board of Directors replaced the chairman and CEO and several other senior executives. Jack Smith, who had been running GM's international operations, became the CEO, and John Smale, former chairman and CEO of Procter & Gamble, became the non-executive chairman of the board. The two men knew they had to take immediate, decisive action to change direction, or risk going out of business. Jack said:

> Our problems had been building for decades, not overnight, as the North American market fragmented, and more and more competitors entered the arena. And we were still blind to the significance of the change.

Taking the first steps – stop the bleeding and lay the groundwork for a change in how GM developed and introduced new products

Jack now had a straightforward task: he had to stop the bleeding before he could even begin to think about positioning the company to grow once again. He took four main steps. He consolidated the organization; he changed product development, segmenting the market based on a clearer definition of customers' preferences; he moved to common processes; and he integrated the enterprise globally.

All of this required changes in my world, because GM had to change the way decisions were made across the organization. We had to respond better to the voice of the market, integrate the deep knowledge in the functional silos and reduce cycle time, if we were to reverse the worrisome plunge in the stock price.

Now that he was CEO, Smith announced the formation of the Strategic Decision Center to, in essence, as he would often say, "Avoid the tyranny of *or* and seek the opportunity of *and*." He wanted research, devoid of GM bias, that would improve management's understanding of how the market was developing, and to help GM engineers and designers look for and bring forward innovative ideas. To change how GM went about developing its vehicle programs, we identified the following five specific actions for our group:

1. Better align strategic and operational business plans

2. Improve management's understanding of complexity, uncertainty and opportunity in the market

3. Determine the required resources for knowledge development and clarify roles and responsibilities

4. Effectively capture ideas for innovative products and services

5. Develop organizational learning as a system.

Jack asked what I needed to ensure the success of the new group. My answer, based on the early advice I received as Census Director from Herman Kahn, as well as my experiences at Xerox and Kodak was: "Those who develop the strategy will implement it." I took this position because, since coming to GM in 1985, I had seen too many talented strategy teams work very hard on developing good plans, and then present them to a management team that was experienced and comfortable in the old ways of doing things. The result was that not many of the strategic plans were implemented.

In some ways this new assignment provided the opportunity to participate in the use of the information I was collecting – which provided insight into what I could do to improve the collection and use of information for decision-making.

The first strategic initiative: vehicle development

To improve our market position we realized that we would have to take on the difficult task of creating the right range of vehicles to meet the needs of each of our customers … at the right time … at the right price. After reviewing the limitations of past processes in addressing cross-functional and cross-marketing brand issues, it became clear that we would require a new way of looking at the problem and its potential solutions. In Ackoff's terms we had a very 'messy' problem, the solution to which would require significant improvements in getting agreement across the enterprise about what we knew and did not know.

Given that it was clear that GM would have to transform the organization's abundant and scattered mental models and functional resources into a unified, coherent course of action, our group worked with experts in Decision Analysis to 'reinvent' the process for GM. We ended up calling it the Dialogue Decision Process (DDP).[27] The DDP involved a series of structured dialogues between the two groups responsible for reaching a decision and implementing the associated course of action. It also dealt explicitly with the uncertainty and ambiguity that go hand-in-hand with decision-making. I made sure that our group would, in part, deal with the uncertainty to ensure we were using relevant information and were keeping track of the underlying assumptions supporting the decision being made.

In the DDP process the first of the two groups was the set of decision-makers that constituted the Decision Review Board. These senior executives were selected by the GM leadership. What they had in common was their authority to allocate resources: people, capital, materials, time, and equipment. In this case, the Decision Review Board was made up of executives representing Finance, Engineering, Manufacturing, Design, and Marketing. To make sure each of them believed their functional perspectives would be fairly considered in the day-to-day activities, they were asked to identify the personnel they wanted to appoint to the Multiple Function Decision Team that would be handling the development and analysis of the specific alternatives.

Once appointed to the decision team, the functional managers and specialists were asked to apply their functional expertise to ensure the problem we were working on was comprehensively framed, in turn ensuring that all of the functional perspectives would be considered in the identification of alternatives and guarantee a fair analysis of those alternatives that were selected. Although each member of the second group embodied the essence of what their functions knew, they were encouraged to work together and share their knowledge to create an improved level of mutual understanding.

---

27   GM Conducted over 50 DDPs. The initial effort was supported by Carl Spetzler and Steve Barrager of the Strategic Decision Group and Dan Owen and managed internally by Michael Kusnic.

This initial effort, called Vision 2000, led to a strategic decision that GM would benefit most by improving its line-up of vehicles in the middle market partition. As we began to implement that strategy it soon became clear that we would need to improve the way in which GM targeted its customers relative to its multiple brands in that part of the market.

Whenever possible, attempt to present the findings of your efforts in the form that is preferred by the decision-maker

One of the things I learned right away from my discussions with GM designers was that you cannot get a true sense from a two-dimensional drawing of what a vehicle will look like when completed… you need to see it in three dimensions. This belief initially led to the use of wooden three-dimensional models, then sculpted clay models and eventually to very dense Styrofoam models carved by computer-directed cutting wheels. This experience of looking at three-dimensional models led many GM executives to be most comfortable with three-dimensional visual models. Realizing that this embedded belief was held by most GM executives, Mike DiGiovanni, the Director of our Market Research group, built a physical market model of the newly developed segmentation scheme using an enlarged version of 'Lego blocks.' The segmentation model was shown in two rows and within each of the needs segments we displayed the age distribution using three colors to describe the baby boom generation and the generations that preceded and followed them. The first row displayed the segments and GM's distribution across the segments as they were at that time. The second row displayed our estimate of how the segments would look in ten years. The two rows were forty feet long, fifteen feet wide and, depending on the number of customers in the needs segment, almost four feet high.

This allowed the executives to walk into and around the segments so they could see how GM's strength in the older pre-boomer generation could become a problem when that generation of buyers was displaced by the baby boomers (who were less likely to choose GM) and the generation following them.

Single- and double-loop learning

We made it a practice that I would serve on all the Dialog Decision Process Review Boards to observe and learn how to improve the process and make sure the content that was needed for future activities would be available as well as making sure that what was learned would be available to the next activity. Again, without knowing it at the time, we were practicing what Chris Argyris called 'double-loop learning.' To Argyris, doing one DDP well would be the equivalent to 'single-loop learning.' Once completed, the errors in thinking and practices were detected and corrected and changes were made to implement the program in an improved manner.

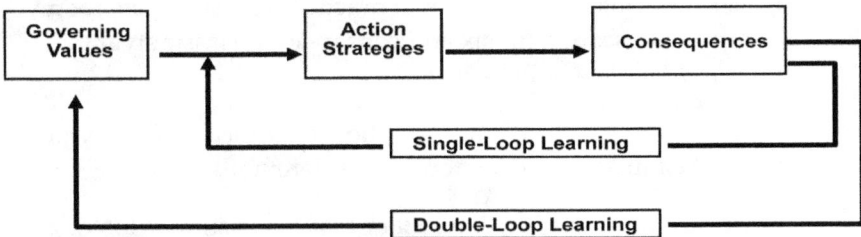

Figure 1: Argyris' concept of single- and double-loop learning

But while this type of learning, as it was in GM's Vision 2000 project, is very important, it doesn't help transfer learning across the organization. Only those involved in the original problem gain anything. And so we also need 'double-loop learning.' Besides detecting and correcting errors, double-loop learning encourages the organization to actively question and modify existing values, norms, procedures, policies and objectives. An example occurred in implementing the first new vehicle program under the new product portfolio.

The MS2000 program… double-loop learning

The first program incorporating the directions determined in Vision 2000 was the MS2000 program. This was a major program that used one vehicle platform to produce cars for multiple brands: the *Pontiac Grand Prix, Buick Century* and *Regal, Oldsmobile Intrigue,* and *Chevrolet Impala* and *Monte Carlo*. Given the success and what we learned from applying the Dialogue Decision Process to Vision 2000 it was determined that we would apply the process and its findings to this program as well.

These vehicles replaced the earlier vehicles that were not as well received by targeted customers, who often purchased the *Ford Taurus*, *Toyota Camry* and *Honda Accord*. Each of the vehicles in the MS2000 program was to be more highly targeted at a group of customers who had expressed their needs in such a manner as to separate them from other customers in the midsize market.

The vehicles introduced in 1997-99 were targeted to needs-based categories of customers as follows:

- Segment Mid 1 – Family Affordability: *Buick Century* – consumers looking for value in a practical vehicle. Open, roomy interior with seating for six and conservative, classic styling. *Chevrolet Impala* would be introduced later.

- Segment Mid 2 – Basic Transportation: *Chevrolet Malibu* – which was to be introduced later and off a different platform.

- Segment Mid 3 – Family Fun: *Buick Regal* – consumers looking for a roomy car that doesn't compromise the appearance and security of a more performance-oriented sedan – it had to provide the power to pass and merge with confidence. *Oldsmobile Intrigue* – consumers wanting elegant, sophisticated styling (not too sporty) with commensurate performance (premium powertrain). They are willing to pay for the right luxury options.
  The *Chevrolet Monte Carlo* – would be introduced as a coupe later.

- Segment Mid 4 – Upscale sports: *Pontiac Grand Prix* – consumers who were car enthusiasts in the mid-size market who want sporty styling, power and the feel of the road (a driver-oriented car). They saw the need for a sedan (easier entry for the occasional extra passenger) but preferred a coupe.

Each of the vehicle development teams immersed themselves in the information GM had collected on each of the segments and went into the field to get a better feel for how existing GM and competitive vehicles were meeting the needs expressed by the consumers for whom they were designing their vehicles.

Sometimes the distinctions between segments were quite subtle. For example, the 'Mid 4 – Upscale Sports' segment epitomized the car enthusiast, the type of person who made it clear that "my car is me!" This type of person felt so strongly about the personalization of their vehicle that they wanted the driver's area to resemble an airplane cockpit, with all the instruments within easy reach of the 'pilot.' The outward appearance had to be sleek. If the outward appearance compromised the comfort of the back seat passengers, customers in this segment would say, "Too bad, if it is too uncomfortable, don't get in." Customers in the 'Mid 3 – Family Fun' segment felt the same way about the performance of their vehicle, but because of their family values they would not compromise the comfort of the back seat for the appearance of the vehicle.

Fred Schaafsma, who at the time was the program manager for the *Pontiac Grand Prix* – targeted at the Mid 4 segment – exemplified the application of the principle that the *value of information is in how the user reacts to and takes advantage of it*. After spending time understanding what distinguished the customers in his segment from customers in other GM mid-size segments, he proclaimed, "I get it... my customers aspire to the equivalent of a four-door *Porsche* at a *Pontiac* price." Staying true to the vision, Schaafsma, working with the Design Staff team, directed that the roof line on the four-door sedan Grand Prix be exactly the same as the *Grand Prix* two-door coupe.

The intense involvement of the vehicle teams in market place settings with targeted customers also revealed several unarticulated needs that were heard by the vehicle engineers. During other on-site discussions with customers, the *Grand Prix* team was able to determine what the customers in their segment meant by the term *performance*. Within their segment, it was primarily about how the vehicle felt when starting out, or, as the engineers described it, 'launch feel.' The engineers rode with customers to understand the feel that customers actually wanted, instead of trying to attempt to translate their words into performance characteristics.

What the MS2000 program did for GM

In 1990, GM had a 31.3% share of the market for mid-size cars. That was the good news. The bad news was that the costs required for the 20 different models to achieve that share made the entire segment unprofitable. GM was violating an important rule of thumb. That rule says that a company's percentage share of a market segment should at least equal the percentage of the product entries the company has in that segment. But, in 1990, GM's 20 mid-size cars represented 42% of the mid-size cars on sale in the USA, far exceeding its 31.3% share of sales. As we learned in the Vision 2000 project, GM was not making effective use of capital and human resources, because it was developing GM cars that competed with other GM cars.

By 2001, because of changes relating to the MS2000 program, GM reduced its mid-size product entries from 20 to 7, resulting in GM having just 21.1% of the cars on sale in the U.S. market. As expected, GM's market share dropped – from 31.3% to 23.4%. But GM's ratio of vehicle entries to market share effectiveness had improved dramatically from .75 (31.3% market share divided by 42% of entries) to 1.1.(23.4% market share divided by 21.1% of entries). The change to highly differentiated cars targeted at specific customer needs not only helped GM operate more efficiently but also hurt competitors that pursued a 'one car fits all' approach, as the following chart shows:

MARKET-SHARE-EFFECTIVENESS RATIOS (Market Share/Share of Entries)

	GM	Ford	Toyota	Honda
1991	0.75	1.73	1.38	2.19
2001	1.10	1.44	1.31	1.36
Differences	+.35	-.29	-.07	-.83

Tradeoffs needed to be made here. No one wanted to cede that much market share, but it was so important at the time to cut costs that the focus on efficiency was appropriate, and cutting to seven mid-size models produced other important benefits. The models, by focusing on customer needs, were more attractive than their predecessors and helped produce major improvements in productivity and quality.

Determining the value of the 'quietness' attribute

Between 2001 and 2003, Andy Norton, who had become the head of GM Market Research, worked with the Vehicle Performance Engineering staff to conduct a series of three studies that attempted to measure the impact of 'quiet' interiors on vehicle preference, and tried to quantify the willingness of consumers to pay for reduced sound levels. To execute these studies, consumers were invited to a facility with a driving simulator which allowed the team to vary the level of interior sound, and to vary the ride characteristics of a vehicle. Consumers evaluated different sound and ride characteristics in the simulator, and participated in a conjoint exercise to identify preferences and willingness to pay. In some cases, only one variable was changed in the simulator, but consumers were still asked to rate all variables, even ones that did not change.

The results of these studies were quite powerful, and surprising. First, the studies showed that in the segments tested (Large, Mid and Luxury Cars as well as Mid-Size SUVs) consumer preference for vehicles overall was strongly affected by the level of sound in the interior. Quieter cars had significantly higher share in the conjoint model results. Additionally, the estimated price that consumers were willing to pay for a quieter interior was up to $500 dollars. This seemed logical to the team. What was surprising, however, was that when only the level of sound in the simulator was varied, other attributes that did not change also received significantly changed ratings from consumers. Consumer ratings for vehicle ride moved almost in lock step with the ratings for vehicle sound, even when the actual ride attributes in the simulator were unchanged ($R2 = .94$). Additionally, consumers rated the vehicle with the quieter interior as a higher quality vehicle. Clearly, changes in sound levels had an impact on several important attributes for consumers.

The first application of these insights was in a mid-sized Buick SUV (*Rainier*) which received several engineering changes that made the interior quieter. This added cost to the vehicle over similar SUVs, but the price achieved in the market was significantly higher than the cost of these changes. Additionally, following its introduction, the *Buick Rainier* won the J.D. Power APEAL award in its first year in the market.

This first application was so successful from a cost/value/profit perspective that GM began to apply this new level of understanding to all new vehicle programs. Today, virtually all of GM's vehicle offerings are significantly quieter than their predecessors and competitors, and it has been a significant factor in driving the volume and profit success of GM's new entries in the marketplace.

The value of information is found in its use!

The successful MS2000 experience and determining the value of the quietness attribute does not mean that understanding customer segmentation or preferences leads to improved sales and greater profitability. What it does mean is that information about customer needs, combined with the creative minds of an enterprise's human resources, can assist decision-makers in determining what a future product and service portfolio should be across a full range of possible operating environments.

The value of double-loop learning

The value of double-loop learning was further exemplified when Joe Spielman, who headed up Vision 2000, was put in charge of developing the 1997 model year *Corvette* with the added management challenge to build the "Best *Corvette* Yet." In this case Joe was faced with resolving differences between three groups. One group (the engineers) wanted a vehicle that in their terms "had the right stuff." They wanted a *Corvette* that would perform as well as any other sports car – even those that cost considerably more. Another group (the marketing organization) thought that they would be able to sell more of a "kinder, gentler" *Corvette*... like one that had a trunk to carry things and was easy to get in and out of. A third group (the finance organization) wanted to keep the costs down so that GM could continue to make a profit on each *Corvette* sold as it had been doing for some time.

In this example, Joe's experience with MS2000 led him to adapt the process to allow the three perspectives to demonstrate the value of their position. The discussion that ensued, when each party better understood why the other two groups took the position they did, produced a solution that was far greater than the sum of each of the initial strongly held individual perspectives. Making full use of their previous experience with the process, the team met the challenge placed on them of building "the best *Corvette* yet." In March, 2000, the Society of Automotive Engineers selected the C4 *Corvette* "the best engineered car of the 20th Century." Incidentally, GM also made a profit on the program!

These lessons apply to many other industries where competition is intense and market segmentation and customer preferences are more complicated than it may have appeared in the past.

In the next Episode we discuss the steps that Jack Smith and Rick Wagoner started to take when it began to look like GM would, for the moment, 'stop the bleeding.'

The primary lessons learned from working on transforming the vehicle business

Lesson	Description	Addressed in Part 2
27	There are significant benefits to be gained in the concept of double-loop learning. Observing the results of previous experiences, particularly how people with deep functional knowledge improved their use of market information, suggested effective ways to determine the purpose of the research project and to improve the eventual use of market research activities.	The Decision Loom
28	If it is fully engaged with eventual users, market research can provide timely – but approximate – information… rather than more time-consuming, detailed reports designed to demonstrate the market researcher's knowledge and command of the standard procedures.	Capability 4

Episode 9: Because the Future is Uncertain...
Learn to create the future you want.

As GM was working itself through the 'Stop the Bleeding' process, we created an organization within the Strategic Initiatives Group called the Envisioning Network. We did so because of what we had been seeing and hearing about the emergence of the 'digital economy' while attending conferences like TED (Technology, Entertainment and Design). In discussions with Jack Smith and his leadership team, we decided we needed to consider changes in society at large, including customer needs, political realities, economics and many other factors. Given that GM had made a partial recovery, based on cost containment and a more focused vehicle development process, we would look into the implications of what an uncertain future might mean to GM.

The process started with the development of four future scenarios that represented a full range of possible external environments that could affect GM. The eventual goal of the process was to evaluate the extent to which GM's long-term plans were sufficiently robust and flexible to let it operate profitably in any of the scenarios. Management would determine the extent to which current long-term plans were sufficient and would identify actions to strengthen any weak spots. The four scenarios GM developed in 1994 were:

- *Momentum* – The key assumption was that the market would stay unchanged for 30 years; only incremental changes would have value. The basis for this assumption was that historically the future has been evolutionary. Only occasionally is it revolutionary.

- *Technology Reigns* – The key assumption was that society would come to expect all problems to be solved by technical innovations. 'Highest Tech' products would be valued by customers, who would expect any limitations of existing products to be overcome. This scenario further assumed environmentally friendly innovations and decreased travel time, despite having more vehicles on the road.

- *Environmental Domination* – The key assumption was that CO2 emissions would be socially unacceptable and that alternatives to fossil fuels would not prove to be feasible. It was further assumed that scientists would demonstrate that CO2 was causing the environment to deteriorate and that pollution reduces human longevity.

- *Geopolitical Realignment* – The key assumption was that economic factors would drive the formation of new geopolitical trading groups throughout the world and that, in general, business and trade considerations would increasingly drive the actions of national governments.

The purpose of including a 'Momentum' strategy (or, as some described it, the Status Quo) was that it forced the group to make an explicit documentation of the assumptions underlying the current strategy.

Based on the scenarios and considerable follow-up work, particularly on the 'least likely' environmental domination scenario, GM established some long-term priorities, including work on successors to the internal-combustion engine.

The Envisioning Network process did help prepare GM for the high gas prices of recent years, by getting management to consider circumstances that they wouldn't have otherwise considered likely and by getting them to invest in research that would otherwise not have been approved. This led to R&D investments like low-cost hybrid propulsion, fuel cells, and clean fuels. GM engineers and product developers say the initial work, started at the end of the 20th Century, contributed to the development of the Chevrolet Volt. The Volt is an extended-range electric car that has put GM in the forefront of environmentally friendly vehicle transportation.

Sometimes it's not the answers but the process of reaching them that reveals an unarticulated need that you're in a position to satisfy

While the Strategic Analysis Scenario effort was going on, GM participated in a consortium research project study led by Patti Hawkins on key factors that drove buying decisions. The study measured both the importance consumers placed on these factors and their current level of satisfaction with how these factors were being addressed in the market place.

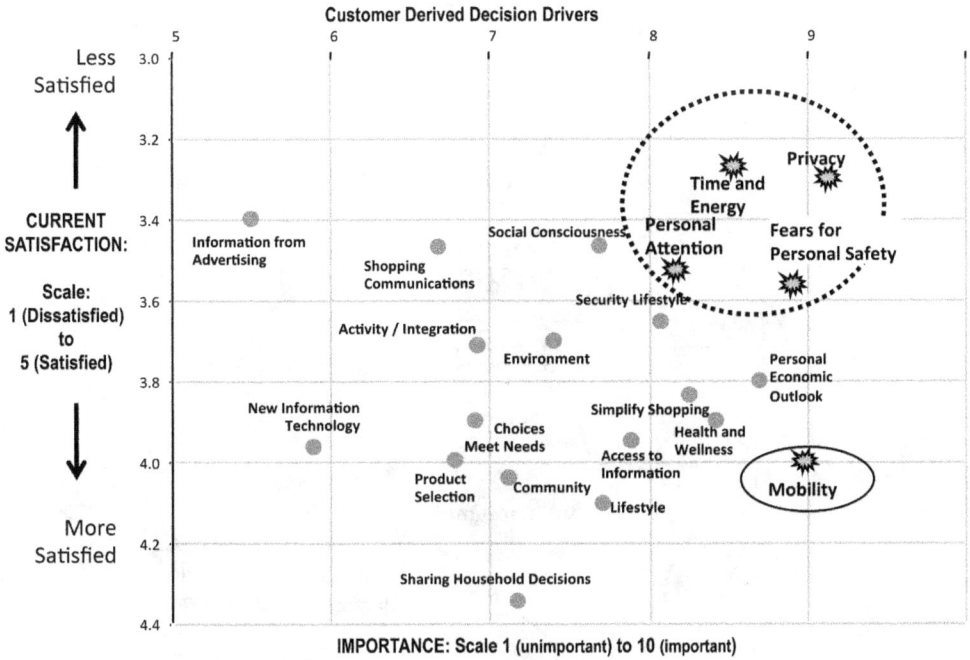

Figure 2: Developing a hypothesis from what appeared to be unrelated facts

The results revealed 22 key factors. Figure 2 displays how consumers rated those factors on two dimensions – importance on the horizontal dimension and their current satisfaction on the vertical axis. Because GM was interested in identifying important areas for which customers were dissatisfied, the vertical scale puts dissatisfaction at the top of the vertical axis. The position of these factors led us to infer a potentially unarticulated need – though not at first glance.

Mobility, the ability to go where you want to go, when you want to go – a factor at the heart of GM's traditional business – was located in the lower right corner. Consumers rated it an important need that was being well met. When presented with this type of information, the traditional response at GM – and probably many other companies – would have been, "We have done a very good job in meeting customer requirements. Let's stay focused on what we are currently doing, because it works. If it's not broke don't fix it!"

However, there were four other, interesting factors located in the upper right corner, meaning they were also among the most important but not well-served. They were:

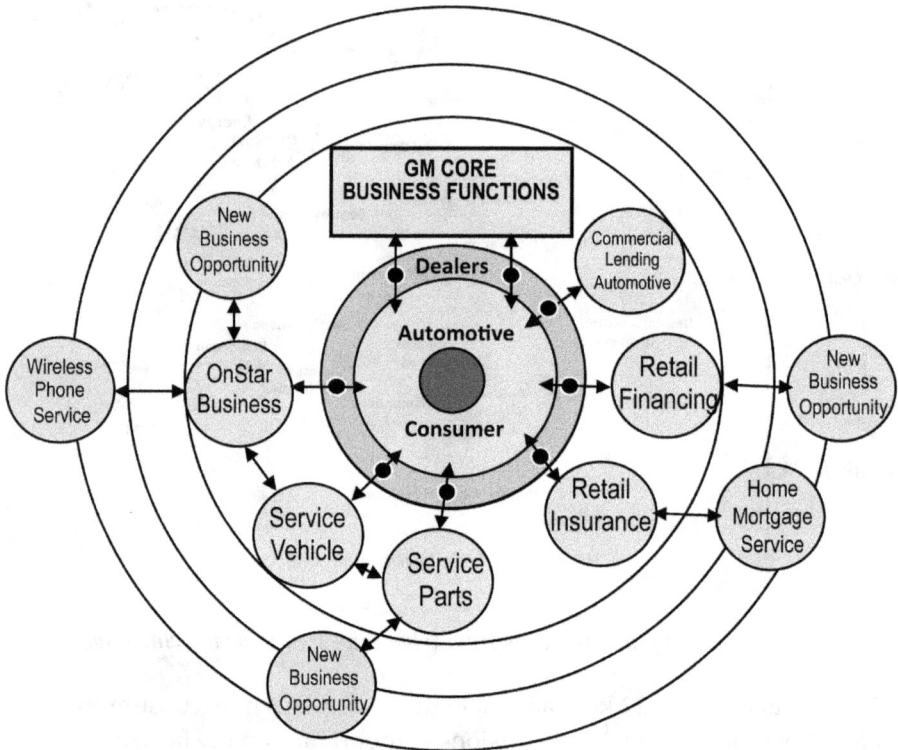

Figure 3: Extended customer relationship business design

With the concept of an extended customer relationship in mind we then conducted an analysis of total spending in the acquisition and use of a vehicle. The analysis indicated that there was almost twice as much total revenue and profit opportunity in moving downstream after the vehicle was sold than there was in staying where GM currently did the majority of its business. But Rick Wagoner made it clear that in no way could this strategy relieve anyone from improving the manner in which we currently performed the core business. This point was highlighted in a presentation which included the statement, "The worst thing that could happen is have a potential customer say, I want the services, but do I have to buy your car to get them?"

In all, we now had four strands that we were trying to weave together into a more meaningful fabric to present to potential customers:

- The four scenarios (Momentum, etc.) that had prompted us to think about alternative investment opportunities.

- The knowledge that showed what customers valued but weren't receiving from car companies, which led us to think abductively[28] about opportunities for mobile services.

- The model of an extended business design, which was helping us sort through new opportunities, especially for services closely tied to our core automotive business.

- Recognition of the possibilities for easy sharing of information and for collaboration with other enterprises, as well as the growing power of information.

Having been introduced to the concept of digital killer apps by Chunka Mui, it was now time to implement a digital strategy.[29]

Testing the water with an external review

To test the value of our proposed strategy we shared it with Peter Drucker, who provided an analysis of a new operating business he called 'GM the Merchant.' Several important trends were highlighted in his 26-page response which highlighted what he saw as the value of migrating from manufacturing to services.

> *The steady decline in terms of trade for manufacturing. Manufacturing is now where Agriculture was around 1950… The trend is clear. It means that manufacturing is producing less and less wealth.*

---

28   While reviewing material and discussion around Design Thinking I heard Roger Martin use the term abduction for the first time. It is a form of logical inference that generally precedes induction and deduction and for which the colloquial term is a 'hunch.' It is often associated with viewing a set of seemingly unrelated facts whilst armed with an intuition that they are somehow related.

29   Downes & Mui, 1998, p. 54

As I read your memorandum, it proposes to complement GM the Manufacturing Company with GM the Merchant. A Manufacturing Company makes products and then sells them. A Merchant is a buyer for the customer…

The Realities strongly support your proposal to add to GM the Manufacturer the new business of GM the Merchant. In fact, the Realities imply that this is one way in which GM can convert the demographic trends, the trend in the terms of trade for manufacturing, and the saturation of the market, into sources of profitability and in fact into sources of growth.

Drucker concluded with some ideas on how to get started.

In fact, I would say the uncertainties of the new venture are so great – and so unprecedented – that further 'studies' would be futile. Only the actual experience of a number of pilots can show what the real problems are, where the real decisions have to be made, which specific structures, procedures and policies are likely to be most successful, and which, no matter how intelligent they look, do not meet the test of reality.

Overall, there was a strong emphasis on being customer relationship centric, focusing on the consumer experience, and establishing a dialogue with the consumer and communities of interest.

The first prototype – OnStar

Under the basic strategy of extending GM's relationship with the customer, the *OnStar* customer service was the most successful of the initial steps taken by GM in implementing its downstream revenue strategy. In its final form, *OnStar* has provided Personal Attention, while Saving Time and Energy, reducing Fears for Personal Safety, and operating within customers' comfort zone on Privacy. Today it is addressing many of the needs of GM's customers and the challenges identified by our external consultants.

Keep a decision record of the reasons why you choose not to do something – if some of them change, revisit the decision

The history of *OnStar* can be traced back to 1993, when EDS and PacBell proposed that GM build a land-based, microwave mobile communication system that would partner GM with an information services company and a cellular company. We put together an evaluation team headed by Steve Carlisle. Steve and his team evaluated the opportunity and their initial analysis found customers to be interested, even though they weren't quite sure exactly how the system would benefit them. They also determined that the capital costs of installing the necessary microwave towers would be so high that the decision was made not to proceed.

In 1994, EDS came back; this time with GM's other subsidiary, the Hughes Corporation. The new idea was to provide a space-based infrastructure that required significantly less capital to get started because the necessary satellites were already in orbit. We decided to proceed on a limited basis.

The initial *OnStar* prototype was introduced on the 1997 Model Year *Cadillac Seville* and Deville as a dealer-installed product that connected the vehicle to a live advisor at a call center. From the very beginning the *OnStar* customer benefit was focused on safety and security, one of the four factors identified as being important but not well served. *OnStar* automatically alerted emergency services if an airbag deployed, indicating an accident. GM's externally mounted and larger antenna, as well as the higher power output of the *OnStar* system, allowed the driver to connect to distant cell towers in areas where normal handheld phones could not get service. The factor of personal attention would be addressed by other services like finding and making reservations at hotels and restaurants.

With some innovative ideas it is sometimes better to ask, "What will it take to make this product successful?" rather than, "Given what I can 'estimate,' what are the chances this product will be successful?"

During my discussions about *OnStar* with Peter Drucker, he reminded me of an observation that he made in, *Managing in a Time of Great Change*: "One cannot make decisions for the future. Decisions are commitments to action. And actions are always in the present, and in the present only. But actions in the present are also the one and only way to make the future." (I have taken this same observation as the theme for Capability 3 in *Part 2* of the book.)

By the same token we decided that *OnStar* had the potential to be a success – perhaps even a great success – but we would have to put the service in place and let customers actually use it to determine its true potential. In a sense we had decided to use the approach used by Steve Jobs as described by John Sculley earlier: Jobs took the position that product design "…always started with the user's experience."

Knowing that consumers would have little to no experience with the *OnStar* concept, it was clear we would have to develop prototypes. We weren't going to know enough if we just interviewed potential customers, describing *OnStar* to them in ways they seemed to be having trouble understanding. I suggested to then COO Rick Wagoner that, in essence, he would need to expend some resources to obtain an 'option' on a future activity that had the possibility of becoming quite valuable. Rick accepted the option rationale and directed that we determine the most efficient and effective way to get *OnStar* into our future vehicles. To ensure *OnStar* kept both an internal and external perspective, GM selected Chet Huber from the GM locomotive division to head *OnStar*. *OnStar* established the following objectives:

- To provide these new services at prices low enough to attract a large subscriber base, GM would factory-install the hardware in many of its vehicles, rather than making *OnStar* an option that dealers could add (resulting in much higher installation costs). We made this decision knowing that many who bought cars equipped with *OnStar* capability would not subscribe to the service.

- GM would create within *OnStar* the resources to encourage and develop alliances with third parties.

- To maximize the use of the *OnStar* call centers and to maintain consistency in the manner in which mobile services were being provided throughout the industry, GM would encourage other companies to install *OnStar* in their vehicles.

- GM and Toyota would work together to build a consortium that would ensure that there were industry-wide standards for telematics hardware, software and communications.

With basic objectives identified, Nick Pudar was given the assignment to put together a team to develop a Factory Installation strategy that would meet the objectives and create a basis for the option on a 'future' business model I had discussed with Rick Wagoner. Pudar, with Ackoff's teachings as background, began the process by getting multiple functions within GM and *OnStar* to describe the idealized design of what a factory-installed execution should be. In addition to the elements listed above, Pudar also focused on the implementation timing as a factor in the idealized design. We aimed to have *OnStar* fully factory-installed on all GM vehicles for the 2000 Model Year lineup. This seemed unrealistic as the product development community could not conceive how they could possibly meet the timing requirement. Experience led them to believe that one vehicle model might be ready for factory installation for the 2005 model year; the product development cycle was too intensive, and the *OnStar* electrical architecture integration made this a much more challenging problem. However as appreciation of OnStar's value to GM increased, there emerged a strong desire by almost everyone to bring it to market as soon as possible.[30] The team came to appreciate that the *OnStar* service could serve as the basis of a 'platform' of extended services that could improve our return on the capital already invested in the vehicle. As one of the engineers described it, "It's like having a cash register in the car. Every time someone uses the service the cash register rings and GM gets an incremental return on its investment."

If GM had limited itself to traditional capital-based budgeting, it never would have been able to justify the investment in *OnStar* that made it such a success. Taking an option on the future visualized through the principles of Ackoff's concept of idealized design produced a business of nearly six million subscribers. Since *OnStar's* inception 15 years ago, *OnStar* Advisors have:

- Unlocked nearly 6 million car doors

- Delivered more than 95 million Turn-by-Turn navigation routes

- Responded to nearly 200,000 vehicle crashes

- Provided nearly 3 million subscribers with roadside assistance

- Located more than 59,000 stolen vehicles

---

30   Barabba, Huber *et al.*, 2002.

In addition, 4.2 billion minutes of hands-free calling have been purchased.

In 2009, *OnStar's* market value was estimated at between $2 and $4 billion. Not a bad return on the approximately $150 million option that GM's executives placed in 1996.[31]

The second prototype – MyProductAdvisor

As noted earlier, GM's participation in conferences like TED provided insights into the emergence of the digital economy. But in addition to generating ideas about creating new opportunities like *OnStar*, we also learned how to improve our approach to finding out customer preferences.

In 2000, I attended a conference where Mohan Sawhney, of the Kellogg Business School at Northwestern University, introduced the concept of a Metamarket. He said these "markets in our minds" are clusters of related activities that consumers engage in to satisfy a distinct set of needs. He said the Internet, by lessening the need for buyers and sellers to have close physical proximity, was creating the opportunity for new Metamarkets like Web MD, and Edmunds.com. He laid out some characteristics of Metamarkets:

- They derive from activities that are closely related in the minds of customers.

- They are not created by firms in related industries because firms are not always organized to provide joint services and figure out who receives what percent of the profits.

They can be organized around major assets, major interests, major life events or major business processes. There could be a Metamarket for weddings that would include the clothes for the bride and groom, wedding reception arrangements, the trip and hotel accommodations for the honeymoon, etc. Edmunds.com serves as a Metamarket for automobile sales and after sales activities.

---

31   In two Harvard Business School Case Studies (Christensen & Roth, 2001), Clay Christensen and Erik Roth provide an external assessment of *OnStar's* development.

He also offered a keen observation about why businesses often miss the opportunities in Metamarkets: "Consumers think in terms of activities, while firms think in terms of product."

It was encouraging that Sawhney's observations were congruent with GM's thinking about new businesses. What was different and quite challenging, however, was that Sawhney took the position that the best way to gain the consumer's trust – to fully engage the consumer – was to have a third party act as an intermediary between GM and the customer – firms like Edmunds and Kelly Blue Book. He referred to that intermediary as a 'Metamediary.' This raised some profound questions, given that GM believed it could be a trusted agent making the life of our customers easier. Mohan's insistence on a 'Metamediary' eventually led us to ask the fundamental question: What would it take for us to be a trusted intermediary?

Applying Buck Weaver's principles (developed in the early 20th Century)

To move GM to a position where we would be perceived as a trusted advisor, in this case for the purchase of the vehicle itself, we took a radical conceptual step: we began to think, as Drucker suggested, like a Merchant Company. Rather than setting up a selling proposition for just GM vehicles, we would help the customer buy what he or she wanted – even if it wasn't a GM vehicle. Because even if it wasn't a GM purchase, we'd learn a lot about what customers wanted and why some weren't buying from us. We'd know more than our competitors did and be able to fix problems and spot trends sooner than they could.

Getting from an idea, no matter how good the idea, to an effective implementation of the idea is not always easy

After some discussion it was recommended that a 'Trusted Advisor' group develop a solution that directly challenged the assumption that an independent party is required to achieve a level of trust in the acquisition of a vehicle.

We also supported the work of Glen Urban at MIT in his development of a system called Truck Town. It was an Internet-based system in which a customer could call up a virtual advisor and discuss with the advisor their preferences and, based on the information, the advisor would recommend a particular truck.

One of the key findings in Glen's work was participant's reaction to interacting with the virtual advisors. More than 75% of Truck Town's visitors said that they trusted these virtual advisors more than the traditional communication methods. This finding was instrumental in GM coming to the conclusion that honesty implied by the unbiased conduct of the virtual advisors would be a critical component in any Internet trust-building program.

In a later article,[32] Glen pointed to the benefits of 'listening in' as customers communicated with the virtual advisor their preferences for certain attributes. This reinforced an evolving concept that was being developed internally within GM.

The eventual recommendation technology was developed by Dick Smallwood using a new application of Bayesian inference to the modeling of shopper values.

Once some basic questions have been answered, the advisor asks users to rank their priorities. Do they care most about price range, or are other attributes most important? Is body style an important consideration, or would they prefer better fuel economy?

To guarantee an unbiased response to the shopper's answers, the measurable characteristics of each vehicle in the system come from an independent company that provides these services to the automotive industry. Furthermore, the information on vehicle quality comes from J. D. Power & Associates, a market research company specializing in measuring customer satisfaction.

Because trust is so important, the site makes it clear that the information consumers provide will remain confidential. No representative will contact them about their responses unless they ask for the contact. The individual information is aggregated so that personal information is anonymous – the site had no persistent cookies and required no registration.

---

32   Urban & Hauser, 2003

AutoChoiceAdvisor.com becomes MyProductAdvisor.com

To address the initial and lingering concerns about any publicity that our service (called *AutoChoiceAdvisor*) could possibly cause GM to recommend a competing vehicle on its own website, and to reach out to a broader consumer base, a decision was made in 2004 to transfer the management of the website to the Market Insight Corporation and it was named *MyProductAdvisor.com*, since it would now allow the consumer to consider additional product categories like television sets, lap top computers, and digital cameras.

The advisor allows shoppers to rate the desirability and importance of product attributes and then uses the Bayesian inference techniques developed by Dick Smallwood to transform these ratings into estimates of 'willingness-to-pay' for the attributes. This inferential process uses an amalgamation of past shopper ratings as the starting point for characterizing the shopper's willingness-to-pay. These willingness-to-pay estimates allow the advisor to rank approximately 400 vehicle models.

In September 2008, the American Marketing Association presented the EXPLOR award for "the best research application that leverages technology in the most innovative fashion" to GM and the Market Insight Corporation because of *MyProductAdvisor.com*. Harvey Bell, at the time Executive Director, Global Advanced Vehicle Development at GM, commented:

> The system provides the Advanced Vehicle Development group at GM with an unprecedented and timely view of consumer preferences as well as accurate market performance simulations for projected new products. It has guided many major product design and development decisions by allowing us to move directly from consumer research to product design. It is now widely used throughout the corporation.

Using Dynamic Modeling to look at expected changes in the distribution channel

Our group took on a very important assignment to determine the impact that new and used-car superstores like AutoNation and CarMax could have on GM. These stores offered a large selection of new and nearly new, low-mileage cars that had warranties, roadside-assistance plans, and services normally available to new car buyers. Sales for these new stores, only six years old, grew to $13 billion in 1998.

The superstores and Internet companies were claiming they would alter the relationship between the automotive producer and the customer, and GM management needed to know how to respond to inquiries from the press and analysts. GM, like most automotive manufacturers, considered itself to be in the new-vehicle business and felt others would handle the sale of used cars. This attitude was based on the fact that most buyers of new vehicles, up to that time, were keeping their cars, on average, for more than six years and that most used cars were, thus, poor substitutes for new cars.

We were given very little time to complete the analysis. I said we would take on the assignment, but we would need continuous access to the key managers working on the problem. With that commitment, we started what was referred to as the '20 Day' project.

For the project, Nick Pudar put together a team that gathered all the previous information and knowledge that was available and, based on his work as a student with John Sterman at MIT and with the assistance of Mark Paich, developed an initial simplified systems dynamics model – including the ability to observe the interactions of new and used cars. The model also tracked the movement of vehicles from production through initial sale or lease, trade-in, the used car market and, ultimately, scrapping. It also tracked customers moving into and out of the market and included a simple consumer choice model for the new/used purchase decision.[33]

As the management team reviewed the model, it was puzzled as to the source of superstores' large inventories of attractive, late-model cars. Making full use of the updated, more comprehensive model that had been developed, the team ran simulations that revealed an unexpected finding – GM was providing the inventory. It was a classic example of what can happen when management is not focused on managing the interaction of the parts, but on managing the parts taken separately.

GM's sales organization used GM's then finance arm, GMAC, to provide attractive leases. Rates on these leases were dropping, partly

---

33   Sterman, 2000. This example is more comprehensively covered in Barabba, 2004, pp. 135-139.

because improvements in vehicle quality meant that the cars lost less of their value during the lease. Customers also liked the idea of transferring risk to GM – while they could buy their cars at the end of the lease period, they didn't have to do so. Leasing as a share of total sales increased from 4% in 1990 to more than 22% in 1997. The other important change was that the mix of leases was changing. Because of decisions made by the sales organization, leases generally went from four years in 1992 to three years in 1993 and two years in 1994. While the sales organization was motivated and rewarded for using this technique to sell more vehicles, no one had noticed that GM had created a situation where a high percentage of the cars on the road would be coming off lease in 1996 and 1997 and would be available for resale in good enough shape that they would compete against GM's new vehicles. By not managing the interaction of the parts, GM was solving a short-term problem and stimulating revenue in early years, while at the same time creating a problem for itself further out.

Because Nick's team had made a really significant innovation – configuring the model as an interactive 'dashboard' that provided information on the full range of factors critical to a comprehensive strategy – managers could test their own ideas and get nearly instant answers. Managers came up with their own, deep understanding of what needed to be done. The importance of his lesson led to the suggestions found in Capability 4.

They made two compelling observations:

- First, GM would need to shift incentives to favor longer leases.

- Second, it was imperative in the future to conduct a formal analysis to determine the impact of any pricing or marketing proposal on the used car market and the resulting effect on the new car market.

Our market research organization was directed to develop and maintain research studies to better understand consumer behavior and to design the research program so that data would be continuously available.

GM acted faster than competitors, saving quite a bit of money as a result. Sterman reported that profits at Ford Credit fell 28% between 1996 and 1997, "largely due to losses on off-lease vehicles." Meanwhile, "at GMAC, net income from automotive financing operations fell only $36 million, less than 4%. . . . In 1998, GE Capital dropped its partnership with Chrysler to finance leases because. . . GE Capital Auto Financial Services got burned on residual-value losses in 1997. . . . In 1998, net income at Ford Credit rose $53 million over the depressed level of 1997 but remained 25% below the net for 1996 (excluding one-time income from asset sales). GMAC's net on auto financing rose $74 million over 1997, a rise of 4% over 1996. . . . In 1998, Ford and other carmakers belatedly followed GM's lead and began to move away from short-term leasing."[34]

The general principle that is illustrated in this example is that complex problems almost always involve interacting elements. Remedying one element does not remedy the problem if it fails to take into account the interacting effects of other elements. Additionally, simulating the potential effects of these interactions over a prolonged period alerts the decision-maker to possible unintended consequences.

GM was making progress, but…

With GM making better decisions based on better data and better decision tools – and with Jack Smith moving on many other fronts – GM was hitting on all cylinders in the early 2000s. The $4.3 billion loss from 1992 had become a $3.5 billion profit in 2003. The pension fund, $21 billion in the red in 1992, showed a surplus of $3 billion in 2003. Productivity had improved so much that GM had become one of the most cost-effective producers, having been one of the least effective in the early 1990s. Quality was above average, having been below average before. GM was maintaining market share, and gaining in profitable segments; it was no longer losing share. GM was innovating in many areas of its business.

2009: GM's Centennial did not turn out the way it was planned

In 2009, GM entered into a government sanctioned bankruptcy. The easy thing for me to say would be that, well, GM was fine when I left in 2003. The honest answer, though, is that the whole car business got ugly – no one, not even highly vaunted Toyota, escaped the problems that came from over-capacity, higher fuel prices, a credit crisis and an

---

34   Sterman, 2000, pp. 54-55

economic recession that crushed consumers – reducing overall vehicle sales in the United States by nearly 40%.

I will provide some brief comments on what occurred to GM and why, in my judgment, it happened, in the epilogue that follows this journey of 50 years.

The primary lessons learned from participating in the development of a new business design

Lesson	Description	Addressed in Part 2
29	There is great practical value in using systems dynamics simulation tools to test out new ideas and to challenge the future implications of what appear to be very good short term benefits.	Capability 4
30	The most useful and useable new information augments, in either a positive or negative manner,the intellect, intuition, and experience of decision-makers.	Capability 3 Capability 4
31	Develop a Decision Record for every major decision. List the expected outcomes of the decision and the underlying assumptions that support and rebut the expected outcome.	The Decision Loom

GM Epilogue: An Opportunity Missed – from near bankruptcy (1992) to profitability (2003) and then into Government-Assisted Bankruptcy (2009)

A retired employee's perspective

So what happened between 2003 and 2010 to cause GM to go into a government-assisted bankruptcy? As pointed out in the previous three Episodes, GM made a number of significant advances in globalizing the organization, achieving success in China and implementing major product improvements, some of which are just being seen today. At the same time GM also had a number of problems including the failed Fiat alliance, continuing losses in Europe, a Yen exchange rate driven by the foreign exchange carry-trade that inflated competitors' profits, and a heavy reliance on incentives to sell vehicles in the USA.

The most compelling issue that needed to be resolved centered on GM's legacy costs. These were the pension and health care obligations that had accumulated over 50 years of labor agreements, a decade of zero stock returns that affected pensions, the cost of health care that increased 46% (vs. general inflation of 26%), and dramatic productivity improvements that resulted in early retirements and led to having one working employee for every four retirees receiving benefits.

By 2005, it was clear that GM's legacy costs were unsustainable. Rick Wagoner determined to address the issue once and for all, but he had to move slowly as the UAW leadership needed time to gain rank and file acceptance. His cautious approach was based on the experience of a strike in 1998 that cost the company billions; he believed a jointly developed cooperative approach to be the best way forward. To help the UAW leadership in their effort to gain rank and file support, he took the unprecedented action of opening the company books to the union so that they could see for themselves that without change there would soon be no company. The importance of this strategic decision is reflected in this section of a letter from the UAW to its retirees on December 20, 2005:

As we have seen recently with other major corporations, employee and retiree benefits which had been thought secure can be lost if the company becomes insolvent. Were GM forced to file for bankruptcy, it is likely that health-care benefits for its UAW retirees would be reduced in ways far more drastic than required by the proposed settlement - if not eliminated entirely. Keeping GM alive and preventing a bankruptcy filing is essential to protecting the health-care benefits to which we believe you and your family are entitled.

We want to stress that, in agreeing to this settlement, we did not take GM's word about the threat to its continued viability. During the negotiations, UAW had full access to GM's financial data, and it engaged a team of internationally respected firms - financial advisers, lawyers, and health-care actuaries - to help evaluate this information. The analysis made it clear that in order to provide UAW-represented GM retirees and surviving spouses the strongest possible long-term protection for their health-care benefits, action had to be taken sooner rather than later.

Rising fuel prices added to the crisis for GM. Large trucks and SUVs were the last large profit-hold for domestic automakers. The decline in sales of both hurt profits tremendously. The changing market conditions and the changed economic conditions led to an opportunity to reach an unprecedented agreement with the UAW on dramatic changes in health care.

The UAW for its part, through the leadership of Ron Gettlefinger, reset its members' expectation that the rise in benefits would continue. This resolved a problem that many public employee unions are faced with today. Together the UAW and GM were able to get a new health-care deal approved by the rank-and-file mid contract; this set GM on the path to end its legacy health-care problem.

Because it took so long to overcome the legacy of the past, before the benefits of the combined efforts of the UAW and GM could be felt, the automotive industry was hit with a financial collapse and the largest recession since the Great Depression. The freezing of financial markets and the fall of nearly 40% in industry sales created a crisis for everyone. Even mighty Toyota would go from making billions to losing billions.

Ford, either by luck or prescience when Alan Mullaly took over in 2006, borrowed against the full value of the company assets which provided them with sufficient cash to make it through without assistance.[35] GM and Chrysler were forced to go to the government for financing to restructure, in a government-assisted bankruptcy.

In the end, the changes resulting from the careful and cautious approach taken by Rick Wagoner did not achieve their potential in time to overcome the new economic conditions of 2008 and 2009.

An interested outsider's perspective

Writing this account of what happened between 2003 and 2009, I was concerned that it would leave the impression of a biased statement prepared by a defender of the past actions of GM – many of which are documented in the earlier Episodes.

Fortunately, Malcom Gladwell's review[36] of Steve Rattner's book *Overhaul*, provides an informed perspective, in this case through the mind of a thoughtful, unbiased outside observer. Rattner was the person selected by the U.S. Government to oversee the transition of the 'Old GM' to the 'New GM.'

In his review, Gladwell makes the point that, in his initial assessment of the situation, Rattner did not have a positive view of Rick Wagoner, GM's CEO. The problem, according to Gladwell, was based on Wagoner's testimony before the Senate, on November of 2008.

"I do not agree with those who say we are not doing enough to position GM for success," Wagoner said, in his testimony. "What exposes us to failure now is not our product lineup, is not our business plan, is not our employees and their willingness to work hard, is not our long-term strategy. What exposes us to failure now is the global financial crisis, which has severely restricted credit availability and reduced industry sales to the lowest per-capita level since World War II."

Gladwell points out that Wagoner's comment highlighted what Rattner thought was wrong with GM. "Its leaders were arrogant and out of touch. Their sales forecasts were bizarrely optimistic... Rattner

---

35   Woodall & Krolicki, 2011

36   Gladwell, 2010

looked in vain for a sense of urgency." It was his impression that Rattner believed that Wagoner was the heart of the problem – pointing out that Wagoner seemed to rely more on his direct reports than on commenting on the key issues himself. With these observations and having met him only once, Rattner decided that Wagoner was not the right person to run GM. Given that decision, Gladwell points out that Rattner's book did not discuss, "Whether Wagoner was any good at the job he was hired to do – that is, run General Motors – which is a critical omission, because by that criterion Wagoner actually comes off very well".

Gladwell lists several Wagoner lapses such as not building up cash reserves for a possible economic downturn and sticking with SUV vehicles in lieu of creating a credible small car. He then mitigates those lapses by listing the accomplishments that were achieved, even with the inherited difficult conditions within which he was operating – the most prominent being "the inherent difficulty of running a company that had to pay pension and medical benefits to half a million retirees."

Gladwell points out that Wagoner:

> ...cut the workforce from three hundred and ninety thousand to two hundred and seventeen thousand. He built a hugely profitable business in China almost from scratch: a GM joint venture is the leading automaker in what is now the world's largest automobile market. In 1995, it took forty-six man-hours to build the typical GM car, versus twenty-nine hours for the typical Toyota. Under Wagoner's watch, the productivity gap closed almost entirely.

> Most important, Wagoner – along with his counterparts at Ford and Chrysler – was responsible for a historic agreement with the United Auto Workers. Under that contract, which was concluded in 2007, new hires at GM receive between fourteen and seventeen dollars an hour – instead of the twenty-eight to thirty-three dollars an hour that preexisting employees get – and give up all rights to the traditional retiree benefit package. The 2007 deal also transferred all responsibility for paying for the health care of GM's retirees to a special fund, administered by the UAW. It is hard to overstate the importance of that second provision. GM has five hundred and seventeen thousand retirees. Between 1993 and 2007, the company paid out a hundred and three billion dollars to those

former workers – a burden unimaginable to its foreign competitors. In the 2007 deal, GM agreed to make a series of lump-sum payments to the UAW over ten years, worth some thirty-two billion dollars – at which point the company would be free of its outsized retiree health-care burden. It is estimated that, within a few years, GM's labor costs – which were once almost fifty per cent higher than the domestic operations of Toyota, Nissan, and Honda – will be lower than its competitors'.

In the same period, GM's product line was transformed. In 1989, to give one example, Chevrolet's main midsize sedan had something like twice as many reported defects as its competitors at Honda and Toyota, according to the J. D. Power 'initial quality' metrics. Those differences no longer exist. The first major new car built on Wagoner's watch – the midsize Chevy Malibu – scores equal to or better than the Honda Accord and Toyota Camry. GM earned more than a billion dollars in profits in the last quarter because American consumers have started to buy the cars that Wagoner brought to market – the Buick Regal and LaCrosse, the Envoy, the Cadillac CTS, the Chevy Malibu and Cruze, and others. They represent the most competitive lineup that GM has fielded since the nineteen-sixties. (Both the CTS and the Malibu have been named to Car and Driver's annual '10 Best Cars' list.)

Gladwell's review of Rattner's actions notes that at one point Rattner wrote: "GM's day-to-day workings were solid. It was the head that was rotting." Gladwell's telling question of Rattner's position is, "… if the head was rotting, how did the day-to-day operations become solid?" Gladwell's observation is reinforced by his reference to the evaluation conducted by Kristin Dziczek, of the Center for Automotive Research, in which she estimated that after the exit from bankruptcy "the 'new' GM is roughly eighty-five per cent the product of the work that Wagoner, in concert with the UAW, did in his eight years at the company and fifteen per cent the product of Team Auto's (Rattner's group) efforts." Dziczek's assessment of the contribution of the 'old GM' is driven home by the statement of Angus McKenzie, Editor of *Motor Trend* Magazine when he announced the Chevrolet Volt as the 2011 Car of the Year:

In the 61-year history of the Car of the Year award, there have been few contenders as hyped – or as controversial – as the Chevrolet Volt. The Volt started life an Old GM project, then arrived fully formed as a symbol of New GM, carrying all the emotional and political baggage of that profound and painful transition. As a result, a lot of the sound and fury that has surrounded the Volt's launch has tended to obscure a simple truth: This automobile is a game-changer.[37]

The price of not positively interacting with its containing system

My assessment, given this background, is that during the 1992-2009 period GM did a good job on identifying a strategic plan to overcome the issues it was facing. Although the plan to generate increased income from customers after the vehicle was sold had the potential to set it apart from other automotive companies, GM did not, however, move fast enough to alter the existing traditional approach to decision-making to take full advantage of the plan. Also, although it started to improve the way it managed the interaction of the parts over which it had control, it did a poor job of managing the enterprise's interactions with its containing system; that is the communities in which it worked, the global society which had concerns over its perceived actions, and elected officials, some of whom tolerated the enterprise while others saw it as an appeaser of organized labor.

A very early warning

Peter Drucker wrote an epilogue in the 1972 edition of *Concept of the Corporation*. In that epilogue he took a 25-year retrospective look at what he said about GM and how GM reacted to the publication of the initial 1946 edition.

Drucker rated GM (in 1972) a success as a *business* – it became stronger within its industry. He rated GM a failure as an *institution* – it became the target of attacks from many areas of society and was perceived by many as the 'perfect American villain.'

In the epilogue he reflected on the changes that he suggested be taken by GM and the results of GM's actions since that time:

And yet, up to this day [1972], the GM model has remained the one general model of organization for large institutions, and, of course, especially for large businesses. One may argue that GM should have

---

37   McKenzie, 2011

taken the critical look at itself that I proposed twenty-five years ago. But,
in retrospect, my critics within GM at that time have been proved right.
Not to have changed anything has been the foundation for GM's success
in terms of sales and profits.

But it also clearly has been the source of GM's failure as an institution.
For today GM is clearly in deep trouble – not because its cars do not
sell or because it lacks efficiency. GM is in trouble because it is seen
increasingly by more and more people as deeply at odds with basic needs
and basic values of society and community.[38] *[p.305]*

Summary

On balance, GM was not the disaster it was made out to be. It made
its share of mistakes and these were compounded by the severity of
the economic recession. It went to the government seeking financial
help in the form of a loan – not a 'bailout.' After all, in addition to
having played a major role in developing and leading the 'arsenal for
democracy' during World War II, and establishing between 1947 and
1973 an industry-wide wage pattern that created the middle class,[39] it
also had paid hundreds of billions of dollars to its retirees over the last
50 years instead of having a major portion of those expenses paid for by
the government, as was the case with its overseas competitors. Instead
of support based on past contributions to society, it received a verbal
thrashing and was ordered to change at the direction of government-
appointed 'advisors.'

The good news is that, because of the speed at which the government
allowed it to go through bankruptcy, GM was able to lower its
operating costs further than it already had by working with the UAW
to reduce legacy costs associated with retirement and medical care
expenses.

The bad news is that it received a significant battering from
government and the press over its competency. Its current product
line-up and resurgence in the North American marketplace, some of
which was developed before the bankruptcy, provides some evidence
that portions of the solution imposed by the government, through their

---

38   Drucker, 1972

39   Lichtenstein, 2004

designated government-sponsored team assigned to fix the problem, may have been more severe than was required.

A suggestion for the New GM

Given that GM is again a private company and its new management team has demonstrated its ability to continue to build and market great cars that generate profits, the enterprise needs to learn from the criticism it received when it was forced into bankruptcy. When GM asked for the support that was needed, the request was soundly rejected. The cause of the rejection was clearly articulated by Peter Drucker when he so prophetically provided an early warning forty years ago in his epilogue in the 1972 edition of Concept of the Corporation:

> *The major lesson we can learn from revisiting General Motors is that an institution, like an individual, is not an island unto itself. It has to solve the basic problem of balancing the need for concentration and for self-limitation with concern for its environment and compassion for its community. General Motors' success is clearly the success of the "technocrat." But so is General Motors' failure.* [40]

My suggestion is to take a portion of its budget for promoting the benefits of acquiring and using GM products and services and develop a clear and concise communication program that points to the many past, current and future contributions of GM that demonstrate a "concern for its environment" and "its compassion for its community." Additionally, in reviewing any current action, GM should assess the extent to which that decision over time will contribute to winning the support needed from the society in which the enterprise performs its function. To ensure the company learns from these future actions, the review should be recorded as a decision record (discussed in Capability 4).

---

40   Drucker, 1972, p. 310

Summary of Lessons Learned

Episode 1:

Lesson	Description	Addressed in Part 2
1	Avoid the Silo Problem. Be careful not to let your area of expertise restrict your willingness and ability to interact with and learn from others who are experienced in fields in which you are not.	Capability 2
2	Avoid starting out with a specific point of view which may cause you to look for and find only information that supports that position. Appreciate the wisdom found in concepts like selective perception, cognitive dissonance, and convergence theory.	The Decision Loom Capability 1 Capability 3
3	When presenting a point of view, make sure that all aspects of the underlying arguments are revealed and understood.	The Decision Loom Capability 4
4	Do not put variables of which you are uncertain in Alfred Marshall's pound called *Ceteris Paribus*. Make uncertainty explicit.	Capability 3 Capability 4

Episode 2:

Lesson	Description	Addressed in Part 2
5	Communicate effectively the results of the information you collected… even when, for the wrong reasons, they are not likely to be well received.	The Decision Loom Capability 1 Capability 4
6	Continually test and assess the extent to which things that worked in the past still work.	The Decision Loom Capability 1 Capability 2
7	Learn to step back and take a holistic look at the conditions surrounding the activity you are working on.	Capability 2 Capability 4

8	Make sure you go beyond what respondents answered to your survey questions and find out why they answered in the manner they did – walk in the respondent's shoes.	The Decision Loom Capability 4
9	Determine whether there is some technology (old or new) that will help augment, not replace, the application of what is already known.	Capability 4

Episode 3:

Lesson	Description	Addressed in Part 2
10	Involve the leadership of the organization throughout the entire process when developing strategic concepts that will have to be implemented by them.	Capability 2 Capability 3 Capability 4
11	Learn how to help people (more competent, in their special skills, than yourself) to apply their skills so as to improve the overall capability of the entire organization. In the words of Russ Ackoff, "Manage the interaction of the parts and not the parts taken separately."	The Decision Loom Capability 1
12	Engage practicing academics who are actively seeking opportunities to test out, under real-world conditions, new ideas that address both current and past problems.	Most of the ideas discussed in Part 2 came, in part, from practicing academics
13	There is a lot more to having people adopt an innovation than just inventing it – it helps when you design your invention so that those who you want to adopt it can reinvent it for their purposes.	Why a Sketch? Capability 4

Episode 4:

Lesson	Description	Addressed in Part 2
14	Engage mid-level management in the process of ensuring the information gathered and analyzed is relevant to the needs of the enterprise. Ensure that they assist in preparing their senior managers for receiving, accepting and acting on the results.	The Decision Loom Capability 1 Capability 2
15	Make sure that understanding and appreciation of business conditions exists throughout the enterprise and reaches deeply into places where specialists, engineers, and scientists formulate and assess ideas.	Capability 2 Capability 4
16	Whenever possible, make sure your market measurements allow information users to see the effects of alternative strategies and how individual customers respond and are not limited to observations based on averages of all customers or segments.	Capability 3 Capability 4

Episode 5:

Lesson	Description	Addressed in Part 2
17	Surface and make explicit the underlying assumptions that would have to be true for your particular problem-solving approach to prevail – even in a court of law.	Capability 4
18	Engage and inform those who will be affected by a decision – about both the process and the basis upon which the decision would be made before the decision is made.	Capability 4

Episode 6:

Lesson	Description	Addressed in Part 2
19	Reach out beyond senior managers and actively engage engineers and scientists in the design of market research projects to improve their understanding and acceptance of those projects.	Capability 4
20	Follow Barabba's Law – "Never say, 'the model says...'"	The Decision Loom Capability 4
21	There is more to making a contribution to the enterprise than just pointing out what the future holds. Put in place the tools to ensure that the subsequent decisions of the enterprise take those findings into consideration.	The Decision Loom Capability 4
22	It is far better to build models of individual behavior than to combine individual responses into data for an aggregate respondent. This provides a rich source of data about individual consumers each with their unique set of preferences and biases. (Provided by Dick Smallwood)	Capability 4
23	You cannot sell sophisticated quantitative analysis directly to a client in the first project. You must first gain their trust before moving on to more complex – and valuable – approaches. (Provided by Dick Smallwood)	Capability 4

Episode 7:

Lesson	Description	Addressed in Part 2
[19] modified	Reach out beyond senior managers and actively engage engineers and scientists in the design of market research projects to improve their understanding and acceptance of those projects. Engage individuals who are willing to reach out to other engineers and designers to translate what you are finding into terms that they can not only understand but actually work with and suggest improvements to.	Capability 2 Capability 4
24	Walk in the shoes of an eventual user of information. The value is similar to the benefits of walking in the shoes of the respondent (as I did in Georgia).	Capability 1 Capability 4
25	It is OK to find out that some of your basic ideas are not new, as long as you seek ways to improve on the old ideas by understanding how they were used and employing new technology to further improve on them.	All of Part 2
26	Breaking an organization's habits developed during a successful past period requires direction from the leadership of the enterprise and a lot of hard work.	Capability 2 Capability 3

Episode 8:

Lesson	Description	Addressed in Part 2
27	There are significant benefits to be gained in the concept of double-loop learning. Observing the results of previous experiences, particularly how people with deep functional knowledge improved their use of market information, suggested effective ways to determine the purpose of the research project and to improve the eventual use of market research activities.	The Decision Loom
28	If it is fully engaged with eventual users, market research can provide timely – but approximate – information… rather than more time-consuming, detailed reports designed to demonstrate the market researcher's knowledge and command of the standard procedures.	Capability 4

Episode 9:

Lesson	Description	Addressed in Part 2
29	There is great practical value in using systems dynamics simulation tools to test out new ideas and to challenge the future implications of what appear to be very good short term benefits.	Capability 4
30	The most useful and useable new information augments, in either a positive or negative manner,the intellect, intuition, and experience of decision-makers.	Capability 3 Capability 4
31	Develop a Decision Record for every major decision. List the expected outcomes of the decision and the underlying assumptions that support and rebut the expected outcome.	The Decision Loom

Part 2. The Design of an Interactive Decision Loom

In this section of the book, I examine the process by which an organization can design an interactive Decision Loom and provide a description of the four capabilities that are required to enable its implementation in any public or private organization.

The approach taken to describing the Decision Loom and understanding its interaction with the required capabilities

The call for an interactive process to address complexity and dynamic change is not new. Robert Waller pointed to the problem in 1982 at a conference in which I participated at the University of Pittsburgh: [41]

> *This comes down to a design problem. On the one hand is complexity in all of its richness. On the other hand we see the human, restricted in terms of short-term memory, but with marvelous capabilities for long-term information retention, for judgment, for utilizing experience, for intuition, and, yes, for passion.*
>
> *In engineering terminology, an interface device must be sought that will link humans and complexity, while preserving the original properties of each. Anyone who regularly deals with real problems in government and industry can testify that such a device has not yet been found and perfected. In fact, a dominant feature of organizations in both the public and private sectors is a continual shadow boxing with problems.*

The purpose of this part of the book is to address the problem that was so insightfully identified by Robert Waller nearly 30 years ago. The reason it has taken me so long to develop a response is that I had to finish the Journey described in the first part of this book in order to fully comprehend the extent and complexity of the problem he had identified and to test and eventually provide a viable solution.

---

41   Waller, 1983

The basic design: it's not just about a decision-making process and its capabilities

As with a conventional loom, we need to look not just at the threads but also to remember the importance of understanding how the loom works and how the weaver manages the interaction of the loom's parts and the threads.

The transformation of traditional business and public decision-making processes into a more systemic process suited to the complexities of the 21st Century is not simple. It requires an organization to develop an interactive decision process interlinked with at least four important capabilities, around which this part of the book is structured. This section outlines and explains how the capabilities and the decision process interact and enrich each other and provides a sketch of how they can be translated into an effective decision-making design for any organization. Here are the capabilities:

- Having an enterprise mindset that is open to change

- Thinking and acting holistically

- Being able to adapt the business design to changing conditions

- Making decisions interactively using a variety of methods

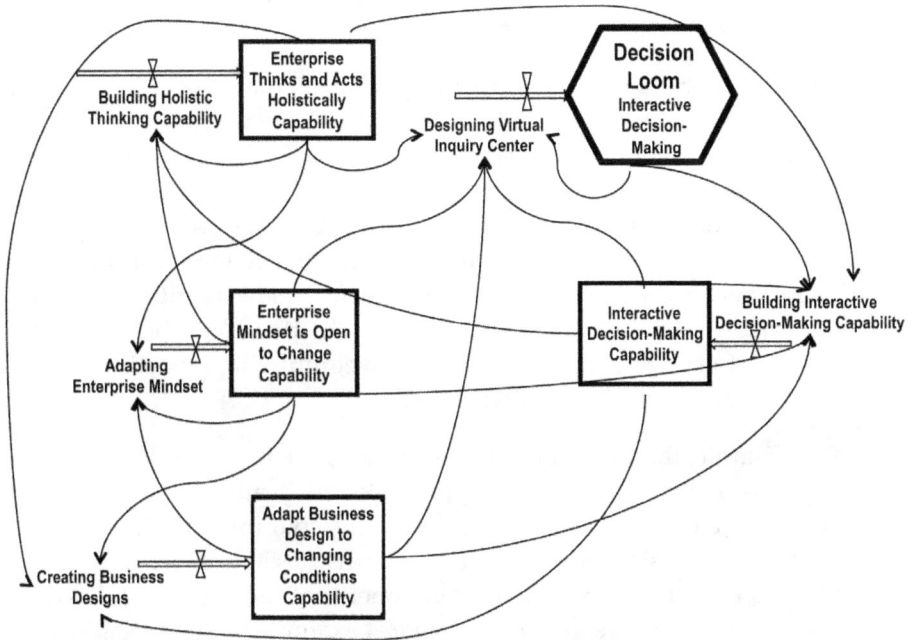

Figure 4: A stock and flow model of the Decision Loom[42]

This modified stock and flow chart displays the four capabilities and the Decision Loom as described in this part of the book. Kim Warren[43] defines capabilities by using a portion of Robert Grant's definition[44]:

> *As Grant observes, resources are things a firm has, while capabilities are things it is good at doing. Common English usage too implies that a capability is about getting something done, while a resource is some useful thing (whether tangible or intangible) that can help to get those things done, but is not the activity itself.*

This stock and flow diagram illustrates the interaction of the four things a firm must be good at doing. They are shown as four rectangles

---

42 I have taken some artistic license in modifying a traditional Systems Dynamics Stock and Flow Diagram to illustrate the extent to which the five activities of this part of the book interact with each other.

43 Warren, 2008: p. 629

44 Grant, 2005

representing stocks. The purpose of the four capabilities is helping to develop and improve the Decision Loom as an interactive decision making process that is shown as a Hexagon.

The most important point of this illustration is that the Decision Loom and the capabilities form an interdependent system. The rate at which a capability is built depends on its own level and the accumulation of other capabilities. The dependence on its own level creates a positive feedback loop in which the capability bootstraps its own development. The interdependency between these capabilities requires an enterprise effort to ensure system-wide balanced growth. This is critical because a shortage of one capability could create a bottleneck in the growth of another. In systemic terms the slowest accumulating capability can limit the improvement of the overall system.

For example, the capability to create innovative business designs depends on the firm's capability to think holistically and to provide an effective mindset. Without the capability to think holistically, the business designs are likely to ignore the possible beneficial interdependencies between the components of the enterprise. This point is clearly made in the hypothetical example of the 'Reliable Computer Company' discussed in Capability 2 where the entire system is negatively affected because individual functions within the enterprise optimized their own performance at the expense of other functions – eventually leading to a dissatisfied customer who purchased a competitive product.

An additional purpose of this chart is to show the reader that there is no prescribed set of rules as to where to start reading or implementing your version of the process. A lot depends on the enterprise in which you are attempting to improve the decision-making process. For example, should you start with improving your understanding of how to create an enterprise mindset capability? Or, are you in an enterprise that is more likely to want to start with a demonstration (pilot project) of the value of thinking and acting holistically? There is no single key to unlock the vault of benefits. A deep understanding of these capabilities (accumulating stocks) and an appreciation of their interaction is more likely to provide the most value.

A brief description of the required four capabilities:

1. **Having an enterprise mindset that is open to change:**
   This capability is a necessary preparation for successfully
   achieving the other capabilities; unless the enterprise mindset
   is sufficiently open and willing to accept necessary changes,
   essential learning cannot take place. Assessing this capability
   is a useful reality check: in some cases the mindset of the
   enterprise is simply so fixed on what worked in the past that
   it is difficult for it to even understand, much less consider, a
   truly systemic design.

2. **Thinking and acting holistically:** Here we are concerned
   with the development of systemic thinking tools; this
   approach does not come naturally to most organizations
   as many managers and staff have learned to apply linear,
   either/or thinking and action while holistic approaches
   require both/and thinking. In this vein it is important to
   understand that logical and analytical approaches are not
   excluded from the design toolset, and some will indeed
   reappear in Capability 4. Holistic thinking means that logic
   and analysis are not the dominant modes of thought but
   are only used when appropriate. In particular, they are not
   appropriate to designing the decision-making process of an
   entire organization; a key lesson of design thinking is that
   the strategy of separating out and then optimizing different
   functions usually reduces the effectiveness of the whole.

3. **Being able to adapt the business design to changing
   conditions:** Here we look at three different business designs
   along a mechanistic and organismic continuum: make-and-
   sell, sense-and-respond and anticipate-and-lead. Although
   the capability uses the term 'business design', this should not
   be interpreted as meaning that the designs only reflect private
   sector activities. In the more detailed description of this
   capability that comes later, several examples of public sector
   applications of the different business designs will be shown.

   The dominant mindset of the 20th Century was focused on
   the make-and-sell design, and the dominant approach was to
   predict what would be purchased and by how many people.
   With the conviction that the estimate of potential participants
   was correct, the enterprise built the capacity to achieve

economies of scale. Today, in a more complex and dynamic environment, the ability of the enterprise to predict future desires based on past behavior has been severely diminished. This does not mean that the make-and-sell design no longer has a place in our approach to decision-making. However, because of the costs associated with incorrectly estimating the demand for future preferences, other designs are assuming increasing importance. See also Episode 6 in *Part 1*, which describes how Eastman Kodak's unwillingness to change its large and highly efficient ability to produce film in the face of developing technologies lost them the chance to adopt an anticipate-and-lead design which could have secured the company a leading position in digital image processing.

The success of a business design depends on how well it addresses the critical elements of the entire marketplace in which it operates. But it is much more difficult to predict with any certainty how those critical elements will unfold. In Capability 3 we show how considering different future scenarios provides a way to evaluate the business potential of different designs. For example, a make-and-sell strategy will not succeed well in an environment where customers expect to have a significant role in the design of the products they want to buy. A sense-and-respond strategy would be much more appropriate in that environment. On the other hand, a sense-and-respond strategy might be a costly failure if customers are not able or willing to participate. Finally an anticipate-and-lead design can flop if the direction chosen is not perceived by consumers or constituents as something new that better meets a need (even an unarticulated need) or if the enterprise cannot meet the technical challenges of developing the new products. A famous set of counter examples of this were the failure of Apple's Newton PDA and the success of its iPhone.

4. **Making decisions interactively using a variety of methods**: Here we provide a sample of decision support tools available to make decision-making more interactive and attempt to classify them according to the three dimensions: creativity & imagination, logic & analysis and collaboration & dialogue.

Use of these tools must be a capability found in the Decision Loom, if the threads of knowledge are to come together in a meaningful answer to complex and dynamic problems. It is vital to understand the potential and limitations of these tools when it comes to the design of a decision/learning system for the enterprise. The chapter ends with examples of applying some of these decision support tools in the development of successful solutions to complex business problems.

The four capabilities, acting as interacting parts, all contribute to the development of the interactive decision process which facilities integrating decision-making across the enterprise

The Outcome: Greater interaction across the enterprise leading to an enterprise that is greater than the sum of its parts.

The Decision Loom becomes a central function designed to serve the entire enterprise. As was pointed out in Part 1, the concepts of single- and double-loop learning are crucial; single-loop learning takes place whenever mistakes are identified and corrected, but this process rarely transfers learning throughout an organization as it characteristically involves only those who were involved in the original problem. When double-loop learning is developed, the values and procedures of the organization are also modified by local learning and the process of learning in one place can therefore adapt to what is learned in another. In this sense, double-loop learning is the capability to learn from mistakes and reinforce the actions that led to success; in essence, learning how to learn. A wealth of experience gained during the learning journey has identified the key components of this capability and the steps needed to develop them.

Described here briefly, the Decision Loom and these capabilities do not follow each other in a linear sequence and they can operate at different times at different levels in an organization. Thus every organization will develop them in its own particular way; there is no fixed recipe for this. The key lessons that contributed to my ability to identify each capability as required for this decision-making design are described in the 'Lessons Learned' following *Part 1*.

A little self-reflection on almost failing to understand the importance of interdependencies and an early warning to those who are certain the path they have chosen should not be challenged

An example of focusing on the parts and not the interaction of the parts occurred in my own journey. My initial approach to the thinking about interactive decision-making was based on a presentation at a Marketing Science Institute meeting in Boston around 1980 where one of the speakers quoted the poet T. S. Eliot asking, "Where is the knowledge we have lost in information?" I looked up the poem, 'The Rock', and found that Eliot preceded that question with another: "Where is the wisdom we have lost in knowledge?"

That led me to suppose that if T.S. Eliot had been a Knowledge-Management Consultant rather than a poet concerned with man's relation to God, perhaps he would have added three additional lines, and with some slight modification, developed a decision hierarchy composed of parts that needed to be understood. It went something like this:

Where is the *wisdom* we have lost in understanding?

Where is the *understanding* we have lost in knowledge?

Where is the *knowledge* we have lost in intelligence?

Where is the *intelligence* we have lost in information?

Where is the *information* we have lost in data?

And rather than lines of poetry, he might have illustrated it something like this:

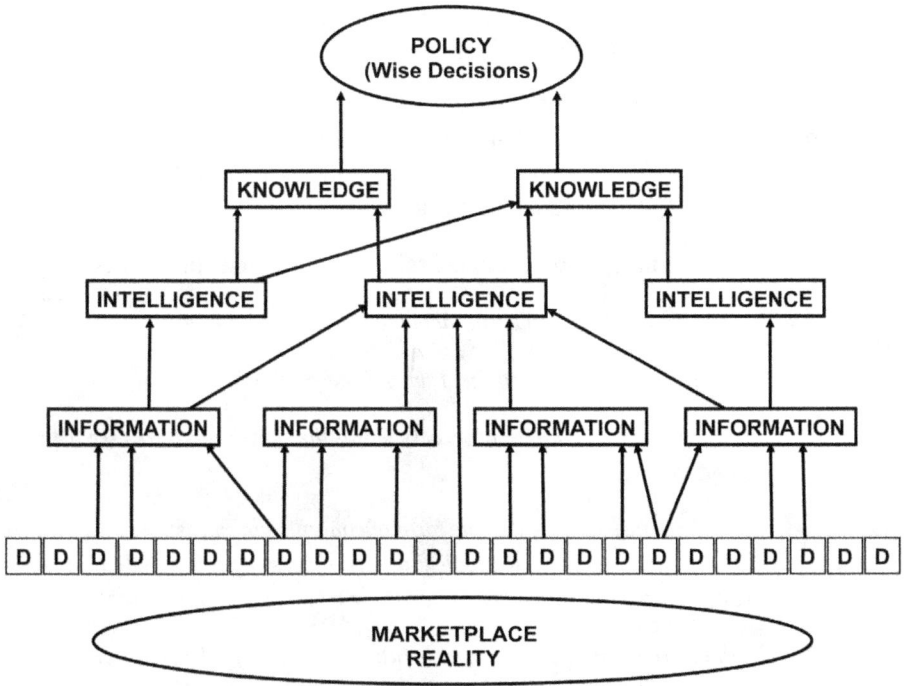

Figure 5: Refinery decision hierarchy

My inclination to use poetry aside, the design of a decision hierarchy is not new.[45] In my case the refinery metaphor of the decision hierarchy fit nicely with my background and training which led me to believe that many facts (represented by the Ds for data) – sometimes collected through interviews, sometimes generated from transactions or records, or through observation – are distilled into information; that the information is then transformed into intelligence, and then knowledge: all of which eventually provide understanding that is used to develop wise decisions.

---

45   Rowley (2007) points to Ackoff's contribution to the current discussion:
      "…authors often cite Ackoff's 1989 paper as a source for the hierarchy."

Thinking systemically: value lies not solely in developing and understanding a hierarchical structure of the elements but also in improving their interaction

The simplicity of the 'parts' hierarchy was challenged by the conclusions of Harold Wilensky from his study of a wide range of cases from international relations, economics, politics, and welfare in the United States and abroad as far back as 1967:

> High-quality intelligence designates information that is
>
> *clear because it is understandable to those who must use it;*
>
> *timely because it gets to them when they need it;*
>
> *reliable because diverse observers using the same procedures see it in the same way;*
>
> *valid because it is cast in the form of concepts and measures that capture reality (the tests included logical consistency, successful prediction, and congruence with established knowledge or independent sources);*
>
> *adequate because the account is full (the context of the act, event or life of the person or group is described); and*
>
> *wide-ranging because the major policy alternatives promising a high probability of attaining organization goals are posed or new goals suggested.*[46]

I found further complications; what happens when the collectors of the information and the users of information do not share the same perspectives? For example, creative personnel in advertising or design believe their ideas cannot be assessed by asking potential customers whether they would use a service or buy the product that is being developed. Market researchers, on the other hand, believe there are methods available to capture the underlying values and preferences of potential customers so that an assessment of the potential value of the new idea can be made. Equally, financial personnel are looking for customers' willingness to pay for a new product or service so they can calculate an expected rate of return to justify the use of enterprise capital.

---

46   Wilensky, 1967

Faced with these complications, I became uncomfortable with studying the parts of the decision hierarchy that I had portrayed with a refinery metaphor that transformed raw data into wise decisions. Jerry Zaltman (now marketing professor emeritus of the Harvard Business School) explained my discomfort. He introduced me to 'knowledge disavowal':

> *Knowledge disavowal refers to the avoidance of knowledge in order to maintain the status quo or to avoid a difficult choice or threatening situation. It does not include the avoidance of information for reasons related to its perceived lack of relevance, timeliness, expected utility, or the cost of acquiring it. Knowledge disavowal is as systematic and pervasive as pro-knowledge phenomena and is found in all settings.*[47]

An example of knowledge disavowal is given in Episode 6 of *The Journey* when Kodak's management accepted the solid evidence that their silver halide chemistry was likely to be replaced in ten years by digital technologies. The knowledge disavowal took place in their selective decision, based on strongly held beliefs, to use digital technology to enhance silver halide technology rather than adopting a straightforward plan to replace it with digital technology. In this case knowledge disavowal proved to be extremely damaging.

On a more personal level, Jerry's insight reminded me that, after developing the refinery decision hierarchy (Figure 5), I had received overwhelming support and commendation from my peers for developing the simple and easily understood hierarchy. This very positive reaction led me to 'avoid' considering alternative approaches that could challenge the direction I had taken and was the basis for continued commendation from my colleagues. In essence I fell prey to Leon Festinger's theory of 'cognitive dissonance.' Here's the brief version:

Festinger identified key behaviors that individuals will use to avoid being put in the uncomfortable position of finding out they may be partially or completely wrong.

> **Selective Perception**: Once we take a position on an issue, we will avoid information that is likely to increase dissonance. This selected behavior results in our making choices in what we read or see and includes finding or being associated with

---

47   Barabba & Zaltman, 1991

like-minded people who will help buffer us from information or ideas that contradict our belief and/or position.

The More Important the Decision – The Greater the Dissonance: The importance of the decision (in my case a significant amount of time I devoted to developing my version of the hierarchy) leads to greater internal resistance to conflicting information once the fallacious decision has been made.

I had also conveniently 'forgotten' the findings of Ian Mitroff's 1983 book *The Subjective Side of Science*. Ian conducted extensive personal interviews with scientists about their beliefs about the moon before and then after the Apollo mission brought back moon rocks. After studying the before-and-after responses he found that each scientist's prior belief about the geological characteristics of the moon had a significant effect on their observations upon actually viewing the moon rocks.

In my case, the extent of my knowledge disavowal was both wide and deep. I completely ignored all of my experience in political campaigns, government service, and the political in-fighting among functions and departments in large corporations. In each of those experiences I saw the effect of social arrangements and the political context on the development, use and mis-use of information. In essence, the benefits found in the simplicity of the nice, neat hierarchy that had evolved in my thinking had led me to 'avoid' concepts that were inconsistent with the direction in which I was headed.

This does not, of course, mean that the hierarchical relationship is not valid and helpful in discussing the components. It is how it is understood and used that really matters.

Jerry and I attempted to visualize these social and political effects with the following chart incorporating the concept of the 'law of the lens.'[48] We pointed out that the interaction of the parts of the hierarchy is complicated by assumptions, truth tests, expectations and rules about decision-making that create a lens through which managers and researchers as well as information users and information providers get different views of the decision and its context.

---

48   *Ibid.*, p. 44

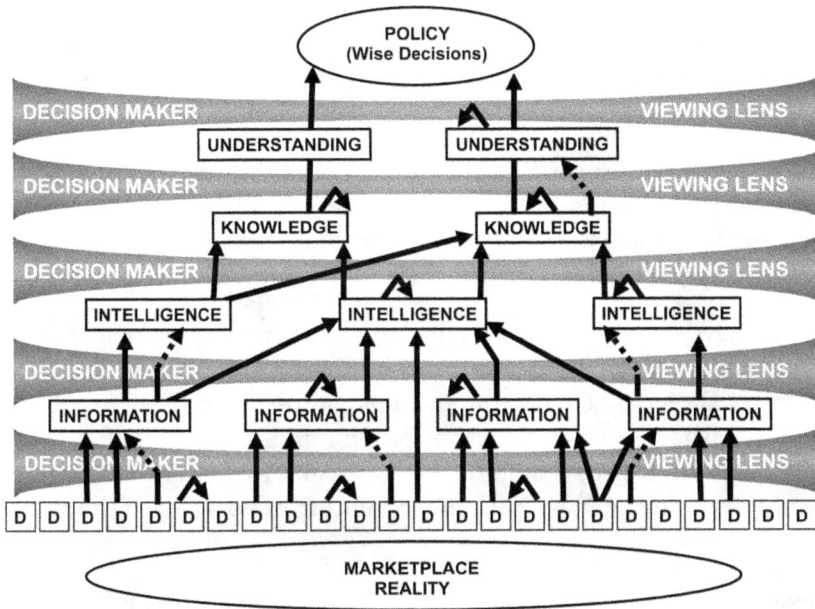

Figure 6: Refinery decision hierarchy modified by the Law of the Lens

In this more realistic illustration, the bent and rejected arrows between the elements illustrate the impact of a possible 'distorted' viewing lens used by the individuals involved in collecting and processing data into information, intelligence, knowledge and understanding, and eventually into a wise decision. The arrows recognize that the viewer's predisposition on the issue directly affects how people see and accept or reject reports from their researchers, and how they determine what is eventually considered in a decision. From the perspective of the person making the final policy or action decision, the chart points to the need to know not only what information was rejected or modified (illustrated by the dotted lines emerging from the filter) but the reasons for the rejection, modification and acceptance as well.

It is important to understand the extent to which individuals in the decision process differ – and not simply focus on who may be right or wrong. For today's complex issues, for which there are multiple 'right' answers, an understanding of why people differ (because of their underlying assumptions) is as important as understanding what might be perceived by many as the 'right' answer.

Today, both analysis and synthesis are necessary, but synthesis becomes more important as we face an increasingly unpredictable future. We need a mindset that understands that a complete system is composed of *interdependent* parts that cannot be divided into *independent* parts.

Each part of the enterprise must rely on, and interact with, the rest of the parts if the enterprise is to succeed. Today, problems are best solved not by breaking them into functional bits, but by carrying them into the next larger system and solving them through integrative mechanisms.

But even 'carrying them into the next larger system' has the potential to lead to bad decisions if they are viewed through a distorted lens. As was clearly shown by Ian Mitroff, the most powerful and dangerous case of the distorted lens is the predisposed mind. That is, a mind that is only prepared to see what it expects to see and that filters out what does not fit comfortably with its understanding of how things should be.

Knowledge creation, dissemination, and application are themselves not separable processes, and the viewing lenses that we use mean that we all have the potential to experience and believe in different realities. This represents both a danger and an opportunity: a danger when the result is conflicted decisions; an opportunity when the sharing of different understandings creates a robust sense of reality and leads to better decisions. What I eventually came to understand is that we need a process that permits the enterprise to accommodate and share different notions of reality. It has also led me to understand that the purpose of a decision-making design is to provide an enterprise with the means to improve the way it inquires about its opportunities and problems.

The lens of learning

These different 'notions of reality' were further explored by Peter Senge, who along with Chris Argyris and others has opened our thinking to the importance of learning and the way in which it occurs. In The Fifth Discipline, Senge describes those predisposed mindsets (mental models) as "deeply ingrained assumptions, generalizations, or even pictures or images that influence how we understand the world and how we take action."[49]

C. K. Prahalad also provided a very active description of the role and importance of dialogue as a method of overcoming the predisposed mind in the learning process:

> *Dialogue means interactivity, deep engagement, and a propensity to act – on both sides. Dialogue is more than listening to customers: It entails empathic understanding built around experiencing what consumers experience, and recognizing the emotional, social, and cultural context of experiences. It implies shared learning and communication between two equal problem solvers. Dialogue creates and maintains a loyal community.*[50]

Prahalad's description provides the basis for a plan of action for both individual and collective learning. The value of his description is that it provides the first step in getting people to listen to others because there is a commitment to share between two equal partners. It implies a faith that understanding is made richer by suspending one's own assumptions and beliefs long enough to consider those of others. Once this understanding is achieved, it prepares us for the really hard work of developing a solution to the problems we now better understand. Managing the interactions of the four Capabilities that follow offers an experienced-based 'sketch' of how to develop viable solutions to the many intractable problems we all face.

---

49   Senge, 1990, Argyris, 1991, pp. 99-109, and Argyris, 1994, pp. 77-85.

50   Prahalad & Ramaswamy, 2004

Background: Why a 'Sketch'?

A critical aspect of a Decision Loom – the concept of inquiry

Inquiry is more than asking questions and hoping for the right answers, on time, and at a price you can afford. Inquiry encompasses both art and science. Identifying the importance of inquiry is also not new. In their 1950 book *Methods of Inquiry*, C. West Churchman and Russ Ackoff attempted to clarify the importance of the continuing need to address the relationship between rational intuition (imagination) and scientific observation (knowledge):

> *If we claim that all true science is based on a rational intuition, then eventually we are obliged to exclude more and more from the realm of science, or else to pursue the course of appealing to common sense or some other faculty beyond pure reason. Or again, if we try to base science solely on sensory observation, we find that we have to exclude certain problems from any possible investigation, simply because there is no way that we can get at their solutions through direct observation. There is no apparent way, for example, of predicating with certainty what future events will occur, for our direct observations are never made in terms of predicted occurrences. As the history of thought developed, the exclusions became more and more significant. To save science from a complete skepticism, some new attitude toward scientific method was required.*

> *It is to be expected that some thinkers, in order to prevent this skepticism, would attempt some sort of a synthesis between the two major positions with respect to the basis of science. One such synthesis would be to insist that both rational intuition and direct observations are essential for science, but neither can exist independently of the other. In other words, every scientist in all his investigations must bring together certain basic rational intuitions and his direct observations... We might express this by saying that rational intuition and observation are each essential or necessary elements in any investigation, but neither alone is sufficient.*[51]

---

51   Churchman & Ackoff, 1950

In 1962, a report by Douglas C. Englebart, one of the founders of personal computing, identified the possible opportunities provided by new technology:

> *By 'augmenting human intellect' we mean increasing the capability of a man to approach a complex problem situation, to gain comprehension to suit his particular needs, and to derive solutions to problems. Increased capability in this respect is taken to mean a mixture of the following: more-rapid comprehension, better comprehension, the possibility of gaining a useful degree of comprehension in a situation that previously was too complex, speedier solutions, better solutions, and the possibility of finding solutions to problems that before seemed insoluble. And by 'complex situations' we include the professional problems of diplomats, executives, social scientists, life scientists, physical scientists, attorneys, designers – whether the problem situation exists for twenty minutes or twenty years. We do not speak of isolated clever tricks that help in particular situations. We refer to a way of life in an integrated domain where hunches, cut-and-try, intangibles, and the human 'feel for a situation' usefully co-exist with powerful concepts, streamlined terminology and notation, sophisticated methods, and high-powered electronic aids.* [52]

In the more than fifty years since these statements were made we have seen a greater appreciation of the need for both rational intuition (imagination) and scientific observation (knowledge). We have also benefited from significant improvements in measuring behavior and attitudes, incredible access to stored information through sophisticated search methods, and access to powerful new analytic methods – some of which may have even surpassed the imagination of these three distinguished minds. Yet, we find ourselves still having difficulty addressing complex problems in a timely and constructive manner.

Part of the problem was later addressed by C. West Churchman who provided a more direct purpose for the need to develop a more effective capability to support the ability to inquire:

> *Inquiry is an activity which produces knowledge . . . by 'produces' we mean 'makes a difference in and of itself.' In other words, for an activity to be said to produce a result, it must really matter, and to test whether it matters one determines whether the absence of the activity would have resulted in something different . . . Knowledge can be considered as a collection of information, or as an activity, or as a potential.*

---

52   Englebart, 1962

However, Churchman also warned us not be trapped into the belief that information collections stored in libraries or file drawers are knowledge:

> ... to conceive of knowledge as a collection of information seems to rob the concept of all its life. Knowledge is a vital force that makes an enormous difference in the world. Simply to say that it is storage of sentences is to ignore all that this difference amounts to.[53]

This is an essential point. The concept of knowledge, as envisioned by Churchman, requires that it be used and that it make a difference to a user in making the right decision and that its value be determined by the extent of use.

Creating a 'sketch' of an idealized design of a Decision Loom that facilitates interactive decision-making – one that is greater than the sum of art and science

Normally when Russ Ackoff would start the Idealized Design process he would start by saying something like, "Assume the system you want to improve has overnight been destroyed. With it completely gone you are in a position to do whatever you want to do without worrying about the impact on the existing system. Now, with that as background what would you do today if you could have access to anything you wanted and could do whatever was necessary?" I invite you to imagine that the decision-making capability of your enterprise has been similarly destroyed overnight.[54]

The approach to be taken

Following Russ Ackoff's Idealized Design approach, I would start by formulating the mess. That is, identifying the conditions which have led to the need to develop an idealized design for developing decision-making process capable of addressing problems and opportunities in a dynamic and complex world.

---

53   Churchman, 1971

54   Ackoff, Magidson & Addison, 2006

Informed by my previous work with Everett Rogers and my own work experience I would also recognize that the actions of any enterprise are driven by its own distinct attributes and behaviors as well as the environmental context in which it operates.

The reason the term 'sketch' was chosen and not 'blueprint,' is that the concept of an idealized design for decision-making is more likely to be broadly adopted if each enterprise is allowed to reinvent the concepts presented for its own purposes. The ability to reinvent allows the enterprise to apply the principles inherent in the concept without being restricted to a set of rigid rules. The eventual user of the concept is better-positioned to consider the suggested activities in the context of:

- The existing organizational structure

- The market and/or societal environment

- The collection and development of the required information

- The selection and implementation of the most useful decision processes.

The value of this approach is discussed in a paper by Michael Porter and Nicolaj Siggelkow. In their paper they provide evidence that:

> While contextuality of activities is an important phenomenon, our research conducted at the firm level suggests that a second type of contextuality is important to further our understanding of the sustainability of competitive advantage: The contextuality of interactions. Whether and how activities interact – for instance, whether they are complements and reinforce each other, or whether they are substitutes – can also depend on other activity choices made by a firm. Thus the nature of the interaction among activities may not be an inherent property of the activities, but a function of the other choices made by a firm.[55]

The essence of the solution to the mess we are trying to solve is to update the ways in which many of us have been taught to think and decide. These are no longer sufficient to address the more complex and dynamic problems of the 21st Century. This will require individuals who are skilled in the old ways to accept additional ways of thinking

---

55   Porter & Siggelkow, 2008, p. 35

that are more aligned with current problems and environments – and will sometimes be introduced into the enterprise by individuals junior to themselves who are more likely to be aware of their existence and potential value.

Dynamic complexity

- What is meant by an accelerating rate of change and increased complexity, and how real is it? I believe almost everyone would accept that today and for some time in the future we can count on:

- Increased customer/citizen and market/community diversity

- A more transparent world – significantly increased information and knowledge available to customers/citizens and competitors

- Market turbulence

- A demand by developing populations to acquire what developed populations and societies already have

We can also expect that...

- We will have less time to respond to market/constituency requests

- We will be less able to forecast market conditions and constituency needs

- The places we normally go to get money and things done will be under pressure to change

- Our ability to find, much less talk to, mass markets through a single communication medium where we control the message content will have decreased.

- We will face a world in which individuals determine what they hear and who they hear it from.

The enterprise, its customers/citizens, and its communities/ constituencies

As an enterprise becomes more systemic in its thinking, it must consider the larger stakeholder system – all those individuals or entities that can affect, or be affected by, the enterprise's decisions. Today the enterprise needs to pay greater attention to the attitudes and behavior of its containing environment.

The mess in which many enterprises find themselves is partially explained by the development of narrowly defined disciplines (organizational functions) which led to highly focused *analysis* of the activities contained within those disciplines. This approach to organization and implementing products and services dominated the later part of the 20th Century. During that period many of us were trained that if we wanted to understand or fix something we would first take it apart so we could examine the parts. We would then attempt to understand the behavior of each of the parts. Based on what we learned about each part we would summarize that understanding to describe the whole. By contrast, systems thinking and design thinking tell us *synthesis* is more important than analysis. Understanding how the parts operate and how to improve them is still important. But, in a more interconnected world, it is no longer sufficient. This important issue is more fully addressed in Capability 2.

And now to an idealized description of the Decision Loom as an interactive decision process and the capabilities that are needed to allow it to take place in your enterprise – right now.

The Decision Loom...an interactive decision-making process

Community knowledge implies careful control and scrutiny on the part of other inquirers; personal knowledge does not. Thus if a scientist undertakes to create knowledge for the community, he must write down what he intends to do, and then, if he is a careful scientist, he must keep a log of what he has done, and finally he is obliged in his reports to present his findings in such a way that any colleague can, if he wishes, observe exactly what the scientist has been doing.

C. West Churchman[56]

Over the last 50 years I have been extensively involved in both providing information to support decision-making and in actually making decisions in the public and private sectors. As important as some of those decisions were, as the stories told in Part 1 make clear, their true value is a combination of what was done and what was learned in making them and observing what happened after they were implemented. The ability to learn from our decisions requires participants in the decision-making process to be fully engaged in the four capabilities that follow this discussion of the Decision Loom. The interactive decision-making process is designed to take advantage of what is accomplished while exercising the forthcoming capabilities and to help the enterprise to systemically understand what has been learned from the actions it has taken.

It should also be noted that I am not suggesting the term Decision Loom should be used as the name to describe this activity in your enterprise. Each enterprise should determine what name is more likely to be accepted by the members of the enterprise involved in its development.

---

56   Churchman, 1971, p. 154

Encourage transparency

The Decision Loom is a learning process that is supported by an interactive decision support system that pumps information freely among employees and across functions in support of a full range of decision processes. A more detailed description of the entire process is contained in the four capabilities that are described in following chapters.

At the heart of this approach is the belief that any enterprise's approach to decision-making needs to be a network of interactive decisions that encourage and reward the sharing and application of information. This systemic approach requires an open dialogue and a focus on learning that is based on accepting that we cannot be as certain about what might happen in the future as we once were.

Like a cardiologist with an angiogram, management must examine the enterprise to find blockages to the free flow of information. Internally, these blockages may exist in any number of forms:

- Inadequate or passive market/constituency understanding capabilities; where decision-makers and information-providers operate in separate functional worlds and information is used only when it is determined that it is needed during the decision-making process

- Intermediaries that stand between the market and the entire enterprise

- Relying exclusively on third parties to provide 'unbiased' reports that are relevant to the enterprise

- Lack of direct feedback mechanisms between customers, suppliers, distributors and the enterprise

- Information systems that fail to detect and properly classify data coming from the marketplace and the community

- Managers who bring forth only the information that supports their decision and withhold evidence that exists and would likely challenge the wisdom of changing.

Prior to making a decision: surface and make explicit the critical assumptions

First identify the stakeholders

There is a relatively straightforward method to ensure that the critical assumptions underpinning each of the enterprise's key strategic and operating decisions are surfaced. Identify the key stakeholders, both within the organization and outside it. Stakeholders can be identified by asking questions like the following:

- Who or what is affected by the decision?

- Who or what has an interest in the decision?

- Who or what is in a position to affect its adoption or execution?

- Who has expressed an opinion?

- Who or what ought to care about the outcome?

The purpose of using stakeholders as the basis of identifying critical assumptions was clearly stated by Richard Mason and Ian Mitroff:

> *A business firm may be conceived of as the embodiment of a series of transactions among all of its constituent purposeful entities, that is its stakeholders. The final outcome of an organization's plan will be the collective result of the effects of the individual actions taken by its stakeholders. Thus a strategy may always be thought of as a set of assumptions about the current and future behavior of an organization's stakeholders.*[57]

Next understand what underlies the assumptions

Conduct a session to surface and challenge the importance and plausibility of the assumptions.[58]

After the list of assumptions has been developed, the extent to which they should be monitored can be decided according to two criteria:

---

57   Mason & Mitroff, 1981

58   This process is described in the Episodes 6 and 9 and Activity 3.

1. The assumption should have a significant bearing on the outcome of the decision.

2. The assumption should be as 'self-evident' and 'certain to be true' as possible – but as Churchman has noted – not all assumptions will be certain.

The key steps for learning from your decisions

In the spirit of developing a sketch, what follows is drawn, in part, from an article I wrote with Russ Ackoff and John Pourdehnad that describes the process in far greater detail.[59]

The process begins with the three components that tend to go into any enterprise decision, regardless of how that decision is made:

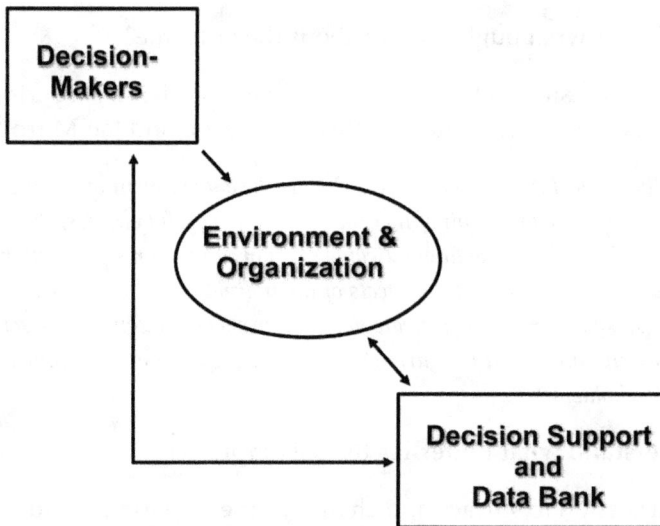

Figure 7: The basic components of most decision processes

There are three basic components to many of the decisions processes with which we are familiar:

---

59   Barabba, Pourdehnad and Ackoff, 2002

1. Decision-Makers – People who use the data bank to make decisions

2. Organization – Receives direction from Decision-Makers and uses and returns information to the Data Bank while implementing decisions.

3. Decision Support and Data Bank – Contains the organization's Decision Process support and its data, information, knowledge and understanding.

In this basic model, a Decision-Maker (someone with authority to allocate resources) gets information from the Data Bank (what the organization knows or can acquire) to make a decision which will be implemented by the Organization in the most efficient and effective manner known to it at the time of the decision.

Inserting learning into the decision-making process

As discussed in Episode 8 (and shown initially in Figure 1), Chris Argyris has provided a helpful view on types of learning. The first type of learning is 'single-loop learning'– the kind that occurs when errors are detected and corrected. This is our most familiar approach to learning. It occurs when someone in the enterprise finds a problem, studies it, makes changes and gets the program back on track.

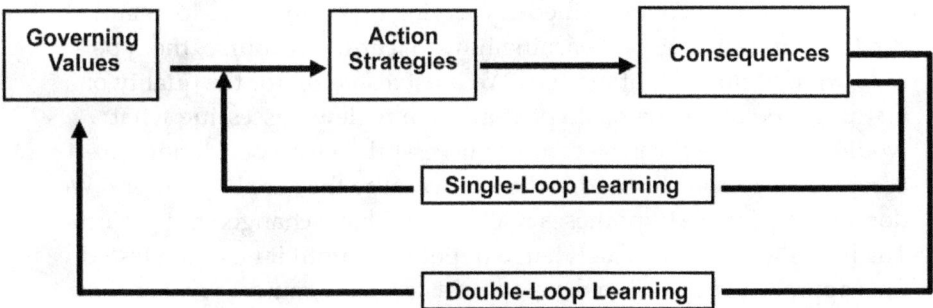

Figure 8: Elements of single- and double-loop learning

But while this type of learning is very important, it doesn't help transfer learning across the organization. Only those who were involved in the original problem have gained anything. And so we also need 'double-loop learning.' Besides detecting and correcting errors, double-loop learning encourages the organization to actively question and modify existing values, norms, procedures, policies and objectives.

Also discussed in Episode 8, the GM MS2000 product team found itself with products on the market that were not competitive enough in its target segment. The team came up with a solution to address the problem. Being a part of a broader enterprise system, rather than just solving their own problem, the team shared its solution with other teams and discovered that the company's overall development process – which assumed an ability to predict customer requirements – was no longer sufficient, in and of itself, for the change in market conditions.

Everyone involved had to step back and look at the entire system, because the problem was not limited to the specific situation in which they found themselves. Rather, it resided in a set of broader systems and beliefs.

Using double-loop learning concepts, a systemic look at the situation might, in another example, reveal that the environment in which products were sold and serviced is changing faster than it did in the past, when the product development process was created. This finding would lead management to consider reviewing all other decisions that were based on the assumptions that have just been determined to be no longer valid.

The ultimate challenge is "deutero-learning,"[60] which occurs when an organization becomes skilled at carrying out both single-loop and double-loop learning, or "learning how to learn." Of course, the type of learning is not all that matters. We must also monitor the quality of learning. Too often, teams do post-mortem reviews, assessing what would have made the project more successful. These speculations are accepted as 'lessons learned,' when in actuality they are hypotheses. We don't know if these hypotheses really would have changed the project. The hypothesis remains just that, a hypothesis, until it has been tested. This approach is critical to developing a company mindset where rigor is applied to testing and confirming hunches in pilot areas, rather than making wide applications based on mere speculation.

---

60 A term coined by Gregory Bateson in the 1940s referring to the organization of learning, or learning to learn.

But in a learning organization, the decision-making process must be more robust and complete than this. If we want to not only make decisions, but also to learn from them, we must add several dimensions. That's where the full learning and adaptation model comes into play. There are three critical concepts underlying this approach:

1. All of the components of the learning process are constantly interacting with each other.

2. Pieces of this system already exist in most organizations. The trick is to integrate and synthesize the decision-making process and the learning functions overall, so as to move from analysis to synthesis without simply 'imposing' a new model on the organization.

3. The Data Bank or Data Warehouse is not static nor is it limited to a physical location. Rather it is an interactive decision process within the organization that varies depending on what type of decision we're making. In other words, Finance has a body of knowledge… Manufacturing has a body of knowledge… as does the Quality group, Marketing divisions, Design Engineers, etc. The Decision Loom is designed to provide methods for each of the functions to share in the knowledge of the other functions.

The goal is to link these resources as much as possible, but we want to avoid the tendency to dump everything into a storage system. The Decision Loom is not merely an IT system that puts everything online. Such systems are useful, and they support organizational learning, but they are not sufficient. Rather, we are looking to sort, codify, and synthesize information before storing it, so that those who need it can find relevant insights, knowledge or decisions.

The Decision Loom can be as high tech or low tech as the organization chooses. Insights may be stored in a traditional library, a file or a computer system. The basis of this approach is found in another long journey, in this case a journey taken by Russ Ackoff, which has evolved into what he called a "learning and adaptation" model to help improve our ability to make strategic decisions, and then learn from them.

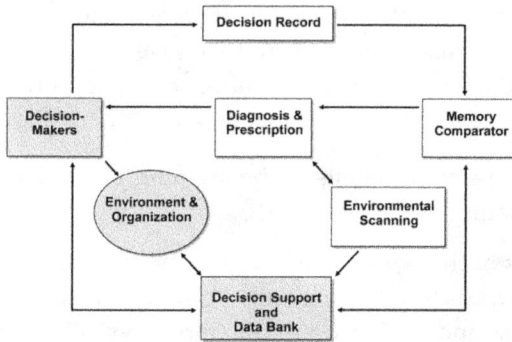

Figure 9: Basic decision-making process, complemented by the learning component of the Decision Loom[61]

The design begins, as we have seen, with the basic three components already described (shaded boxes).

To enable continued monitoring, the enterprise will also have to document the information that was used to support the important decisions it has made.

This can be accomplished through the use of a decision record, which captures the decision, as well as the underlying assumptions that were used, the expectations that were held, and the types of information, knowledge and understanding that were employed in making the decision.

---

61   For a more detailed examination of the Learning and Adaptation (L&A) Support System see Barabba, Pourdehnad and Ackoff, 2002. A brief description of the process described there (and a diagram of the L&A Support System) can be found in Appendix A of this book.

DECISION RECORD	Date:	INFORMATION USED:

The form figure:

Figure content (Decision Record form):

DECISION RECORD

Date:
Identification Number:
Report Prepared by:
Report Checked by:

INFORMATION USED:

KEY WORDS:

WHO PARTICIPATED IN MAKING THE DECISION:

DESCRIPTION OF ISSUES:

THE DECISION-MAKING PROCESS:

IS ISSUE PRIMARILY AN :
____ Opportunity OR ____ A Threat (check one)

OUTCOME (Check One):
____ No Decision   ____ Decision to Do Nothing
____ Decision to Do Something (Describe)

WHO IS RESPONSIBLE FOR IMPLEMENTATION (if anyone)?

IMPLEMENTATION PLAN:

ARGUMENTS PRO:

ARGUMENTS CON:

OBSERVATIONS AND COMMENTS:

EXPECTED CONSEQUENCES OR EFFECTS AND WHEN THEY ARE EXPECTED:

ASSUMPTIONS ON WHICH EXPECTATIONS ARE BASED:

Figure 10: A sample Decision Record format

Every enterprise should develop its own Decision Record to capture the characteristics and the needs of the decision process of the enterprise.

The Decision Record serves as the *memory* to monitor and compare the assumptions and expected outcomes with actual performance. It also makes all aspects of the decision available to future decision-makers. The record is reviewed and agreed upon by the decision-making team, thereby providing the organizational memory of what was decided, why it was decided, and who made the decision.

Once the decision is implemented, we use the *memory comparator* function to track what was expected to happen against what actually happened, as well as the underlying assumptions.

This comparison of 'before and after' reinforces the importance of monitoring and learning from the implementation of our decisions.

When the comparator function finds no significant difference between what is expected and assumed, and what actually happens, then nothing needs to be done, other than to record this in memory for future reference. If, however, a significant difference is found, the *Diagnosis and Prescription* activity tries to find out why. Perhaps the information used in the original decision was in error… or the decision-making process was faulty… or the decision was correct, but was not implemented properly…or there were unexpected changes in the containing environment.

We can go even further, by using *Environmental Scanning* tools. Often, organizations don't clearly state the parameters of their decisions. What were the deliverables? What were the underlying assumptions? Did we assume the economy would remain stable? Did we assume that the competition wouldn't make a counter offer to our customers?

Environmental Scanning is a broad based function, which should be ongoing at all times, and which adds an important additional dimension to our ability to make strategic decisions and learn from them.

It is here that we monitor both the environment and the organization, providing our decision-makers with information and knowledge that tends to exist beyond their daily radar screens. Here we track such things as workforce concerns, company reorganizations, weather that shuts down the distribution system, activity by the competition, and changes in the value of foreign currencies. The list goes on. Without maintaining a constant monitoring the company risks becoming myopic.

I say that because the scanning information is used not only in decision diagnosis, but is also fed *into* the Decision Loom for future reference as well as providing early warning to management of a change occurring in one of their underlying assumptions. This is where the 'Adaptation' part of the Learning and Adaptation Model comes in.

By scanning and assessing the strategic implications of internal and external forces, we are able to focus beyond issues that are merely relevant to a specific decision, and understand what might be happening within our organization or the larger environment that could impact the effectiveness of our overall decisions.

A Personal Example of a Decision Record

In the development of this book there were several critical decisions that were made prior to publication. One of the most critical was whether to include the experiences described in *Part 1: The Journey* or to simply provide the design of the Decision Loom. What follows is a decision record of the decision that was made.

DECISION RECORD

Date: February 1, 2011

Report Prepared by: Vince Barabba

Report Checked by: Triarchy Press

KEY WORDS:
Book Format, Reader Preferences, and Electronic Publishing

DESCRIPTION OF ISSUES:
Publisher felt that Part 1 was autobiographical while Part 2 was more like a business/management guide, and that the two would be of interest to different groups of readers – so they should be published as two separate books. Author felt The Journey was not autobiographical but demonstrated evidence of lessons learned that led to suggested approaches to the Decision-Making Process.

IS ISSUE PRIMARILY AN :
_X_ Opportunity OR ____ A Threat (check one)

OUTCOME (Check One):
____ No Decision ____ Decision to Do Nothing
_X_ Decision to Do Something (Describe)

Decision was made to include a reduced version of The Journey and an index to where lessons were learned and where they were applied. With that as background the reader was provided with information to decide whether they wanted to read the Journey first, second, or not at all.

ARGUMENTS PRO:
The hope was that both sets of potential readers will buy the book anyway, even though one part of the book is of less interest to them.

ARGUMENTS CON:
We may be unduly optimistic and potential readers will not be so indulgent. There is always risk in a compromise.

EXPECTED CONSEQUENCES OR EFFECTS AND WHEN THEY ARE EXPECTED
Initial reviews will have either a positive or negative impact on book sales. This will occur soon after book is released.

INFORMATION USED:
Experience of Both Author and Publisher

WHO PARTICIPATED IN MAKING THE DECISION:
Author and Publisher

THE DECISION MAKING PROCESS:
A rational discussion between Author and Publisher seeking a constructive outcome to what initially appeared to be an irresolvable issue.

OBSERVATIONS AND COMMENTS:
If the reader gets this far into the book… the decision to alter the design of the book to a non-traditional format actually worked! The extent to which it worked will be determined by reviews and final book sales.

Figure 11: Decision Record on the design of this book

Learning how to avoid crises brought on by changing conditions

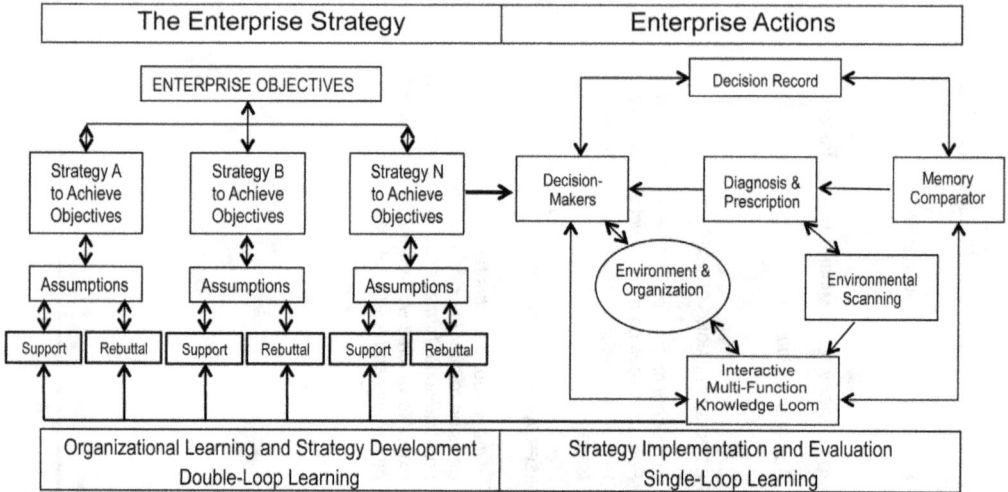

Figure 12: How the Decision Loom helps anticipate problems before they become a crisis

Figure 12 illustrates how the scanning of the containing environment can provide an early warning capability to the enterprise. If the enterprise lists both the supporting and rebuttal information that underlie the accepted assumptions that were used in developing the Enterprise Strategy, those responsible for the interactive decision-making process will be in a position to monitor that information either by evaluating how a current decision has turned out or, through environmental scanning, begin a tracking program of the information that was critical to accepting the assumptions underlying previous decisions. When there is a change, either positive or negative, in those assumptions the leadership of the enterprise is informed of the change and of possible consequences – either to the general strategy of the enterprise or to a specific action. Assuming the enterprise has developed the Dynamic Modeling capability described in Episode 9 and Capability 4, simulations can be conducted to determine the effectiveness of alternative actions available to the enterprise when considering the effect of the changing condition of the containing environment and underlying assumptions.

If the model appears complex, that's because organizational learning and adaption is complex, and there are many interactions between the various elements. This is not a flow diagram. Rather, the model offers a two-dimensional representation of an integrated, cross-functional process that leads to an improved decision-making process that incorporates organizational learning and offers advance notice of problems or opportunities.

Implementation

Implementing this activity will not be easy... but it is certainly feasible. The difficulty will occur, as described in Capability 1, in changing the mindset of the enterprise so that the following occurs:

1. All enterprise functions share their knowledge in a form that can be understood by others.

2. Decision-makers willingly list the reasons why the assumptions underlying their decision should be constantly monitored.

3. The enterprise takes the time to list the reasons behind the decision. This ensures that the enterprise will reinforce its beliefs when the decision turns out to be correct, and learn to question existing beliefs when it doesn't.

4. Discovery. The enterprise determines that the value of learning from past decisions is greater than the cost that might be incurred in litigation that is brought forward because the basis of a decision is now available through discovery.

How do we get from this ideal mindset back to where we are and what decisions do we make right now to ensure that we get to where we want to be. What follows are my suggestions as to four capabilities you should have right now if you want to implement a Decision Loom. If you actually have these capabilities – fine. If not, what follows will provide an indication of what lies between where you want to be and where your capabilities currently are.

Examples of the ideas presented

Following each section of *Part 2* (including this one) I give examples of successful actions taken by enterprises to adapt to changing conditions. The emphasis is on specific examples of the action taken by the enterprise. This is not to say the entire enterprise itself was or is successful. In today's rapidly evolving environment these examples place emphasis on how the enterprise addressed a current and specific situation.

W.L. Gore: Leading without leaders

While it is inconceivable to many that a business might succeed if it lacks titles, bosses, general hierarchies, and a core business, W.L. Gore negates that paradigm: since beginning in 1958, the company has never endured a loss and continues to roll out incredible innovations. The company's products number well above 1000, with successes including the Gore-Tex lining that waterproofs fabric, dental floss that does not shred and Elixir guitar strings that last longer and sound better.[62]

An environment without bureaucracy was Gore's goal when he left DuPont, envisioning a workspace with open communication and a long-term outlook that would allow individuals the freedom to explore new ideas and collaborate across pedigrees.[63] While there are *de facto* leaders in each of the divisions for general administrative purposes, teams do the day-to-day work and informal power is given to those that inspire followers. However, product development is not completely *ad hoc* and new ideas at Gore are subject to continuous peer review. At the outset, employees ask questions and offer contrary perspectives. Gore's leaders acknowledge this is timely on the front end but see the value on the back end when workers buy in and commit to the success of the project after they have been able to voice concerns or add their own 'two cents'.[64] As the project progresses, 'Real, Win, Worth' is employed and more questions arise: "Is the opportunity real? Is there really somebody out there that will buy this? Can we win? What do the economics look like? Can we make money doing this? Is it unique and valuable? Can we have a sustained advantage [such as a patent]?"[65] Gore will take these same questions to potential product consumers, incorporating their feedback to tweak the product or gauge enthusiasm.[66] Should a product fail to meet its intended objective, it

---

62   Deutschman, 2004

63   Ibid.

64   Hamel, 2010

65   Harrington, 2003

66   Ibid.

does not go to waste – the guitar strings resulted only after their use as bike cables failed – and the designer had the freedom to transition the product into a new space. Moreover, with a focus off the short term, lofty yet influential projects are feasible, like Gore's continued work with GM on fuel cells.

With more than 6,000 employees in 50 locations – the company hopes to maintain this structure even as the company grows. In fact, they see their management model as a complement to scaling, since they "push authority out to operating teams", as opposed to consolidating power in several people or geographic locations.[67] In the meantime, it seems only a matter of time before the world enjoys the next big advance from the folks at Gore.

The Black Box – Learning from mistakes

In the following excerpt from his paper[68] on "Building Corporate 'Black Boxes': John Pourdehnad provides an excellent example of the value of a Decision Record in his description of how the National Transportation Safety Board (NTSB) has successfully used decision records to improve airline safety.

Historical data on airline safety shows that, in the early days of commercial aviation, airline fatality rates were approximately 1,500 times higher than those of railroads and 900 times higher than those of bus lines. Today it is commonly known that air travel is safer, in terms of passenger miles, than travel by automobile, bus, or railroad. In 1930, there were 28 passenger fatalities for each 100 million passenger-miles. Today, the number is less than one… [Malcolm] McPherson… wrote the following about the performance of commercial aviation systems:

"Thanks to the high level of professionalism of aircraft manufacturers, (through their entire hierarchy), and especially of the airlines' flight crews, plus the vigilance of the Federal Aviation Administration (FAA) and the attention to detail of the National Transportation Safety Board (NTSB), aviation accidents have (and I apologize for this word) plummeted since the advent of big-jet travel in the early 1960s."

Clearly, the commercial aviation industry is doing something right about safety. Indeed, its progress has been impressive. It exemplifies a successful learning and adaptive (L&A) system. In order to understand

---

67   Hamel, 2010

68   Pourdehnad, 2008

its accomplishment, it is necessary to understand the principal functions of its system.

…the commercial aviation system, in addition to its operating environment, consists of three major components that continuously interact: (1) software (all the regulations, SOPs, policies, manuals, checklists, maps, performance charts, tables and graphs), (2) hardware (the aircraft itself and its supporting system), and (3) liveware (pilots and all the people that they deal with on the ground and in the air). "No [function] is totally isolated from the others; if one element is inferior, it will have a negative impact on all the others."

Detecting and Correcting Errors

Although great effort is directed at raising the competency level of all those who work within the system, mistakes occur. In order for the aviation industry to learn and improve, it must and does have a way of identifying errors. A 'Black Box' is on every commercial aircraft. It consists of flight data and cockpit voice recorders. [Nicholas] Faith wrote that black boxes are the best single source of information for investigators. As a memory, they provide data on the long series of events that occur during a flight. Crucially, black boxes are completely objective. Because they record events as they occur, they are exempt from interference and influence. (As will be discussed later, this is an important requirement for any learning system.) Analysis of the data in black boxes enables investigators to compare expected happenings with what actually happened and to determine where the difference between them has occurred.

Determining what caused deviations from expectations is the responsibility of the National Transportation Safety Board (NTSB). Its main function is diagnosis and prescription – to investigate accidents, identify their causes, and recommend improvements. In order to achieve a high standard of excellence, the NTSB is a professional body with its own investigators and methodology. [Nicholas] Faith… makes this point:

"Air-accident investigators, or 'tin-kickers', are a very special breed. In one sense they're detectives operating in a very specialized field, but, at a senior level, they have to be capable of co-coordinating, and thus of comprehending, a far wider range of professional skills than their equivalents in the criminal field."

Despite its responsibilities, the NTSB has no regulatory or enforcement powers. Once the cause(s) of an accident have been determined, its recommendations for action are sent to the Federal Aviation Administration (FAA), which sets and enforces air safety standards. In addition, the FAA plays a major role in assuring system efficiency, regulatory reform, sharing and analysis of safety information, surveillance, inspection, and accident prevention.

System Memory (Knowledge Repository)

In order to provide high quality input to relevant decision-makers, the FAA has created the Aviation Safety Reporting System (ASRS). It collects voluntarily submitted aviation safety incident reports in order to reduce the likelihood of aviation accidents. ASRS captures information about such things as emergency landings, mechanical/maintenance problems, security, health related fatalities, injuries and illnesses, operational problems, and passenger disturbances. This information is used to identify and remedy deficiencies and discrepancies in the National Aviation System (NAS). Lessons from mistakes are documented and organized for easy access and made available to those who need and are authorized to receive it. In this setting, there is constant support for policy formulation and system improvement. Also, in many instances, expertise is leveraged across the system.

Capability 1: Having an Enterprise Mindset that is Open to Change

Far better an approximate answer to the right question, which is often vague, than the exact answer to the wrong question, which can always be made precise.
John Tukey

In a world of more fragmented markets, extensive social concerns, and digitally accelerated opportunities, all the interdependent components of an enterprise must have direct access to what the enterprise knows about the consumers of its products, services, or policies as well as its competition, the surrounding environment and itself. Traditionally many enterprises have operated in a sequential manner: one group collects the information; another group translates and presents the information to another group, which then decides how to develop a product or service. The product or service design is then turned over to a division that makes it, and in turn releases it to another division, which promotes and distributes the product or service.

Enterprises no longer have the time or the resources to operate in this manner. In order to make a Decision Loom possible, the enterprise needs to take note of Tukey's words and aim for a system of inquiry that provides either approximate or more precise information that can be transformed into relevant answers to the right questions in a timely manner at a cost that decision-makers will feel offers good value. This means avoiding processes that require simplifying the problem so that it appears it can be answered precisely – which often yields a precise answer to the wrong problem.

Thus the enterprise needs to make every attempt to avoid making Ian Mitroff's "Errors of the 3rd and 4th Kind":

> *The Type Three Error occurs when to* **our** *detriment* **we unintentionally fool and trick ourselves** *into solving the wrong problems precisely,* **but we don't necessarily force our definition on others.** *In sharp contrast, the Type Four Error occurs when, to* **their detriment** *and for* **our** *gain and benefit, we intentionally* **force others** *into solving the wrong problems precisely. That is, in the Type*

Four Error we force and trick others into solving **our** *definitions of problems.*[69]

To get to a new mindset, the enterprise may have to re-train many of its managers who have previously been trained in, and are comfortable with, the more functional and linear approaches to managing the process that had worked well, at least in their mind, in the past. Generally these approaches lead to two forms of knowledge misuse:

1.   Satisfying a predisposition

As an example of how the system works in many enterprises, managers preparing to make a decision will direct someone or some organization to gather information relevant to the decision – sometimes focusing only on information that will support their point of view. If the information is consistent with the manager's predisposition, it is quickly incorporated it into the decision process. If it is not consistent it is either ignored or those portions of the research that support the predisposition are highlighted in the final report and any contradictory information is removed.

2.   Finding out you asked the wrong question

Another type of problem occurs when not enough time is devoted to ensuring that the study is designed so that relevant issues are addressed in a form that will be both timely and accepted by the decision-maker. In these cases, many important decisions around the questionnaire and data collection are left up to those responsible for the data-collection process. Often in this approach the manager, when seeing both the data-collection process and the report's results for the first time, finds the results do not provide the information needed to support the decision-making process. If time permits, the decision-maker will request a follow-on study. If time is not available, the decision will be made based on existing, and probably outdated, knowledge or existing predispositions. Finding out that the information you requested is not adequate has been described by Jerry Zaltman as having 'Post Survey Regret.' Although costly and sometimes cumbersome, this approach appeared to work reasonably well when enterprises were not faced with the dynamic and rapidly changing

---

69   Mitroff & Silvers, 2010

environment they now face. Today and for the foreseeable future, however, decision-makers are not afforded the luxury of 'starting over.'

Fortunately, some enterprises and universities have come to understand these problems. New approaches like Prahalad's concept of co-creation[70] and many Internet-based new technologies have provided the impetus to bridge the functional gap between the designers of relevant information and the users who seek support to improve on their new ideas.

A cautionary note

Before starting on this type of endeavor, the enterprise should make sure that all those involved in the change process are sensitive to the existing culture of the enterprise and the practices of its leadership. The following story[71] provides the context for this sensitivity:

> *There once was a tribe of Australian aborigines called the Yir Yoront. The central item in the Yir Yoront culture was the stone ax, which tribe members found indispensable in every activity – from producing food to constructing shelter. For the elders, the stone ax was a symbol of masculinity and respect. The men owned the stone axes, but the women and children were the principal users. Thus, according to a prescribed social system, the tools were borrowed from fathers, husbands, or uncles.*
>
> *Enter some well-intentioned missionaries. They distributed steel axes to the Yir Yoront to help them improve their living conditions. There was no important resistance to the shift to the new tool; the aborigines were accustomed to obtaining their tools via trade with others. Moreover, the steel axes were more efficient for most tasks; as a result, the stone axes rapidly disappeared among the Yir Yoront.*
>
> *The missionaries had distributed the steel axes to men, women and children, old and young alike. In fact, the younger men were quicker to adopt the new tool than were their elders, who maintained a certain distrust. The result was a major disruption of sex and age roles among the Yir Yoront. Elders, once highly respected, now became dependent upon women and younger men and often were forced to borrow steel axes.*

---

70   Prahalad & Ramaswamy, 2004

71   Barabba, 1985

In addition, the trading rituals of the tribe were undermined because stone axes had previously formed the basis of trade. Ties of friendship among traders broke down. Overall, the religious system and social structure of the Yir Yoront became disorganized as a result of an inability to adjust to the innovation.

Naturally, the steel ax alone did not cause all these changes among the Yir Yoront. But researchers concluded that it was central to most of the cultural disorders.

I first ran across this story as a student while studying the work of Everett Rogers.[72] I was trying to understand why some innovations were adopted faster than others. Rogers had defined an innovation as:

An idea, practice, or object perceived as new by an individual. It matters little, so far as human behavior is concerned, whether or not an idea is 'objectively' new as measure by the lapse of time since its first use or discovery. It is the perceived or subjective newness of the idea for the individual that determines his reaction to it. If the idea seems new to the individual, it is an innovation.

Beware of unintended consequences

As an example of what to watch for when adopting an innovation, in many enterprises the younger generation of employees are more likely to see the use of advanced electronic support tools (steel axes) as commonplace and will expect others to look upon these new tools in the same way and with the same enthusiasm they do. To the extent to which older employees or those with strong functional expertise see these new tools as dangerous to their position and ability to perform using existing tools (stone axes) actions may be taken to slow down or reduce the chances of taking full advantage of the new tools.

The important point is that, when attempting to change the mindset of an enterprise, whether it is a profound change or simply a modification, a new practice does not have to be truly new (in the sense that it has never existed before) in order for it to be perceived as new. And in providing something new you need to be aware that the change may threaten an individual's sense of security in their current role or in the way that others perceive that role. The key point is to make sure that

---

72   Rogers, 1962

you have considered whether the benefits you are bringing forward (your steel axes) outweigh the potential negative consequences of the disruption that might arise from either the perception or the reality of their introduction.

The importance of understanding how the enterprise interacts with its containing environment

Today, information providers can no longer be allowed to say, "I'll give it to you fast, accurately, or cheap; take two, because I can't do all three." The mindset must now be, "Given that I know what you really need and how you plan to use it to make the decision, I can acquire or develop what you want fast enough, accurately enough, and at a price you will value."

Managers must also ensure that the enterprise understands the implications and interactions of decisions beyond its organizational boundaries. Today, the enterprise must also understand there are other stakeholders beyond its consumers or constituents who have to know enough about its goals and practices to believe that it is an enterprise worth supporting. These additional stakeholders include the enterprise (which includes other divisions and companies that deliver the products and services to the customer and community), employees, suppliers, investors, and so forth. Additional stakeholders are found in the community, which is made up of consumers in a societal context, the governmental interests that attempt to represent them, the special interest groups that carry strong views on specific issues, and the competition for customer and community attention and resources.

The three main voices of a more comprehensive community of interest are illustrated in Figure 13: the consumer/constituent, the market/community, and the extended enterprise. Needless to say, there are many opportunities for agreement and conflict between these different market participants. It falls to decision-makers to understand the interactions and how they contribute to conflicts and agreements.[73]

---

73 Maslow (1965) elaborates on the internal and external conditions that affect these interactions. His prophetic observations provided an early indication of what was to come.

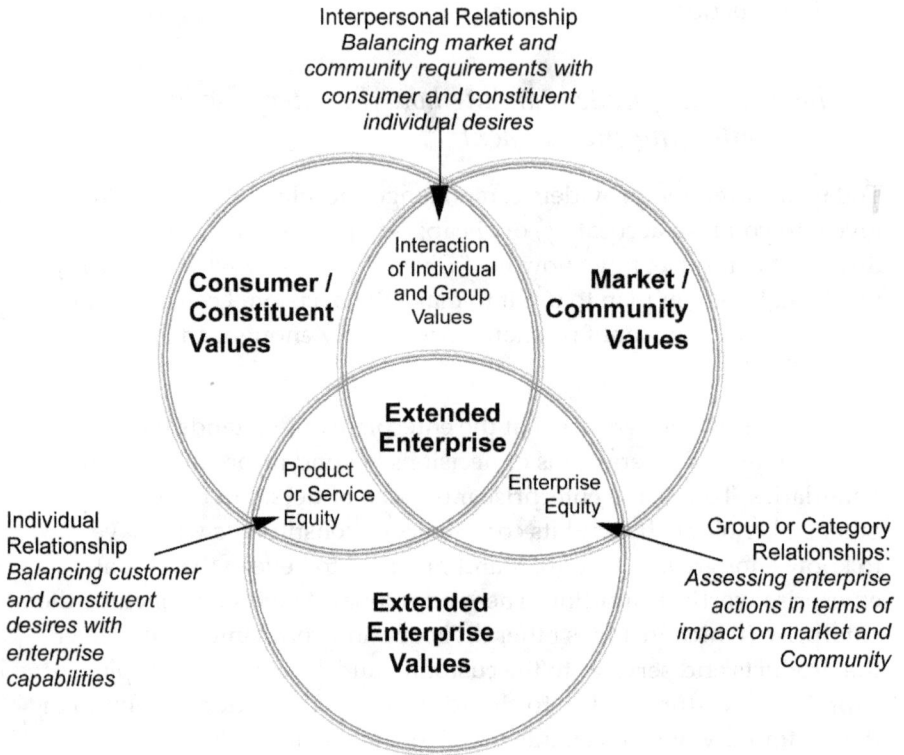

Interpersonal Relationship
*Balancing market and
community requirements with
consumer and constituent
individual desires*

Interaction
of Individual
and Group
Values

**Consumer /
Constituent
Values**

**Market /
Community
Values**

**Extended
Enterprise**

Product
or Service
Equity

Enterprise
Equity

Individual
Relationship
*Balancing customer
and constituent
desires with
enterprise
capabilities*

**Extended
Enterprise
Values**

Group or Category
Relationships:
*Assessing enterprise
actions in terms of
impact on market and
Community*

*Figure 13: The encompassing system of an extended enterprise which must
be comprehended within the Decision Loom*

The position or the view of any member of the total system on issues, as represented in this figure, is not necessarily fixed. For example, vehicle safety used to be solely a community value, reflected in government regulations on safety belts and other features. It is now an enterprise and customer value, as well, to the point that safety features are a selling feature for most vehicles. The same can now be said for environmental issues, which began as a community value and have taken on new meaning for both the enterprise and the customer.

This illustration serves as a visual reminder that customers and constituencies do not live in a vacuum. They live in communities – both real and virtual. Thus, we must simultaneously consider the desires both of the individual and of the community made up of those individuals; people's values in a personal buying situation do not necessarily map to their values in a community situation.

As I wrote at length in *Surviving Transformation*,[74] an enterprise making laundry detergent might find that customers want a 'whiter than white' wash, which the enterprise knows it can provide by using phosphate-based detergents. At the same time, the community – this includes customers, government regulators, and interested organizations – wants 'cleaner than clean' public waters, which are not compromised by phosphates. So, the enterprise needs to produce a profitable product that meets customer requirements and addresses community concerns.

But this is easier said than done. There are trade-offs. The enterprise has to find a way to get an individual to say:

As a consumer: "Non-phosphate detergents clean my clothes almost as well as phosphate-based detergents."

As a citizen: "I'm not sure how much non-phosphate detergents will clean up the environment, but every little bit helps."

Disposable diapers present a more complex problem. Like detergents, they provide real convenience to consumers, yet their environmental cost is less direct and obvious to the consumer because most consumers do not see landfills on a daily basis. The fact that landfills have less direct impact on their personal lives leads many individuals to rationalize their use of the diapers by saying:

As a consumer: "I find disposable diapers extremely helpful, and the thought of returning to cloth diapers and the mess they create in my house is unacceptable."

As a citizen: I'm not willing to give up my disposable diapers for the amount of environmental benefit the government or the environmentalists claim. Besides, what happens to all water that has to be cleaned after I wash the cloth diapers? How much energy do I use to get all the hot water I need to do the wash?"

If you are a manufacturer of disposable diapers, this is not the time to relax. You may have some time, but you had better start working on a solution that maintains the level of convenience while providing a

---

74   Barabba, 2005

more environmentally sensitive solution. If someone beats you to the solution, they will have a significant advantage.[75]

For example, in 2005 Procter & Gamble launched 'Tide Cold Water' to meet the consumer need for cold water washing. They conducted a life-cycle analysis of a range of common consumer goods that indicated that if consumers reduced the wash temperature of domestic laundering it would result in a significant reduction in energy consumption – which, it turned out, was among the largest environmental contributions P&G could make. This move to low temperature washing, enabled by Tide Cold Water allows the consumer to save energy while not compromising on the cleaning results obtained. Each consumer making a small difference makes a significant difference when multiplied across the population.

This approach to thinking about problems and their solutions has the potential to offer a significant competitive advantage, but only if the entire enterprise is brave enough to embrace it. As IDEO chief executive Tim Brown says in his book, *Change by Design*, "design thinking needs to move upstream, closer to the executive suites where strategic decisions are made". [76]

In today's environment, leadership needs to constantly look at the total system in which specific decisions operate and continually ask, "Am I asking people to work more efficiently within their function at the expense of helping the entire enterprise and the community in which it operates become more efficient and effective?" Time must also be found to nurture community support by making sure the many interests (some conflicting) that make up the community are sufficiently aware of the enterprise's behavior that is beneficial to them, not only as customers but as citizens as well.

Ackoff's approach to idealized planning is to start by answering the question, "if you could have whatever you wanted today…what would it be?" With the position you want to achieve clearly stated, Ackoff makes the point that it is easier to find a path back to where you are and then take the actions implied by that path to get you to where

---

75   I am indebted to Pam Pudar for her work in developing the examples used in describing this concept.

76   Brown, 2009

you want to be. In the spirit of idealized design here is an example of an idealized state that can be modified for the use of any enterprise in establishing its own idealized state.

The idealized mindset of the enterprise will have been achieved when:

1. An unambiguous sense of direction permeates the enterprise. The mission of the enterprise is known and understood by everyone including the communities that can affect or be affected by the enterprise – it is the universal premise behind all decisions and tasks, and the enterprise is focused on finding better ways to gain, develop, and – most importantly – maintain customer or constituent support.

2. Strategic and operational plans interact to reinforce each other. There are no downstream disconnects between enterprise functions and the eventual users of the enterprise's services.

3. By understanding how and why their function interacts with other functions, all decision-makers understand how their roles contribute to the total enterprise – their accountability is clear. All the activities are aligned.

4. The interaction of market knowledge with creative product and marketing ideas results in a steady stream of innovative and customer-satisfying products and services that leverage the capabilities and resources of the entire enterprise.

5. There is empowerment throughout the enterprise. Direction and accountability are clear, but there is no micro-management from above. Management is focused on the interaction of the parts and not the parts taken separately.

6. Conflict and differences of opinion are not suppressed. When they surface, they are channeled into a process that seeks a consensus decision. That is complete agreement – not necessarily in principle, but definitely in action.

7. There are no simplistic ideas about how individuals or competitors will respond to the actions of the enterprise: planning and execution recognize the full complexity and uncertainty of the competitive environment and societal context.

8. Existing and retired employees of the extended enterprise are the most effective recruiters of new employees.

9. Other enterprises want to interact with you.

10. When employees are asked, "If this enterprise was a school where people come to learn how to get imaginative ideas accomplished, would you pay tuition for your children to attend?" the universal answer is an enthusiastic "yes."[77]

What follows are two examples of actions taken by enterprises to adapt to changes in the external market or their customer base and which subsequently changed the enterprise mindset accordingly.

Examples of the ideas presented

LEGO: A 21st century universe[78]

In the 1990s, children's tastes were shifting to digital and high-tech entertainment outlets. LEGO, a Danish company built on offering a creative physical outlet for children's imaginations, was struggling with product development. Among other missteps, like an unpopular cartoon show, designers were freely producing ever-more complex amalgamations of the toy without thought to demand and supply costs. This increased the number of distinct components from 7,000 in the 1990s to 12,400 by 2004. Not surprisingly, losses had reached $205 million and debt was nearly $1 billion.

For seven decades since 1932, the Kristiansen family had run the legendary toy company but in 2004 they stepped aside and Jørgen Vig Knudstorp, a former consultant, took the helm. He radically changed company operations by outsourcing production, reducing staff, and divesting the company of failing theme parks. Moreover, designers were newly subject to firm contests in which LEGO only produced the winning design; the number of components returned to previous levels. He also pushed innovation to the forefront, adding more programming options to the build-your-own robotics kit (Mindstorms)

---

77   Michael Kusnik contributed to an earlier version of this description, Russ Ackoff influenced me greatly and Jerry Zaltman had the idea of asking whether employees would pay tuition for their children.

78   Greene, 2010

and allowing consumers to design, build, and order their own LEGO creations through an online design studio. Through the latter, LEGO is gaining untold data on customer preferences. Moreover, new high-tech gaming options starring LEGO became available, like the popular LEGO Star Wars and Indiana Jones series and the highly-anticipated LEGO Universe (a massively multiplayer online game). These efforts to modernize the LEGO product and make it appealing to the 21st Century child have brought the company back from the edge: net profit for 2009 was $404 million, 63% higher than in 2008.

Xyntéo: The benefits of multi-enterprise collaborationError! Bookmark not defined. on a global scale

Spanning three continents and a range of sectors and industries, Xyntéo is an international business consortium that uses the power of collaborative innovation to find new pathways to low-carbon growth. This endeavour was far more than simply networking or cooperating. Member enterprises (many of them international names) came together as partners to develop solutions that were beyond the scope, scale or capabilities of any one organization. As well as benefiting from the creation of new networks and from meeting pioneering leaders, regulators and scientists in diverse fields, this group, under the banner of the Global Leadership and Technology Exchange (GLTE), benefited directly in that participation by:

- Identifying new growth opportunities and trends in the low-carbon sphere.

- Gaining excellent networking opportunities among pioneering thinkers across sectors and industries.

- Participating in practical collaborative projects to identify benefits tailored to individual partners – for example mitigated threats to demand, new revenue streams and enhancement to reputation.

- Improved understanding and access to the world's best practices, knowledge, strategies, and tools for making the transition to the low-carbon economy.

Xyntéo's GLTE process operates on the principle that successful innovation arises from the application of a three-tiered model within each member company, using insights gained from collaborative exchange with other partners and organizations beyond the partnership:

- Understand and interpret the changing context: climate change is creating a new economic landscape. The process helps interpret how the risks and opportunities will affect businesses and industries.

- Build a new strategic agenda: this draws on four areas – technological and operational innovation; policy and regulatory innovation; business model innovation; and collaborative innovation along and across supply and value chains.

- Enhance organizational capacity: determine new organizational requirements in terms of skills, structures and cultures.

To date, this collaborative effort has generated many groundbreaking low-carbon projects, such as:

- **Low-Carbon North Sea Oil Field Development** – Working with the oil and gas supply chain on ways to develop North Sea oil fields while minimizing the carbon emitted in the process

- **IT for Greening** – Seeking ways that information technology can build low-carbon business models

- **A Voice for Gas** – Working with the European Gas Advocacy Forum on the role of gas as a bridging and/or destination fuel

- **Sustainable Consumption and Culture Change** – How to achieve widespread cultural and behavioral change within a business, its supply chain, and its customer base.

- **The Shapers Programme** – Identifies the pioneering business leaders, regulators, innovators and thinkers who will shape the low-carbon economy.

- **Indo-Nordic Partnership for New Growth** – Investigating how collaboration between an industrialized and a rapidly developing region can stimulate strategies for low-carbon growth.

All of the above are designed to give tomorrow's leaders the hard evidence that collaboration can generate real business benefits in a low-carbon economy.

Capability 2: Thinking and Acting Holistically

I have chosen to use the term holistic here to avoid the current discussions around the differences between Systems and Design Thinking, which too often try to convince us to choose one or the other.[79]

Enter the phrase "The whole is greater than the sum of its parts" into a search engine and you get around a million results. But, as often as the term is used, many enterprises do not operate in a manner that allows the parts to interact so that a greater whole is created.

Russ Ackoff offered a definition that is useful in thinking about those interactions. He makes it quite clear that an enterprise is operating as an effective system when:

> The extent to which each essential part can affect the properties or behavior of the whole is known throughout the enterprise.
>
> No essential part has an independent effect on the whole; the effect it has depends on the properties or behavior of at least one other essential part. Thus, the essential parts form a connected set.
>
> Therefore, a system is a whole that cannot be divided into independent parts, and if the whole is taken apart, it – and its essential parts – will lose their defining functions.[80]

Despite the merits of thinking and operating in a systemic manner, many enterprises do not. When they do, the system is often defined too narrowly. For instance, a company may decide to focus on optimizing profit for a single quarter, not the long term, or may let different functions work on optimizing their capabilities, rather than find ways to optimize operations for the enterprise as a whole.

---

79   See Appendix B for an example of how, when asked by an executive who had just been introduced to Design Thinking, I attempted to demonstrate what both processes had in common.

80   Drawn from the work of, and conversations with, Russ Ackoff.

This, of course, leads to the important question: if the Systems/Design Thinking approach is so valuable why is it not in wider use? To my mind, the major reason is that the traditional internal and external performance measurements at the heart of the old management mindset often do not fully capture the consequences of using or not using a design-based systems thinking approach.

How fixing each of the parts can decrease the value of the whole

Imagine a personal computer owner who has been a loyal customer of the Reliable Computer Company (RCC). He has been impressed by the excellent service – an attribute that has been reinforced by the marketing department's advertisements that close with the tag line, "you're never more than 48 hours away from having your problem solved." The customer is considering a new computer and although RCC computers are among the highest priced, because of their reliability and service he believes they offer good value for the purchase price. This would be his fourth Reliable Computer purchase.

The customer, however, is unaware that last year, under pressure from Wall Street to reduce operating costs to industry levels, management set goals for each function to reduce its operating costs. Management was pleased by the following results:

- The service department, following a major benchmarking study of the lowest-cost PC manufacturer, made the decision to outsource field service to the PDQ Service Organization.

- The manufacturing division decided to move toward an 'order-to-delivery' manufacturing process and reduce parts inventories.

- The purchasing department instituted programs to pressure suppliers to reduce cost and carry some of the parts inventory.

Unexpectedly, the customer, prior to making his next purchase, encounters a hardware problem that will require the shipment of his computer to the RCC service center. He calls the service number that came with his computer. The call is intercepted and directs him to an automated set of screening questions.

The recently retained (and less expensive) outsourced service provider, PDQ, uses a less sophisticated customer screening application, forcing him to provide background information he had provided for an earlier repair: service contract number, date of purchase, serial number, type, etc. After sorting through all the screening questions, the customer is connected to an agent from PDQ who informs him that, based on his problem description, it will be at least 7 days before his computer can be serviced and returned. The customer expresses his displeasure and notes that after ten years of being a loyal customer and having purchased three RCC computers, this will be the first time he will not have access to his computer for more than two days.

The PDQ agent expresses understanding of the customer's disappointment and transfers him to the RCC complaint hot line. After again responding to the automated response screening questions, the customer is put on hold (in part due to the combination of a reduction in service operators to reduce costs and an increase in the number of complaints due to the poor durability of the less expensive parts acquired by the purchasing department) to wait for the next customer relationship representative. At 30 seconds into the holding period, a pre-arranged recording of the RCC's award winning advertisement comes on. At the point where the famous tagline "You're never more than 48 hours away from having your problem solved" is played, the customer hangs up and heads out to the local computer store to buy a different brand of computer.

In this instance, each department made decisions that met the cost reduction targets set by management – independent of the interaction those decisions would have on the remaining parts. The service department, through outsourcing, was able to show that service costs were reduced, the manufacturing division showed reduced inventories, and the purchasing department showed reduced parts costs. The financial department was able to book savings, indicating that RCC met all of its financial targets. As a result of meeting its numbers, Wall Street analysts rewarded management's actions by upgrading their recommendation to buy from neutral. Everyone who met their individual target was rewarded with a bonus.

What management (and the Wall Street analysts) failed to do was determine the eventual revenue and cost consequences of those actions, how they would be seen by a very important component of the enterprise's containing environment – the customer – and the effect those independent actions would have on the existing loyal customer's next computer purchase.

And that goes some way to answering my earlier question, "given the obvious negative consequences of not thinking systemically, why is it not more frequently applied?" In many enterprises, the managers of key components are anchored in – and are sometimes rewarded for – operating in a less systemic manner. And many of them are promoted before the consequences of their past actions become evident.

The extent of this mindset was documented when *Strategy + Business* magazine celebrated its 10th anniversary. To commemorate the event, it published the results of a reader survey that identified the ten most enduring ideas that had been published in the magazine.[81] Number one was 'Execution' (cited by 49.3% of those who responded), which was described as follows:

> It is not your strategic choices that drive success, but how well you implement them… To our readers, execution does not mean attention to numbers and metrics, but, as a correspondent wrote, "looking at your whole process, finding small ways to improve each part individually, really implementing the improvements, tracking the results to judge effectiveness, and then repeating the process.

This description of the number one enduring idea is the antithesis of systems thinking, which wasn't even in the top 35 ideas on the magazine's list!

The need to reevaluate the more mechanistic mindset of the Industrial Age

For too long, a generally accepted approach to business, as presented in countless textbooks, has been characterized by fixed boundaries. At the time of its introduction, Michael Porter's approach to strategy was straightforward; choose from among Cost Leadership, Differentiation, and Focus.[82] This approach was well founded since it was based on a world that was less complex and dynamically changing than the world

---

81   Kleiner, 2005

82   Porter, 1985

in which we live today. His recommendation was for the enterprise to distinguish itself from its competitors by how well it operates either as the low cost producer, providing products that have unique attributes that differentiate them from the competition, or by developing a highly focused strategy that seeks a narrow market and attempts to achieve either a cost advantage or to differentiate itself from the competition. An underlying premise of the approach suggested by Porter is that a successful enterprise is able to take full advantage of predictable consumer needs and consistent industry structures, in which change is relatively slow and predictable.

In this earlier view, he was saying that remaining focused on the core business was critical because the firm's profits tend to be limited to its share of the total profits available from the sector in which it operates. This usually leads the firm to focus on understanding the vertical value chain of activities within that industry. It is in this environment that business designs seeking mass markets and the resulting efficiencies found in economies of scale were developed and flourished for decades.

This approach fit very well with the mechanistic mindset that developed in the Industrial Age of the 19th and 20th Centuries, during which we were encouraged to think about managing businesses as if they were made of parts – like pieces of a jigsaw puzzle.

In this mechanistic mindset we were encouraged to think about addressing problems in government and business as if we were solving a jigsaw puzzle. Solving a jigsaw puzzle is relatively simple, because you can assume all the pieces of the problem that are needed are known and can be found in the box. Each of the pieces will interact with only a few other pieces and do so in a very specific way, and there is only one correct solution. Pieces with straight edges provide direction: once all the straight-edged pieces are in place, the boundary of the issue is addressed. To confirm you've solved the problem all you have to do is look on the cover of the box and the single correct solution is there for you to see. This 'solve the puzzle' metaphor was generally used to illustrate how to approach many of the issues we faced during the early part of the 20th Century and represented to a great extent the way things were approached at many public and private agencies and taught at many colleges and universities.

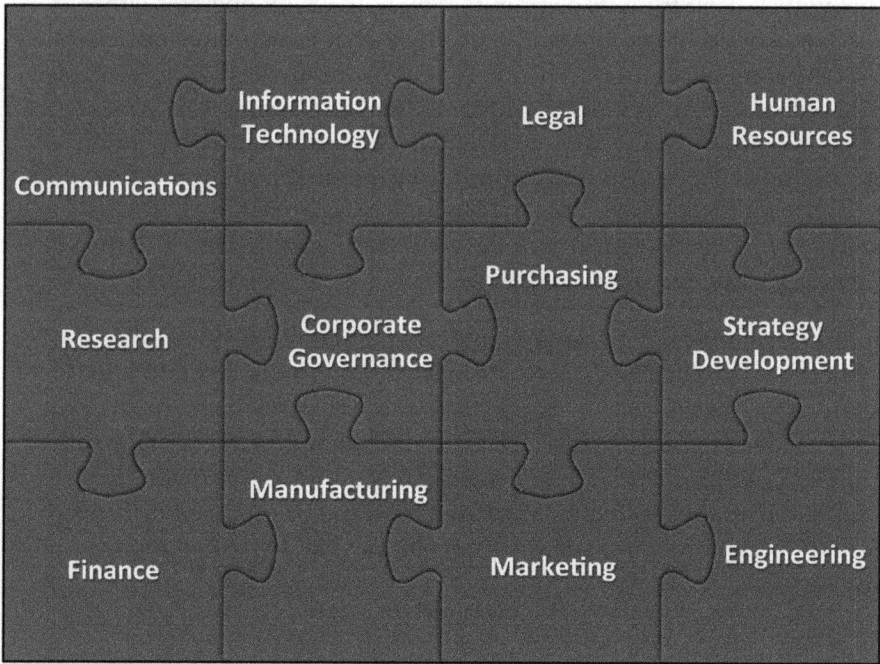

Figure 14: The Jigsaw Puzzle metaphor

In the puzzle metaphor, the illustration indicates that primary functional activities are likely to operate as independent pieces located and managed within the public or private enterprise. Generally, each functional activity is described by how and where it fits into the final picture of the organization. Once this view is approved by management, each function then develops a plan that provides it with the necessary human and financial resources to fulfill its role.

The metaphor worked as long as change was evolutionary. Enterprises could maintain success by continuously improving the manner in which their operations had always been managed and by adopting best practices within their industry. I'm not sure we ever faced problems that were addressed by the simplicity of the jigsaw puzzle metaphor but I am quite sure we are not likely to face so simple a problem in today's environment. Indeed the mindset characterized by the puzzle metaphor leads management away from systemic thinking. Consider the characteristics of the puzzle metaphor relative to those of a system described by Ackoff:

Systemic Conditions as Described by Ackoff	The Jigsaw Puzzle Metaphor
Each essential part can affect the properties or behavior of the whole.	The parts, while essential, do not affect the properties or the behavior of the whole. If one piece is modified or removed you can still see the remaining parts of the picture.
Each part has an interdependent effect on the whole; the effect it has depends on the properties or behavior of at least one other essential part. Thus, the essential parts form a connected set.	The essential parts have more of an independent effect on the whole.
Subsets of the essential parts (subsystems) can also affect the properties and behavior of the whole, but none has an independent effect.	Pieces with straight edges can be considered subsets whose purpose is to describe the boundary of the system.
Therefore, a system is a whole that cannot be divided into independent parts, and when the whole is taken apart, it – and its essential parts – lose their defining functions.	The system can be divided into independent parts (the individual puzzle pieces), and when the whole is taken apart, the role of each puzzle piece is still obvious.

The singular focus on a department/function's own role also led to the creation of impermeable walls surrounding each function, which by nature decreases the ability of management and functional units to improve their interactions. This phenomenon has been described as the silo effect.

Many functional managers, sometimes for good reasons, attempt to maintain complete control to ensure that their function is run efficiently and not influenced by outside forces.

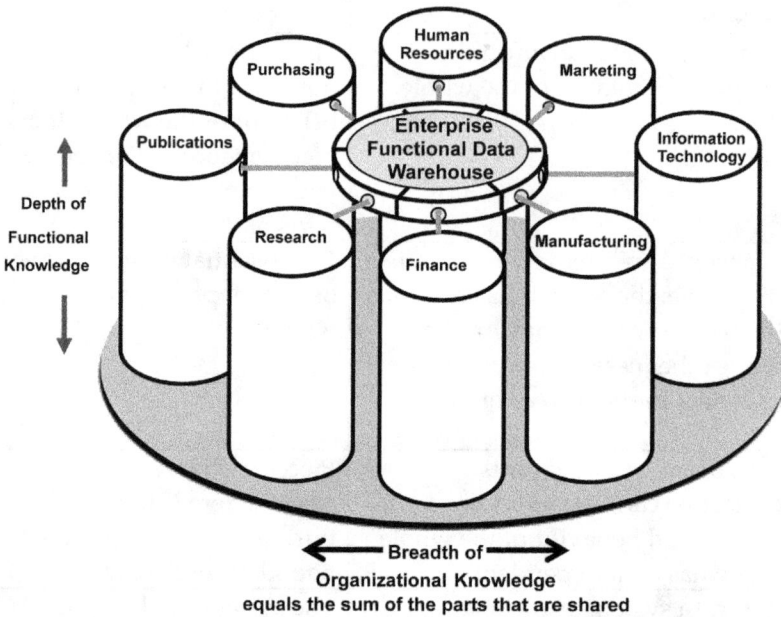

Figure 15: Information storage system designed to improve effectiveness of functional knowledge

These silo walls allow the functions to stay focused and contribute to their ability to use their resources to generate deep and valuable functional knowledge. Indeed, the value of the functional knowledge is critical in the development of innovations that improve many of the elements within the function. The price of limiting the focus of the discipline, however, is that the walls inhibit the ability of the functions to learn what the others know and how they operate. This lack of understanding makes it more difficult for them to determine ways in which they could improve their interactions. It also limits the ability of the enterprise to develop a deeper understanding of the system (the whole) which could facilitate management's ability to manage the interaction of functions (the parts) as well as increasing overall enterprise knowledge.

The negative consequence of the silo effect occurs when major functional areas do not talk to one another in situations where they should. They simply exist side-by-side like isolated silos and, like the Reliable Computer Company, do not find out about the negative consequences of their independent actions until after the customer is lost.

This effect is symptomatic of what could be called the new marketing myopia (the old marketing myopia is defining one's market too narrowly). The misperception is that it is primarily the marketing function that does marketing, when virtually all groups make decisions that affect how customers or constituents, competitors and societal interests view the enterprise's offerings. This more interactive position is consistent with Drucker's observation:

> Marketing is not only much broader than selling, it is not a specialized activity at all. It encompasses the entire business. It is the whole business seen from the point of view of its final result, that is, from the customer's point of view. Concern and responsibility must therefore permeate all areas of the enterprise.[83]

This approach survived as long as the transition from one independent division to another led to successful products and services – in other words, as long as the independent puzzle pieces continued to fit together as expected.

The Organismic Mindset of the Systems Age

In the 21st Century the pieces of the puzzle are not fitting as well as they used to. Businesses increasingly operate across traditional functional boundaries. Rather than achieving a single path to success, many organizations are finding it necessary, not as Porter initially suggested in 1985 to choose among, but instead to address all of the following:

- Be the most efficient and effective producer

- Provide the range of products and services customers require

- Focus on meeting customer needs for specific purchase occasions more efficiently and effectively than the competition

- Focus on customers and reach them in ways they want to be reached.

---

83   Drucker, 1954, pp. 38-39

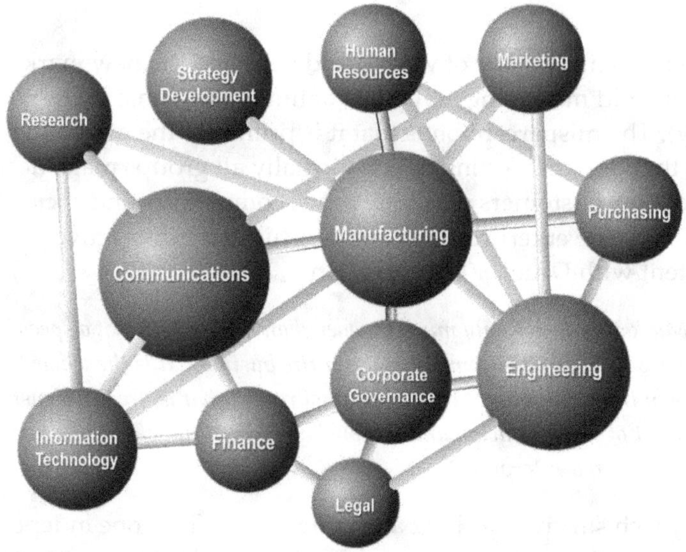

Figure 16: The molecular structure metaphor

In this case, the enterprise distinguishes itself from its competitors by how well it manages the interactions of a, b, c, and d. This type of environment is better described by the metaphor of a molecular structure than a jigsaw puzzle. Depending on how the elements of the molecular structure interact, we can end up with an entirely different outcome than we expected. And when we impose external forces (both positive and negative) on that environment, the elements can change position and even interact in different ways.

In this 'molecular' environment, it makes sense for the walls of the functional silos to be more permeable so the functional experts can better communicate with one another. As Fritjof Capra describes it, "A membrane is very different from a cell wall. Whereas cell walls are rigid structures, membranes are always active, opening and closing continually, keeping certain substances out and letting others in."[84]

---

84   Capra, 2002

Functional membranes – their potential

Figure 17 provides a partial illustration of the value of having functional boundaries that are more like membranes than walls.

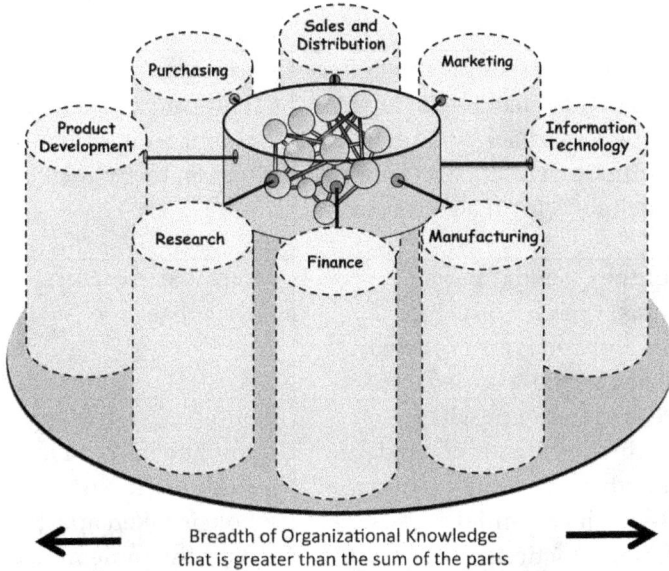

Figure 17: The Decision Loom's information storage system is designed for interactive, cross functional use

In this case, functional managers encourage their employees to gain a broader understanding of the whole and interact with those functions they affect to determine whether they can improve the performance of the whole. They stay focused on developing deep functional knowledge but are willing to allocate a portion of their resources to finding ways to share and learn from others while seeking to address internal and external issues. They also seek synergy in designing information systems that make the sharing of information easier. This allows the enterprise to develop a deeper and broader understanding of how it operates and how to improve the interactions. This approach encourages everyone to look at the containing system of the enterprise and its sub-systems (e.g. the functional silos, particular products or services) as a systemic whole.

Systemic Conditions as Described by Ackoff	The Molecular Structure Metaphor
Each essential part can affect the properties or behavior of the whole.	Each element is essential and can affect the properties or the behavior of the whole.
Each part has an interdependent effect on the whole; the effect it has depends on the properties or behavior of at least one other essential part. Thus, the essential parts form a connected set.	Each element interacts and can affect at least one other element and can have an effect on the whole.
Subsets of the essential parts (subsystems) can also affect the properties and behavior of the whole, but none has an independent effect.	Molecular structures can have subsets.
Therefore, a system is a whole that cannot be divided into independent parts, and when the whole is taken apart, it – and its essential parts – lose their defining functions.	A molecular structure cannot be divided into independent parts. If the whole is taken apart, it is no longer the same molecular structure.

The tyranny of disciplines

C. West Churchman has said that highly focused disciplines whose interests are centered on improving specialized methods are the enemy of Systems Thinking. He describes an enemy, intriguingly, as:

> Someone who is distrusted and admired, loved and hated, respected and feared. Above all, an enemy is someone who holds powers, resources, capabilities that one desperately needs.[85]

Decisions about creating less permeable walls around functional silos within the enterprise and avoiding the tyranny of disciplines (or functions) require the willingness of functional managers to better understand, and appreciate, what is going on in the other areas of the enterprise. To encourage functional managers to expand their view of the enterprise, leadership must ensure that they are both given the opportunities and are rewarded for doing so.

---

85   Churchman, 1979

Senior management should set up capabilities that provide functional managers with improved understanding of what is going on within the enterprise and reward them when they either forgo resources or give resources up to allow another function to perform an activity that improves the overall condition of the enterprise. It might be as simple as creating an award for any function that has provided resources in the form of people, funds, or ideas to another function that took an action that benefited the whole enterprise.

These organizing principles must also take into account approaches and operating relationships that are relevant in a world in which the *past cannot always be translated into prologue*. This, of course, will not come easy. The information that demonstrates the value of making the change must not only be collected, it must also be presented in a format that encourages its acceptance and use. Churchman made this clear when he pointed out, "To conceive of knowledge as a collection of information seems to rob the concept of all of its life... Knowledge resides in the user and not in the collection. It's how the user reacts to the collection of information that really matters."[86]

In a world of increased complexity and an accelerating rate of change, an enterprise must develop both deep functional knowledge and also find ways to make the relevant portions of that knowledge available to other functions within the enterprise when and where they need it, in a form that is consistent with how they will use it, and at a price commensurate with its value to a particular decision.

This requires an environment where the deep knowledge of the functional perspective enhances the understanding of the broader issue being addressed without being diminished by the perception that functional representatives hold biased positions based on their functional ties. An example would be the manner in which Jeff Hartley, as described in Episode 7 of *The Journey*, learned to walk in the shoes of the vehicle designers so that he could develop procedures that improved their use of customer information and the manner in which the market research function performed its function.

This is not a recommendation to inhibit the collection of deep, specific, functional knowledge. On the contrary, the continued development of such knowledge is critical to the enterprise's desire to innovate. But we

---

86   Churchman, 1971

must develop this knowledge in a manner that allows decision-makers access to what Reid Smith and Adam Farquhar call a 'knowledge hub,'[87] which is more valuable than the sum of all the specialized functional knowledge to which it is connected.

This principle applies in business, education, health, or any other specialty affecting the human condition. Even by themselves, these isolated bits of knowledge are valuable, but when combined with knowledge from other sources, they can take on even greater value. In the extreme, as Edna St. Vincent Millay pointed out in 'Huntsman, What Quarry?', like individual threads in a tapestry, single threads of information are of little value. When woven together properly, however, they form a coherent image of greater value.

Just as internal and external knowledge captured by one function tends to be trapped within that function, so the tradition of organizing by functional activities often leads to decisions or external communication that makes it difficult for consumers or constituents to form a coherent picture of what the enterprise, as a whole, is capable of delivering. In the case of government, single working parents do not view the problem of raising a family as the gathering of independent activities such as getting a job, staying healthy, getting to work, getting the children to school, and improving their chances for success by improving their education. To them, these are all interdependent activities, the interaction of which must be managed if they are to survive. The government does them a disservice by forcing them to go to independent units and figure out how to get them to interact on their behalf.

The critical point is that this kind of holistic environment will not happen naturally. Decades of thinking mechanistically (e.g., working or studying the parts independently) must be overcome by the leadership of the enterprise. Those who make decisions and those who will approve them must ensure that the full taxonomy of what is known has been applied to the decision. This responsibility should not be delegated to subordinates. It can only be accomplished by senior managers who, in making or approving decisions, evaluate whether the full capabilities of the entire enterprise have been involved appropriately and are acting interdependently to create a whole that is greater than the

---

87   Smith & Farquhar, 2000

Examples of the ideas presented

Patagonia Cotton Greenfield

Patagonia, the outdoor sportswear and equipment company, was an early pioneer of the green business model, creating a brand whose core values are continually represented in every niche of its decision landscape. Launched in 1972, Patagonia prides itself on its eco-friendly products and sustainable business practices. In 1991, the company was struggling to rationalize its use of non-organic cotton after learning of the environmentally harmful chemicals involved in producing conventional cotton. Yet, customers were not demanding organic cotton and it would have a serious impact on the bottom line: cotton was 20% of total business and at the time, organic cotton cost 50% to 100% more than conventional cotton. (There was little demand for the product and, as a result, few economies of scale for producers.) Part of this margin was that the team would need to re-work supply chains and subsidize the farmers and spinners to incentivize them to go organic.[88] However, conventional cotton was antithetical to the company's core business model and the CEO was adamant: "if we continue to make clothes with conventionally grown cotton, knowing what we know now, we're toast anyway. Let's do it; let's go organic." The board agreed and Patagonia used only organic cotton by the spring line of 1996.

To counteract the rising input costs, Patagonia reduced its margins and the number of cotton items in the store. However, in the subsequent year, rather than struggling with falling sales and customer backlash, "Patagonia's cotton sales rose 25% and... established an organic-cotton industry"; ten years later, bigger retailers were jumping on board and Walmart became the top buyer of organic cotton.[89] While the shift was risky for the bottom line, the switch made sense holistically for the business and its brand – and importantly, customers agreed. The bottom line remains strong today: the CEO suggests Patagonia had solid gains in both 2008 and 2009 despite the economic downturn and sales were up again in 2010, by $25 million.[90]

---

88   Holmes, 2009

89   Casey, 2007

90   Wang, 2010

Capability 3: Being Able to Adapt the Business Design to Changing Conditions

One cannot make decisions for the future. Decisions are commitments to action. And actions are always in the present, and in the present only. But actions in the present are also the one and only way to make the future..

Peter Drucker

In this activity a process is suggested to help business and public sector leaders decide what kind of enterprise they want to lead in the face of an uncertain future. This type of strategic thinking is crucial to helping an enterprise find the most efficient ways to get to where it wants to be from where it is now. It also requires the leadership team to take into consideration the broader societal environment, including customer needs, political realities, economics and many other factors.

Evaluate how alternative business designs would benefit your enterprise

As was pointed out earlier, the use of the term 'business design' is presented in the broadest context possible. That is not only how a private firm would conduct its business, but also how public agencies at the local and global level should be conducting their business.

Adrian Slywotzky, author of *Value Migration* and co-author of *Profit Zone*, has provided a clear and succinct definition of business design. For our purposes I have modified it [using text in square brackets] to demonstrate its more universal application:

> *A business design is the totality of how a company* [or any enterprise] *selects its customers* [and constituents], *defines and differentiates its offerings* (or responses), *defines the tasks it will perform itself and those it will outsource, configures its resources, goes to market [or reaches out to those it wishes to serve], creates utility for customers [and constituents] and captures profits* [or provides benefits to society]. *It is the entire system for delivering utility to customers* [and constituents] *and earning a profit* [and recognition] *from that activity.*

Companies [or enterprises] may offer products [or services], they may offer technology, but that offering is embedded in a comprehensive system of activities and relationships that represents the company's [or enterprise's] business design.[91]

The array of business designs

Digital opportunities are multiplying our options and creating the possibility of a broader range of business designs within which innovation can take place.[92]

The range of possible designs is almost infinite. What follows is a brief classification of possible designs that I have found useful. It is not a complete list but is illustrative of the potential range of opportunities.[93]

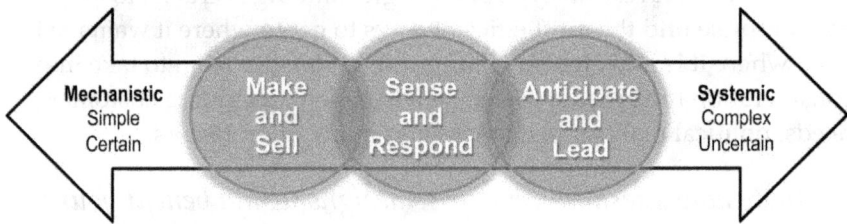

Figure 18: An array of possible business designs

Make-and-Sell

A make-and-sell design does just that. The enterprise predicts, based on its experience and market research, what the market/community will demand. In this design, customers/citizens know what they want and have the means to acquire it. The key to success is to correctly predict demand. The make-and-sell enterprise relies on economies of scale: finding a large market/audience and then setting up a capability to provide what is wanted in an economical way. Performance

---

91   Slywotzky, 1996, p 4

92   The concept of alternative business designs are discussed in Prahalad & Ramaswamy 2004 and in Kotler *et al.* 2002.

93   Barabba, 2005, pp. 17-27 has a more detailed description.

measurements are gathered through benchmarking and best practice evaluation.

David Riesman uses the metaphor of a gyroscope to describe the 'inner-directed personality types' who thrive in this environment.

> *It is what I like to describe as a psychological gyroscope. This instrument, once it is set by the parents and other authorities, keeps the inner-directed person... 'on course' even when tradition, as responded to by his character, no longer dictates his moves.*"[94]

The leadership of the make-and-sell enterprise believes strongly that change will be evolutionary; they assure themselves of success by continual improvement in how they have conducted their business over the years. They challenge all claims of forthcoming radical change and possess interpersonal skills to persuade others they are on the right path. Others see them as conservative traditionalists. Up until recently nearly all automotive manufacturers fell into this category.

In the public sector, a make-and-sell design could be described as 'predict-and-provide.' This design can be found in government agencies that have been providing services over a long period, particularly to public constituencies that are characterized by relatively slow and evolutionary change. Given that sometimes there is little direct contact between those being served and those serving, the ability to sense the possibility of change can be somewhat hampered. This situation is further complicated by the lack of a market mechanism since most of the agencies are funded from general tax payer funds and there is less opportunity for the users of their services to seek those services from another agency. I am not saying that these agencies are failing to perform at an accepted level of service. The essential point is that when change is evolutionary and predictable it matters not whether you are in the public or private sector – there are many advantages to having a continuous production that allows the provider to benefit from economies of scale and continuous improvement. Up until the later part of the 20th Century the United States Census Bureau was a beneficiary of this business design. As will be discussed later, the conditions of evolutionary change were severely disrupted and the Census Bureau found itself in an environment that required a far greater understanding and appreciation of the requirements of the

---

94   Riesman, 1961, p. 16

customers (society at large) that the agency had been established to serve.

Sense-and-Respond

A sense-and-respond design starts with the enterprise believing the future is not easily predicted nor controlled. Therefore, the leadership of the enterprise organizes itself to respond to what is actually happening, as opposed to what is forecast to happen. Sense-and-respond firms seek to provide products or services that satisfy needs or desires that customers are aware of and that are not being satisfied by the current market. This process starts by reaching out to selected markets and saying, "Help me to identify your needs, and let's work together to satisfy them." A sense-and-respond organization sees itself as an adaptive system for responding to an ever-changing, ever-widening range of requests. It is built around dynamically linked sub-processes and relies primarily on economies of scope, rather than economies of scale. The people in a sense-and-respond environment are empowered and accountable and spend their time producing customized outcomes in accordance with an adaptive business design.

The leadership of such an enterprise tends to encourage managers to recognize that the unpredictable environment requires giving up control of procedures and processes. Generally the leadership designs the organization to empower people to improvise and adapt. As with the make-and-sell business design, David Riesman provides a metaphor – this time radar – to describe what he called the 'other-directed personality type'.[95]

> *What is common to all the other-directed people is that their contemporaries are the source of direction for the individual – either those known to him or those with whom he is indirectly acquainted, through friends and through the mass media. This source is of course 'internalized' in the sense that dependence on it for guidance in life is implanted early. The goals toward which the other-directed person strives shift with that guidance; it is only the process of striving itself and the process of paying close attention to the signals from others that remain unaltered throughout life.*

---

95   *Ibid.* p. 21.

This approach encourages staff at all times to seek to know the current needs of individual customers, and invest in understanding the underlying values that drive them. Like the bow-and-arrow game hunter, they aim just ahead of the market, basing their aim on a pattern of emerging knowledge about customers, society, and business practice. Others see them as externally driven internal-change agents. The creative team at Apple Computer serves as a great example of this approach.

Government agencies have found that technology has provided them with improved methods of sensing changes in the preferences of the population they serve. Many agencies of government have developed websites that not only describe the current capabilities of their agencies, but also provide their constituencies with the ability to identify limitations and suggest alternative solutions. The dilemma, of course, is that the agencies face a more complex structure if the suggested changes require additional funding. In this case they are required to demonstrate the value of the improvement and get approval from elected officials who sometimes do not share the same attitude toward altering the way things are currently accomplished. This is further complicated when the funding requires additional taxes from some who will not be the beneficiaries of the improved service.

An example of sensing the need for change and responding based on demonstrated experience and the use of new technology is how the U.S. Census Bureau transformed the way it collects Census data.

From the 18th through the middle of the 20th Century, Census enumerators traveled door to door to conduct the constitutionally mandated Census for the purpose of apportioning the Congress of the United States. The enumerators filled in information on a Census schedule for members of each household. By 1960 the Census began to assess the need for a quicker and less expensive way to complete the Census.

For the 1960 Census, the Census Bureau experimented and mailed out questionnaires to households in urban areas. Given that the Census Bureau did not know how well householders would fill out the form they were asked to complete the questionnaire and hold it until an enumerator came by to pick it up. Based on that experience, in 1970, the Census Bureau implemented a mail-out/mail-back enumeration for households in larger metropolitan areas (approximately 60 percent of the U.S. population). The results of that experience, and the technical development of address coding guides discussed in Episode 3, encouraged the Census Bureau to conduct a national mail-out/mail-back process for the entire country. Self-enumeration by mail has led to improved quality of the resulting data and reduced costs.

As the Census Bureau has found out, in today's more complex and dynamic environment it is no longer acceptable to wait for decades to sense a change and make improvements. For example, during the 1990s, the Census Bureau further developed the use of electronic data collection methods. They employed new interviewing techniques, including computer-assisted personal interviewing (CAPI) and computer-assisted telephone interviewing (CATI), complemented mail-out/mail-back procedures and helped cut costs. Electronic reporting, employing computer tape, diskettes, e-mail, and electronic questionnaires, made it easier for businesses to respond to economic surveys and Censuses.

Anticipate-and-Lead

An anticipate-and-lead design assumes the future is largely determined by what the enterprise purposefully does to change things – not how it responds to signals from the market place. The mindset is different from make-and-sell in that the anticipate-and-lead enterprise accepts that it cannot predict what the market is likely to want. The anticipate-and-lead enterprise focuses on the future it wants to create. Once that future is determined, the enterprise attempts to lead the consumer to new ideas based on identifying both articulated and unarticulated consumer needs. In conversation, Russ Ackoff suggested that this design should be called Anticipate-and-Create, which was more consistent with his concept of idealized design.

The deep understanding of these needs is sometimes gleaned from direct observation of consumer behavior, including what the individual would prefer that is not now available. The ability to anticipate and lead is facilitated by emerging digital technologies, which allow decision-makers to observe real-time behavior by markets and consumers. Although the techniques used may be similar to those used in the other business designs, the purpose is profoundly different. Performance is measured by the enterprise's share of truly new and profitable products. Evaluation of best practices is replaced by the determination to develop the next practice.

Sometimes an invention can lead to an anticipate-and-lead design. In 1981, the distinguished statistician of the University of Michigan, Leslie Kish, introduced the concept of a rolling sample design in the context of the decennial Census. During the time that Kish was conducting his research the Census Bureau also recognized the need for more frequently updated data.

Anticipating that change in society would soon be occurring so fast that the long-form detailed information supplied by the decennial Census would be of less value, and based on Kish's research, the Census Bureau developed a research proposal for continuous measurement as an alternative.

Based on that earlier research and in-field experimentation, the Census Bureau now conducts the American Community Survey, which provides annual estimates of population characteristics for areas of more than 20,000 residents. Anticipating that users would demand information for smaller areas, the survey is designed to provide a five-year rolling average report allowing the Census Bureau to report less precise, but more current and frequent information on Census block groups with populations of between 600 and 3000 people.

Trait	MAKE-AND-SELL
Attitude toward knowing what the future holds	Over the time in which we expect to gain a profitable return on our investment, we can accurately predict what kind of products and services we need to produce, and how many.
Mental model and strategy	Business as an efficient mechanism for making and selling offers to well-defined market segments with predictable needs.
Process	Mass Production. Emphasis on repeatable procedures, replaceable parts, and standard job definitions to efficiently mass produce products defined by the company.
Product and service design	Design for consumers. Intuition and market knowledge lead to products and services that satisfy enough targeted customers to meet investment objectives. Customer involvement is passive.
Knowledge management perspective	The most efficient knowledge management is to store precise measurements of what the enterprise knows and what it will need to know in an efficient and accessible warehouse.

Trait	SENSE-AND-RESPOND
Attitude toward knowing what the future holds	We cannot predict the future, so we must design our business to quickly adapt to changing conditions, which we will identify earlier than our competitors by continually assessing market conditions.
Mental model and strategy	Business as an adaptive system for responding to consumer requests in less predictable environments.
Process	Selective Customization. Modular products and services, produced by modular capabilities, inside and outside the company, which are linked to create customized responses to requests defined by customers.
Product and service design	Adaptive Design. Constant monitoring and surveillance of consumer attitudes and behavior leads to products and services designed for efficient adaptation to frequent changes in customer requirements. Customers can be active participants in the design of the changes.
Knowledge management perspective	Primary knowledge is know-why (systems knowledge) as opposed to know-how (process knowledge). Knowledge must be available to all those who need it.

Trait	ANTICIPATE-AND-LEAD
Attitude toward knowing what the future holds	We cannot predict the future, but we can largely determine what it will be by what we do. We must anticipate what will be required that is currently not provided and do so in a way that is in the interest of the firm, its customers, and the containing system in which we operate.
Mental model and strategy	Business requires creative approaches that lead to the development of entirely new products and services that customers desire and believe to be a fair value.

Process	Causing the future we want to create. Determination of how to cause that future to occur. Design and implement a plan of action to bring about the necessary changes as quickly and as innovatively as possible.
Product and service design	Design to cause change. Design is idealized. It is based on intuition and market knowledge. Products and services are designed to cause selected customers to change from the accepted way of doing things to a better way of doing things. Interested customers can be actively engaged in the idealized design process.
Knowledge management perspective	The goal is not management of information; it is quick acquisition. The enterprise needs knowledge about the future it wants to create. Storing what worked in the past is less useful. The plan is to design a system that will adapt as strategy develops based on prior success in changing the way things happen.

Table 1: Distinctions in the Alternative Business Designs.[96]

The Importance of 'and'

Depending on your responsibilities, experience, skills, and current mindset, it is highly probable that one of these business designs will seem better than the others. For example, someone with an interest in improving the efficiency of the manufacturing process would see the economies of scale associated with the make-and-sell business design as, on balance, more valuable than the other designs. But it would be a serious mistake to assume that one business design is inherently better than the others. Depending on the business conditions that exist, the ability to predict future actions, and the ability to think creatively, it is more likely that a hybrid model, taking advantage of the most appropriate traits of each design, will be most beneficial.

In a world of increased complexity and accelerated change there is great peril in choosing one strategy or the other. Serious consideration needs to be given to using traits of one strategy and traits of another.

---

96   Much of the original thinking regarding the make-and-sell and sense-and respond business design descriptions grew out of collaborative work with Stephan Haeckel. While developing these concepts, Jeff Hartley contributed to the personality traits of all three business designs.

In 1995, Nicholas Negroponte made a strong case for how we would move from an industrial world of products made up of *atoms* to a knowledge-based world of products made up of *bits* of information. Since that time, the remarkable growth, eventual decline, and current expansion of purely *bits*-based business has given way to the belief that the opportunity is not a future world of solely atoms or bits, but a future world of atoms and bits.[97]

Today's successful business design could fail for you tomorrow

This problem of understanding the effect of customer benefits is compounded by the fact that consumers are being asked to choose from among a vast array of products and services. Consumers increasingly do not have the time and energy to sort through them all. Meanwhile, enterprises are finding that direct and indirect competitors are developing alternative ways (as pointed out by Clay Christenson – sometimes using surprising and disruptive technologies[98]) to meet the needs of traditional customers. This competition has put pressure on profits right at the time when the enterprise needs additional resources to develop innovative ways to address the competitive threats that it faces.

Unfortunately, many enterprises are organized and managed in ways that make it hard to form an undistorted picture of what customers would be willing to purchase. This is particularly true of products and services beyond what is currently in the market. Knowledge and market information captured by one organizational function tends to be discussed within that function but seldom enriches the understanding of others. These functional 'silos' often lead to arguments about this approach or that approach, instead of finding what combination of approaches will be seen positively by the ultimate consumer. Leadership must adapt its business design to more effectively create a dialogue with its chosen customers across the enterprise.

Adapting to – and changing – the environment

In nature, species that survive do so because they have evolved to meet the challenges of their environments. Humpback whales survive

---

97   Negroponte, 1996, pp. 11-13

98   Christenson, 1997

because their mouths have baleen – fibrous strainers that catch the available krill and plankton. Hawks survive because their combination of vision, soaring wings, and talons help them prey upon the small birds and mammals that live in open fields and meadows. These animals have evolved in a way that allows them to respond to the challenges they face every day. If their environments change faster than they can biologically evolve, however, they are out of luck. Few animal species have the capacity to adapt to accelerating rates of change.

Human beings and their organizations are quite different. Although they, too, must adapt themselves to the environment, they also have the capacity to *change the environment*. Jacob Bronowski describes this difference between human beings and other animals quite simply: "Man is a singular creature. He has a set of gifts which make him unique among the animals: so that, unlike them, he is not a figure in the landscape – he is a shaper of the landscape. In body and in mind he is the explorer of nature, the ubiquitous animal, *who did not find but has made his home in every continent*. (Emphasis added.)"[99]

In the foreword to the *Adaptive Enterprise*,[100] Adrian Slywotzky addresses the issue of adaptation in business designs. "Adopting a sense-and-respond orientation produces multiple benefits for an organization. I'd like to point out three benefits over and above those articulated by Haeckel: new business building, solving the medium-term growth crisis, and preempting future competitive opportunities."

After elaborating on the first two benefits, Slywotzky addresses the third benefit as follows:

> The third benefit grows out of the second. Playing sense-and-respond reinforces itself. Once an enterprise gets into a dynamic mindset, it learns, it gets better. Its know-how extends beyond archery, aiming at a static target, to include skeet shooting, taking on a moving target. As the enterprise develops its sense-and-respond skill set, it elevates sense-and-respond from listen and comply to **anticipate and preempt**. (Emphasis added).

Slywotzky further points out that "Sense-and-respond helps us be on time – on market time. Very good sense-and-respond helps us be early. But a superior ability to sense and interpret signals about changing

---

99   Bronowski, 1973

100   Slywotzky, 1999, p.*xi*

customer needs before they mature into formal requests helps us get there sooner still, soon enough to preempt the next major opportunity and to create an unassailable leadership position."[101]

With this as background, each enterprise should attempt to lay out the right mix of business designs for the alternative futures it has considered – including its plans to address the organizational and cultural changes that may need to take place.

The impact of digital technologies on business design

The digital economy's primary effect has not been change itself, but an increase in the rate of change. Just as an organization begins to understand customer wants and needs, those wants and needs change, in both subtle and dramatic ways.

As computing and communication technologies improve – along with the understanding of their applications – so do the abilities of businesses to acquire deep and broad external knowledge of *current* and *potential* markets, thus allowing them to better sense changes in customer requirements and to begin to anticipate additional changes. These technologies are also helping to reconfigure and make better use of internal knowledge of a company's capabilities as an extended enterprise, enabling it to serve those markets innovatively. Technology is redefining the nature of competition.

In the face of the unprecedented speed of change in the business environment, it's essential that businesses learn to approach transformation in a different way.

Lacking a crystal ball, we can only assume that the future will be different from the present. The degree of difference is, of course, what every enterprise would like to know. Pursuit of a single answer to this question, however, has led to approaches that require a significant amount of simplification of the future's true complexity – such as point estimates of the growth of GNP, price indices, population, and the cost of raw materials.

The inherent futility of these point estimates is that the more one lists, the higher the probability that one or more of the assumptions

---

101   *Ibid*, p.xiv

underlying the point estimate will be wrong. Yet in spite of such faulty logic, this is the approach that underlies the long-range planning and thinking of many enterprises. A more realistic approach is to accept that we cannot know with precision what the future holds and to learn how to design business plans and strategies to deal with that uncertainty – strategies that allow the enterprise to adapt when the unexpected occurs.

This understanding, in the context of a shared corporate business design, can enable a company's decision-makers to decide how to, "craft a business model that is not only superior, but *unique*," as Slywotzky and David Morrison suggest.[102] This step suggests that the enterprise choose from among alternative business designs by determining which of those designs is robust over a range of possible alternative future scenarios.

First: identify realistic alternative business designs

To demonstrate the process I will use the three business designs just described – *Make-and-Sell, Sense-and-Respond,* and *Anticipate-and-Lead.*

As discussed earlier, any enterprise is likely to determine that a hybrid model, taking advantage of the positive traits of each design, is most beneficial.

Many enterprises grew successful by using customer research to efficiently predict, then make-and-sell products in cadence with changes in customer needs. In many cases, they even defined those needs by creating innovative products, then communicating the benefits of those products to prospective customers. In those instances when the enterprise didn't get it right, the discrepancies were generally resolved by adjusting prices. The brand new widget isn't exactly what the customer wanted? Let's 'deal' with that discrepancy by marking its price down – until someone buys it.

On the other hand, some companies, like Cisco, have grown successfully because they organized themselves to respond flexibly and economically to individual customer requests in the required time frame.

---

102   Slywotzky & Morrison, p.8

Some successful companies are notorious for believing that they know what's best, regardless of how the world is changing around them. Central planning staffs and long-range business plans based on a long list of single-point assumptions have traditionally been the norm.

However, discontinuous change has raised questions about the value of forecast-based, long-term plans. Hence, a framework for strategic thinking is more important than ever to help approach options with intelligence and insight. But instead of expressing the results as a plan, the enterprise must consider a range of alternatives linked to a set of possible responses. Strategic thinking, in comparison to traditional planning, can only operate within a business design that is knowledge-based and adaptive to unexpected change.

Second: envision alternative future scenarios

To make good decisions in the face of the longer term, where the unexpected is to be expected, requires a decision process that evaluates how robust a business design would be in an uncertain future.[103] This is no small challenge. For example, while everyone agrees that digital technology will continue to change the way businesses operate, there is little agreement on precisely how, nor on the extent and timing of this change. Dealing with this uncertainty requires an envisioning process that senses and interprets a broad expanse of technological, societal and demographic trends, in order to gain understanding about what could occur in the future and the implications it may have on current decisions.

The envisioning process enables better understanding of the assumptions that underpin possible future business environments, especially in scenarios where the enterprise perceives it will have only some, or very little, control over the conditions under which it will be making its decisions. It is most important to remember that scenarios are not developed to limit the range of possible actions. Instead, the benefit of the process is in revealing alternative approaches that could be taken now to create more beneficial future conditions.

The envisioning process begins by gathering together experts from a variety of key fields and providing them with whatever information

---

103   Barabba, 1998. It is also discussed briefly in Episode 9.

is available to enable them to develop a set of scenarios – plausible, challenging stories about what might happen in the future. These are not forecasts. They do not predict by extrapolation. Instead, these scenarios reveal a state of understanding possibilities, allowing for the condition of not knowing exactly what the future might hold.

Many business decision-makers like to sort out and simplify things and get to know the things (problems) themselves. But in doing so, it is important to be aware that what we see is based on our perceptions and on our personal and, many times, functional organizational experiences. These perceptions provide no more than a reflection of market reality. Although decision-makers must stay close to reality, they must do so understanding the interaction with the broader system which contains the reality they are attempting to address. Breaking things down into their parts is about analysis and not synthesis. To operate as a system, we need to remember Ackoff's definition of a system:

> A system is a whole that is defined by interdependent parts in which the function of each essential part affects the functions of the whole, and the system as a whole cannot be divided into independent parts or it will lose its defining function.

The envisioning process attempts to maintain as much of reality's complexity as possible, while allowing management to make decisions in the context of an uncertain future.

The possible scenarios that emerge from the envisioning process, combined with the appropriate decision process, help prepare for, not avoid, discontinuities and sudden change, and help one recognize and interpret important events and new developments as they occur. For the purpose of determining the value of using scenarios and to gain an appreciation that portions of the prospective scenarios can actually occur, assume we are back in 1990 and have developed a set of alternative scenarios designed to reflect what could occur in the year 2010. This 'retrospective' scenario set is found in Table 2. Although these 1990 scenarios might sound quite predictive in retrospect, it is important to emphasize that as used in this process, a scenario is not a prediction of what will happen. Scenarios are descriptions of *possible* futures that *could* occur. The key to a successful process is to make sure a full range of possibilities is presented to increase the likelihood that whatever may occur is captured in one of the scenarios. Again these are descriptive scenarios and are presented only to illustrate how scenarios and alternative business designs can be used by an enterprise.

SCENARIO 'A' Manufacturing Economy: Today's (1990) Dominant Model	SCENARIO 'B' Hybrid Economy: Convergence between Scenarios 'A' and 'C'	SCENARIO 'C' Digital Economy Achieves Promise
Key Element: Buyer and Seller Role RelationshipAssumptions		
TILTING SLIGHTLY TOWARD SELLER POWER: Product differentiation minimizes overcapacity. Firm holds product information. Hard for buyers & sellers to interact. Mass advertising is main form of customer communication. Tailoring products is expensive.	TILTING TOWARD BUYER POWER: Buyer diversity causes oversupply of some goods and services. Better buyer access to data and contact with sellers in placing orders. Sellers can communicate with previous owners of firm's products. Ability to tailor products.	BUYER POWER DOMINANT: Market fragmentation leads to oversupply of goods/ services. Enhanced ability to interact with sellers and buyers when ordering. Much more ability to communicate with previous owners of enterprise products. Enhanced ability to tailor products.

SCENARIO 'A'	SCENARIO 'B'	SCENARIO 'C'
Enterprise Direction		
FIRM-DRIVEN: Marketing forecasts customer demand tempered by assessments of regulatory/societal concerns. Using forecasts, management specifies products the firm designs and makes and which of its outlets will distribute them. Mass advertising used to promote the product.	CUSTOMER-BASED: Buyers assess availability of products/services from all firms. Networking with trusted individuals and using other sources, buyers specify attributes and components, delivery, price and finance arrangements.	WEB-DRIVEN: Web tools screen all products by relevance. The customer orders the 'best match' to be delivered. Executives focus on creating best-in-class products and a trusted Web interface for customers. Firms build alliances to ensure they have access to products wanted by buyers.
Definition of Marketing		
Marketing forecasts customer needs, persuades customers to buy the firm's products, and distributes them in the most effective manner.	Senior executive uses the marketing concept and oversees all the functions of the firm in its delivery of what the customer ordered.	Firm develops systems to allow interactive, trusted relationships with each customer. Data is gathered so the firm can tailor its offerings to that customer's specific needs and interests.
Places of Customer Contact		
Firm has many outlets. Customer must come to an outlet to buy product.	Outlets let customers experience the product. Firm distributes globally using customer's preferred distribution channels .	Firm sells the product to the customer and delivers it to the customer anywhere, anytime, any way the customer desires.

SCENARIO 'A'	SCENARIO 'B'	SCENARIO 'C'
Primary Method of Communication to Customers		
The firm advertises using mass media or direct mail without the customer's consent and presumes that it represents a main source of product information.	Firm invites the customer to ask for more information and asks permission to send the customer ads. Firm knows it is only one source of product information.	Interactive trust-based communication with customer (who can easily detect false claims). Information delivered when the customer is interested. Less conventional advertising.
Pricing Practices		
Firm sets initial price to attract customers, then offers rebates. It offers higher-price options and may make some options standard so the base product is more appealing.	Customer proposes a price and negotiates to agree the price. Firm may reduce price if customers take extra services (insurance, maintenance plans, etc.)	Firm specifies a mechanism by which the customer's price will be discovered (e.g., auction, dynamic pricing etc.). The buyers use that mechanism to set price they are willing to pay.

Table 2: Examples of hypothetical alternative scenarios developed in 1990 deemed likely to occur between 2000 and 2010.

Putting the scenarios to good use

The scenarios allow decision-makers to consider which combination of the three business designs (make-and-sell, sense-and-respond, and anticipate-and-lead) to adopt in case any of these scenarios actually occur. To appreciate the risks and rewards associated with each of the alternative business designs, the decision team can view possible outcomes of the three business designs under all three scenarios in a decision table, as seen in Table 3.

It is important to point out that, if the decision tree were completed by others, the interpretation of the expected results could very well be different. The value of the process is to help the decision team reach a consensus decision based on a synthesis of all the information they have available at that time.

For this hypothetical analysis, the decision involves choosing between the make-and-sell, sense-and-respond, and anticipate-and-lead business designs. The criteria for selection are limited to two items: 1) Which business design will increase the number of customers with whom the enterprise will have a long-term relationship? and 2) Which business design will increase the enterprise 'share of their wallet?'

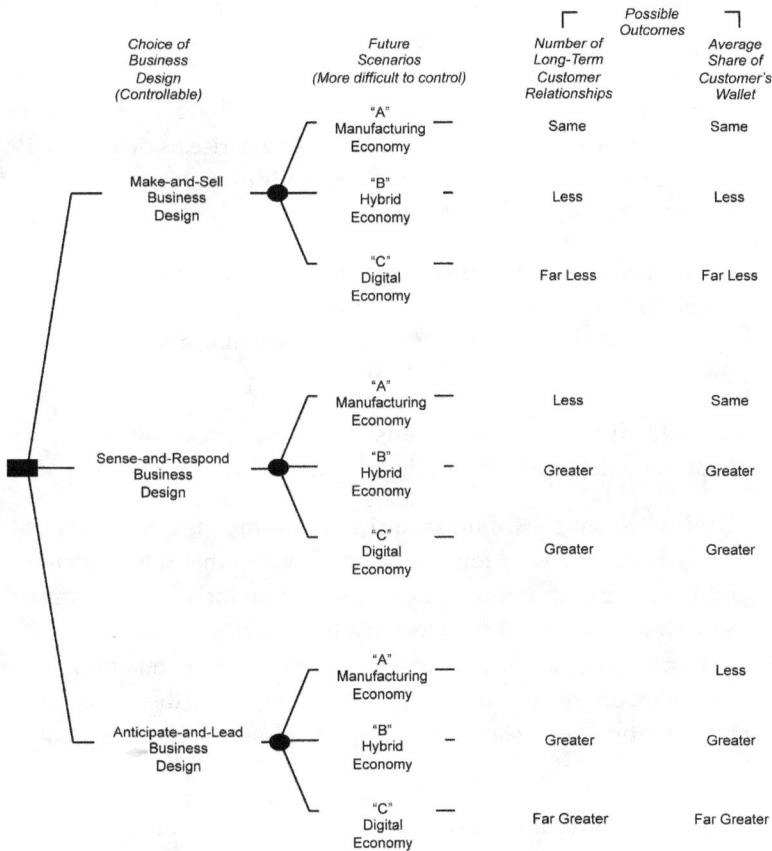

Choice of Business Design (Controllable)	Future Scenarios (More difficult to control)	Possible Outcomes	
		Number of Long-Term Customer Relationships	Average Share of Customer's Wallet
Make-and-Sell Business Design	"A" Manufacturing Economy	Same	Same
	"B" Hybrid Economy	Less	Less
	"C" Digital Economy	Far Less	Far Less
Sense-and-Respond Business Design	"A" Manufacturing Economy	Less	Same
	"B" Hybrid Economy	Greater	Greater
	"C" Digital Economy	Greater	Greater
Anticipate-and-Lead Business Design	"A" Manufacturing Economy		Less
	"B" Hybrid Economy	Greater	Greater
	"C" Digital Economy	Far Greater	Far Greater

Table 3: Overview of alternative scenarios on business design choice

- As shown in Table 3, if the enterprise chooses the make-and-sell business design, it could expect the following to occur:

  Under Scenario A (Manufacturing Economy), the enterprise is likely to end up with the same customers, given its ability to forecast customer needs and continue to take advantage of economies of scale. They will likely achieve the same share of customer wallet, since it will continue to limit its product portfolio to the same products.

  Under Scenario B (Hybrid A&C Economy), the enterprise is likely to end up with fewer customers. This would be the result of developing products for which the demand is less likely to meet enterprise forecasts. This will drive operating costs up and require price reductions to convince consumers to buy products that do not meet all their requirements. The share of wallet will be less because customers will see the enterprise as dealing on price alone and not able to provide additional products or services that the customer prefers.

  Under Scenario C (Digital Economy), the same conditions as for Scenario B will occur except that they will be exacerbated by the speed at which customers are able to determine alternatives to the enterprise's products and services.

- If the enterprise chooses the sense-and-respond business design, it could expect the following to occur:

  Under Scenario A (Manufacturing Economy), the enterprise is likely to end up with fewer customers, given that it may incur added costs in trying to achieve flexibility which is of less value since the firm can actually forecast future sales. The increase in costs could put the firm at a price disadvantage resulting in lost sales. Share of customer wallet is likely to be the same, with the possibility of a slight increase if customers seek additional services.

  Under Scenario B (Hybrid A&C Economy), the enterprise is likely to end up with more customers. This would be the result of developing products for which the enterprise is more likely to meet consumer requirements. Although the investment in flexibility could drive operating costs up, the ability to meet their requirements will allow the firm the opportunity to increase prices. The share of wallet will be greater because customers will see the enterprise as being more responsive to their needs, and they may therefore be willing to entrust more of their expenditures to the firm.

Under Scenario C (Digital Economy), since predicting customers' future needs will be extremely difficult for everyone in the industry, the enterprise is likely to experience a competitive advantage if it moves to sense-and-respond before major competitors, thus allowing it to gain more understanding about each customer's unique profile of preferences, and the value that the customer attaches to each preference.

- If the enterprise chooses the anticipate-and-lead business design, it could expect the following to occur:

    Under Scenario A (Manufacturing Economy), if the enterprise chooses this business design, it will face similar results to the sense-and-respond business design – only worse. This will occur because competitors who maintain the make-and-sell business design could be at a significant cost advantage because they do not invest in digital technologies and flexibility. By contrast, this enterprise will have spent considerable sums on equipment and on training people to accomplish unnecessary tasks.

    Under Scenario B (Hybrid A&C Economy), the enterprise is likely to face the same improvement in number of customers and share of wallet as under the sense-and-respond business design.

    Under Scenario C (Digital Economy), the enterprise is likely to gain far more customers and share of their wallet. It could provide the full range of products required by these customers and, because they have anticipated their requirements early, it could meet these requirements where, when, and how customers desired. This would create an environment conducive to the products and services that the enterprise has introduced.

Although limited in scope, a review of the expected outcomes of this hypothetical analysis clearly shows that the decision surrounding which business design to choose is affected by which of the possible future scenarios is expected to emerge.

Decision-makers under these circumstances are left with several choices:

1. Do what they want to do and hope the future environment goes their way

2. Try to develop a business design that is robust for all scenarios

3. See what they can do to encourage the desired future environment that is most conducive to their strategy.

If the decision-makers choose to encourage the desired future environment, they must first determine, given their current and potential competencies, which of the future scenarios they would prefer. They must then determine the likelihood that they and potential alliance partners could cause that scenario to occur.

When reviewing alternative strategies for addressing a problem in this manner, a hybrid strategy generally emerges which is superior to the initial strategies used in conducting the analysis. In this case, one might choose to create an anticipate-and-lead organization with sense-and-respond characteristics, or vice-versa. In the future it will not be wise to choose one over the others. There is great value in developing a business design that avoids the tyranny of 'either/or,' and takes advantage of the opportunity presented by 'and.'

GM's introduction of the *OnStar* mobile communication system and XM Satellite Radio in 1996-1997 is an example of operating within three business designs. If automobile development and manufacturing in the 1990s is the epitome of the make-and-sell offering, how does an auto company create a customized sense-and-respond or anticipate-and-lead value proposition for the customer? When faced with this question, GM took what it learned from Chunka Mui's concept of the Killer App and applied that thinking to GM's position in its current market place and its connections to technological advancement being worked on at its then component organization Hughes Electronic and Electronic Data Systems (EDS). The basic thinking is captured in Figure 19.

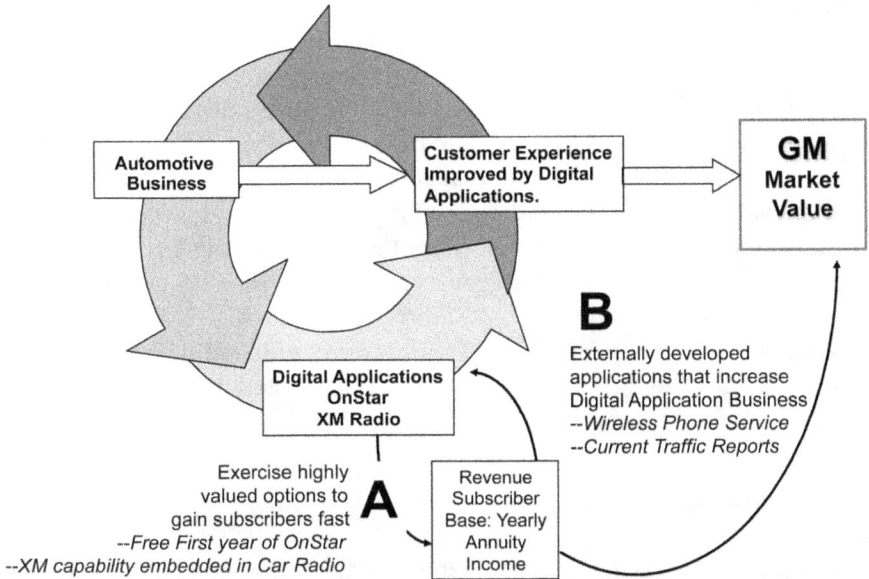

Figure 19: Illustration of OnStar business design

The primary metric to be used to determine whether GM should move to a new business was the extent to which the new business would improve GM's market value.

The basic premise was that GM could get there faster and more economically by [A] leveraging its traditional automotive business into an integrated set of downstream, digitally-based subscriber businesses. The strategy was to transform GM's existing served market into a set of subscriber-based, digital businesses that would generate annuity income.

The next step was to use the large digital subscriber base to attract [B] new, third-party application providers like wireless phone service providers and providers of current traffic reports. Today, GM is the largest wholesaler of wireless phone service in the United States.

In this context GM was responding to expressed customer preferences relative to safety and security and improved mobile communications. By establishing an embedded digital platform in the vehicle that could be modified when additional opportunities became available the company was able to keep up with the digital economy's rapid pace of change.

The introduction of XM Radio, the first satellite radio system in a vehicle, was more an anticipate-and-lead business design. In this case, GM determined that satellite radio would only be successful if sufficient vehicles had radios that could receive the satellite signals. The availability of these radios would provide enough potential subscribers to warrant the investment required to develop and deliver the appropriate programming at an acceptable price. By creating a strategic relationship with XM Radio (now SeriusXM), GM changed the environment by installing satellite compatible radio in a large percentage of its vehicles. In this case GM invested in XM Radio and also benefited from its stock value.

The value of learning to live with uncertainty

Recent experience has shown that, regardless of how much analysis is conducted, one still cannot always predict which future will emerge. It could be one of the scenarios envisioned or another entirely unexpected alternative. However, if the enterprise knows what conditions could occur, it is then faced with at least two options: it can determine how much it wants to spend to ensure its plans are robust across the range of possible scenarios, or take action to allocate resources to try to bring about the scenario that offers the best competitive position.

Using the actions suggested in the description of the Decision Loom shown in Figure 12 to monitor assumptions underlying the scenarios that the enterprise has identified is one way of minimizing the chances of being 'surprised.'

Although planning for a 'certain' future based on past experiences may have worked in the past, this activity provides a way to choose among business designs and to minimize the negative impact if the future turns out to be different than expected.

Examples of the ideas presented

Nintendo: playing a different game

In the 1990s, Nintendo was the unchallenged leader of the gaming industry until the release of the revolutionary disc-based platform that offered crystal-clear graphics and improved memory storage. Sony's PlayStation was among the first of these new consoles in 1994 and Microsoft and Nintendo soon followed with the Xbox and GameCube, respectively. By 2005, Nintendo held a distant third in market share and the former star was fading.

Lead strategists at Nintendo considered their position and the two problems that were plaguing the current market: 1) as the target demographic (young consumers) aged and incurred time deficits, they stopped playing and 2) more powerful processors meant more expensive consoles and games (at the time, PlayStation 3 was $600), and only serious gamers were buying. The strategists concluded that rather than continuing to compete over the same problematic consumer base, they would play a new game altogether. They decided there was room for a cheaper and more casual gaming experience that could appeal to a wider audience, including families. A new game controller that was remote with motion sensors might also bring a nontraditional gamer, who enjoyed an interactive experience, to the mix.[104]

The price point ($250) and the revolutionary hand controller of the Wii were an immediate success – Nintendo fought to keep up with demand for nearly a year after its launch. With its multi-player feature and simple yet engaging games, both families and women also embraced the Wii. Moreover, while competitors depended on strong margins from their games, the Wii console was profitable on its own.[105] In its first year it outsold both the Playstation 3 and the Xbox 360 combined. In addition, as the ultimate proof of success, new consoles with motion sensors arrived in 2010 from both Microsoft (Kinect) and Sony (PlayStation Move Controller).

A successful action does not last forever

As an example of how fast things can change, Ben Fritz of the Los Angeles Times in December of 2010 reported:

---

104 Gaudiosi, 2007

105 Kohler, 2007

Just three years ago, Nintendo's video-game device was nearly impossible to find, as hard-core gamers clamored for it along with novices, including families with young children and grandparents drawn to its easy-to-use wand. From January 2007, just after it launched, until last May, the Wii was the top-selling game console nearly every month in the U.S. But things have taken a decided turn. The Wii fell to No. 3 from No. 1 this year, with U.S. sales down 24% in the first 10 months compared with the same period in 2009. Sales of Microsoft's rival Xbox 360 are up 34%, and Sony's PlayStation 3 has risen 15%.

Fritz went on to identify what he thought to be the reason for the Wii's success:

That success came largely from an untapped market: infrequent game players. But infrequent game players by definition don't make for repeat customers when it comes to buying new Wii games. Their attention has also turned to online social games such as 'FarmVille.'

Qualifying the negative nature of his report on Nintendo, Fritz quotes Marc Jackson, of Seahorn Capital as saying:

Nintendo is contrarian by nature and they always seem to have a longer-term plan than their competitors. I'm sure they're figuring out what to do next, and it's going to surprise everyone. [106]

Cisco: Video venture

Cisco CEO John Chambers made a big bet on video. During 2010/11, the company made numerous acquisitions in the video media industry (e.g. ExtendMedia, CoreOptics Inc.), including purchasing the makers of the Flip video camcorder. The device allows users to record nearly an hour's worth of video and then easily upload the file to online sites like YouTube. This decision comes as smartphones and tablets increase demands for streaming video, which chews up massive amounts of bandwidth. While these demands are mainly consumer-driven at present, there are prolific opportunities for professional services including videoconferencing or provision of remote medical care.[107]

---

106   Fritz, 2010

107   Fortt, 2010

Facilitating the use and ease of video will mean big business for Cisco, because the company's core strategy to increase consumption of network resources – and more consumption means more business. To bring together these complementary strategies, it has already built a platform to optimize new traffic with its Medianet architecture, which is essentially a 'smart' network device that can customize the video to the intended recipient device (adjusting costly bandwidth along the way). Next up was the release of its tablet, the Cius, in the spring of 2011. Built on an Android OS, the device is designed for professionals as "a mobile collaboration business table", with HD video conferencing options.[108] Users can also use clouds to share, produce, and edit documents through a more secure connection than most other current tablets. While the pieces seem to be in place, success will depend on the rate of adoption and whether Cisco networks prove ready for the increased traffic. Regardless, video phones, once relegated to futuristic movies, now seem poised to be the next widespread commercial device. Whether Cisco leads this industry in the future will depend on its ability to encourage demand by creating a future with the right technology to make it happen.

---

108   Cisco Corporation, 2010

Capability 4: Making Decisions Interactively Using a Variety of Methods

Today, the challenge for a manager is not to focus enterprise resources to seek a single approach to address all the enterprise's decisions. Rather, it is to manage, through the Decision Loom, a comprehensive process of decision-making to increase the chances of making the best decision among the available alternatives, including those that surface at the last minute. The process must also make explicit the rationale for the decision and allow tracking of the assumptions upon which the rationale was based.

The portfolio of decision processes embedded in the Decision Loom needs to be designed to help manage the interactions between the choice of decision support tools, the expertise of the enterprise, and the involvement of creative people in the decision process. The decision system must be adaptable to its environment and draw on the energy and the imagination of those who will affect, or be affected by, the outcomes.

Addressing perception and reality

In Plato's Republic, a magnificent discourse takes place between Socrates and others in their attempt to envision the perfect political state. It turns into a discussion of what people are able to know with certainty. In the allegory of the cave, the acquisition of human knowledge is likened to the shadows and reflections seen on cave walls. People and objects passing outside the cave may have different appearances because of the way the light shines into the cave at any given point in time. For people sitting inside the cave, it would be naive to interpret the shadows as the real world. As Socrates says:

> The forms which these people draw or make . . . are converted by them into images. But they are really seeking to behold the things themselves, which can only be seen with the eye of the mind.[109]

---

109   Sterling & Scott, 1985

For today's decision-makers, the point is still relevant: while we strive to move closer to reality, we must remember that the design of the Decision Loom to support decision-making, like the cave images, can provide no more than a reflection of the reality of the society and the marketplace or of internal enterprise conditions.

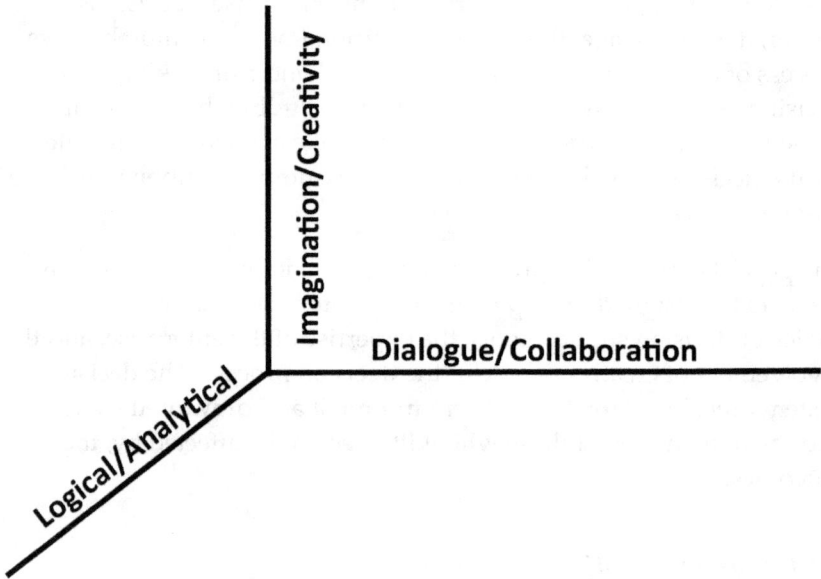

Figure 20: Three organizing dimensions of the interactive decision-making process

The initial dimension of the Decision Loom is logical/analytical. In our Western culture, we are accustomed to this approach to decision support tools, which involves breaking up any whole into its parts so as to discover their purpose, proportion, function, and interactions. If we are to make the best use of this dimension we must avoid this common mistake. For example we have been taught that to better understand a problem, we need more information. To deal with more information, we need more people, more sophisticated techniques, more state-of-the-art technology. Although there are times when more is better, that is more likely when the more provides additional insight – not just numbers. We are, in fact, learning an old lesson, which good senior managers have known for a long time – you can't run a successful corporation by the numbers alone. We need to ensure we are dealing with reliable and relevant approaches to improving our understanding of the issue we face.

The second dimension is dialogue/collaboration. Decision-making and implementation in virtually any organization is a collective process. Sharing of information from various perspectives is a start. However, the goal should be not only to share ideas but to have better ideas come forward and to implement them promptly and effectively.

The third dimension is imagination/creativity. People with access to diverse experiences and viewpoints can be the key to generating the best possible range of alternatives to solve an important, complex problem. These people need to draw on intuition, fantasy, inner imagery, inspiration and everything else that is creative about the human psyche.

And that's the challenge. The Decision Loom must provide decision-makers the capability to move beyond the realm of facts and analytical thinking… to one of collaboration and intuition to achieve insight into alternative ways of achieving objectives. They must somehow integrate the three dimensions by creating a thinking and observing space representing a more modern concept of Plato's cave.

It's not a data warehouse… it's a Decision Loom

> *In much of the popular literature about research and science, the authors often assume that the meaning of a 'systematic collection of known facts' or 'collection of information' is a clear concept to most readers. Apparently they think of a collection' in terms of a library, and a systematic collection to be like a well-run library with an adequate indexing and cataloguing system… It is true that stored in it are strings of meaningful symbols. But it has no adequate way of showing which strings are meaningful and which are true.*

> C. West Churchman[110]

---

110   Churchman, 1971, p.9

To address Churchman's desire to bring meaning and an assessment of credibility to what is stored will require a variety of tools, expertise, and innovative ideas. To ensure that it has the most appropriate set of tools, unique where necessary and shared where appropriate, an organization should have a systematic approach to developing and advancing its decision-making process. The strings of data, information, intelligence, knowledge, understanding, and wisdom need a structure and process to ensure that, as implied by Churchman and called for by Edna St. Vincent Millay; there is the equivalent of a Decision Loom to weave them into a useful fabric.

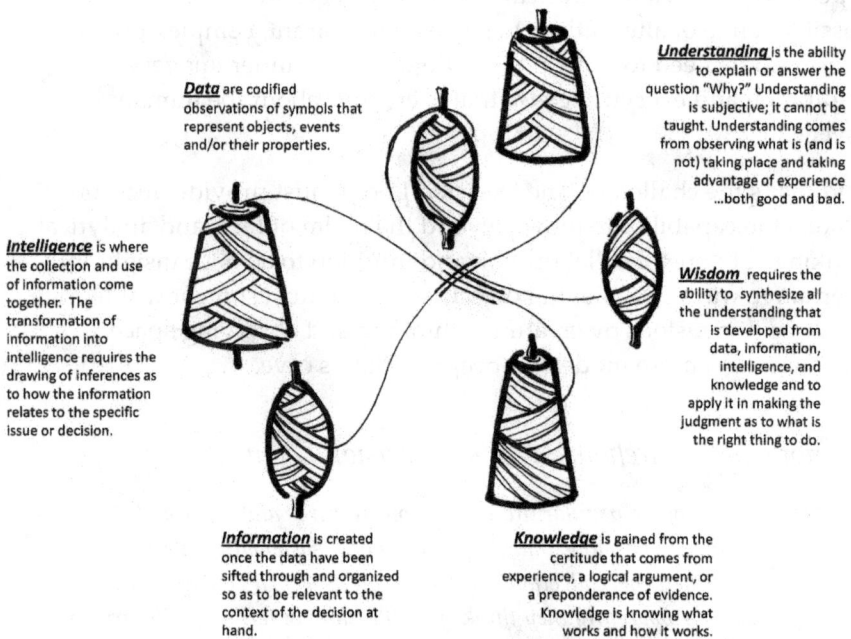

Data are codified observations of symbols that represent objects, events and/or their properties.

Understanding is the ability to explain or answer the question "Why?" Understanding is subjective; it cannot be taught. Understanding comes from observing what is (and is not) taking place and taking advantage of experience ...both good and bad.

Intelligence is where the collection and use of information come together. The transformation of information into intelligence requires the drawing of inferences as to how the information relates to the specific issue or decision.

Wisdom requires the ability to synthesize all the understanding that is developed from data, information, intelligence, and knowledge and to apply it in making the judgment as to what is the right thing to do.

Information is created once the data have been sifted through and organized so as to be relevant to the context of the decision at hand.

Knowledge is gained from the certitude that comes from experience, a logical argument, or a preponderance of evidence. Knowledge is knowing what works and how it works.

Figure 21: Components of a Decision Loom

The challenge to the designers of decision support systems is to enable dynamic interaction between people and systems and to provide individuals with the most appropriate tools and processes for sharing. For example, the threads of an enterprise Decision Loom are represented as an interactive component of all forms of input into a decision. It is not something that can simply be stored in a warehouse of what is known about what to do. In today's enterprise, knowledge is itself a dynamic entity, changing faster than ever. Knowledge – representing what is known – is created by people using information to make decisions or testing out potential ideas. At the same time, enterprise knowledge will change and it will alter the relevance of information and data. It's not about what comes first in a hierarchy… it is about how the components interact as they come together in a decision process.

As an example of the importance of not letting my earlier refinery metaphor of the decision hierarchy dictate the flow of information, assume that an engineer is working on the next version of a successful product. In this instance, based on the experience of working on the current product, the engineer is quite comfortable about the 'knowledge' of what to do. But the engineer also wants to ensure that some factors that contributed to previous knowledge have not changed or been altered. In this situation the engineer will want to connect with other contributing spools and determine if any of the information or data that were used in the past have changed, or whether any new data have been collected that could indicate a need to reconsider the knowledge upon which the previous decision was made.

In operation, the enterprise decision process requires a variety of tools, techniques, and processes, reflecting the variety of activities across the organization. Some environments will require sophisticated analytical capabilities, while others operate in a more creative manner and require decision support tools that support more qualitative approaches. While appropriate tools and processes would be developed, the decision-making loom would also consider the organizational perspective to ensure there is commonality among the spools wherever appropriate. Maximizing commonality will greatly advance our ability to share knowledge and create an efficient and effective decision support system.

Determining the appropriate decision support tools

> I suppose it is tempting, if the only tool you have is a hammer, to treat everything as if it were a nail.[111]

---

111   Maslow, 1962, p.15

Visualize a carpenter walking around a roughed-in house and suddenly noticing a nail not fully hammered down. One experienced and swift blow with a hammer and the problem is neatly solved. Given his success and since the hammer is in hand, the carpenter looks for more loose nails; after all, if one nail had not been fully hammered down, who is to say that there are not others? With a keen loose-nail-seeking sense, the carpenter expertly tracks and pounds many more nails. He becomes quite skilled at spotting loose nails and confident at wielding his hammer. Soon, however, no more loose nails remain. No matter; our carpenter can simply 'squint' a bit and switch to pounding in loose screws, staples, and other hardware.

The same hammer-and-nail syndrome can cause us to try forcing the problem at hand into a preferred analytic process or framework with which we have had positive experiences. We choose not to see (sometimes wearing psychological blinders) certain aspects of the problem to the point where we can almost see the 'right' answer, only further reinforcing the 'correctness' of our favored approach. In essence, the potential problem with successful decision support tools is that we can become so accomplished at, and accustomed to, using them that we forget to consider whether they are appropriate for addressing the problem at hand. The true power of analytic processes and frameworks comes from our being aware of both their strengths and shortcomings.

Ideally, understanding the nature of a given problem should determine which analytical approach to take. Prior to deciding on the right decision support tool(s) there is great value in developing an understanding of the nature of a problem in its organizational setting and the level of technical detail required to support a final decision. The framework that follows reminds us that the tools we select can influence outcomes and that we need to first understand the nature of the problem and then determine the approach, or approaches, that we should take.

A suggested framework for considering approaches to decision-making

When examining decision support tools for the Decision Loom, one must consider both their organizational and technical aspects.

Organizational aspects include, but are not necessarily limited to:

- the extent to which the decision requires collaboration among different functions within the enterprise

- whether we are improving an existing activity or developing a new idea and will require creative individuals who need freedom from rules and processes

- the extent to which the stakeholders share a vision of the problem and its linkage to the organization

- the number of decision-makers involved – is there a single decision-maker, or will multiple stakeholders be required to allocate resources?

- whether the eventual decision-makers will be involved in the process or will assign subordinates to work out a solution for them to approve.

Technical aspects include, but again are not necessarily limited to:

- the required specificity – how broadly and deeply into the issues of the problem will the analysis probe – will the decision be made on the basis of general observations or will very specific information elements be required?

- how significant is the system behavior over time, and how interdependent are the issues across time and space?

- how much uncertainty exists in the data assessments?

- how much uncertainty lies in the relationships that exist in the problem?

- how much time is available to develop an answer that will be accepted and acted on – can completeness and specific answers be traded off for approximate and more timely answers?112

---

112   Mike Jackson (2003, pp. 17-28) provides a more detailed and comprehensive framework called System of Systems Methodology.

PROBLEM SOLVING ASSESSMENT TOOL

ORGANIZATIONAL ASPECTS	TECHNICAL ASPECTS

Collaboration Across Functions
Minimal ———————————————— Extensive

Allowance for Creative Thinking
Minimal ———————————————— Extensive

Shared Vision
Weak ———————————————— Strong

Number of Decision-Makers
Low ———————————————— High

Management Involvement
Minimal ———————————————— Extensive

Required Specificity
Minimal ———————————————— Extensive

Dynamic Complexity
LOW ———————————————— High

Data Uncertainty
Low ———————————————— High

System Component Interaction
Minimal ———————————————— Extensive
Initial   *Actual*
Assessment   Implementation

Timing Requirement
Right Now ———————————————— When Finished

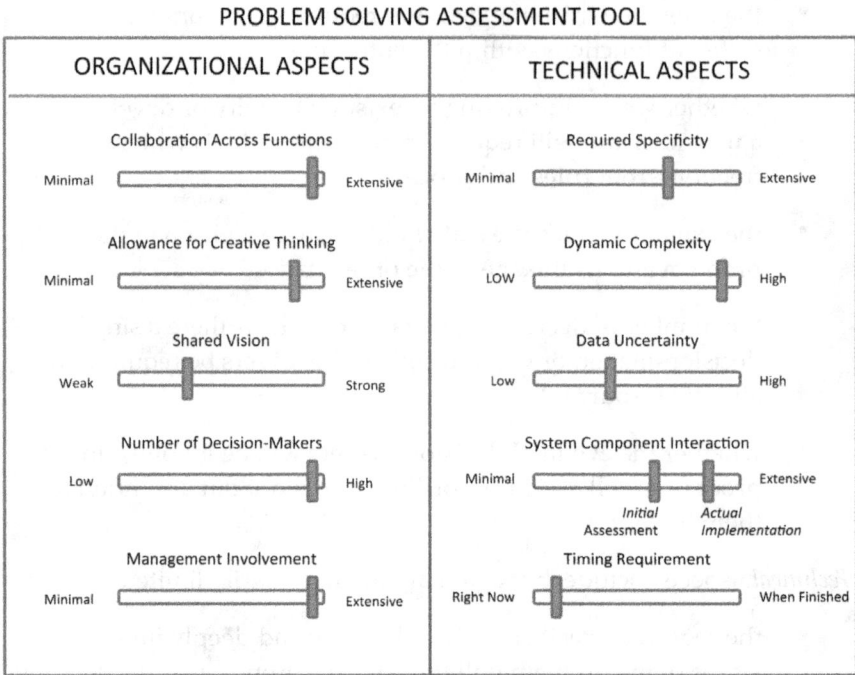

Figure 22: Characteristics of a decision process

As an example, consider the nature of the problem GM faced when looking at the potential impact of very large new and used-car superstores on GM's distribution channels (discussed in Episode 9 in *Part 1*).

From an organizational perspective:

- it was determined that the eventual solution would require extensive collaboration across organizational functions with the involvement of many decision-makers from those functions – all of whom were likely to come to the problem with varying points of view

- since used car superstores were new to the industry, addressing the problem would require some creative thinking

- there was no shared view of the problem

- since the solution had the potential to affect many functions there would be a number of involved decision-makers

- because of the nature of the organizational aspects of the problem the assignment was accepted on condition that those managers affected by the eventual decision would participate in the problem's formulation and throughout the entire process.

From a technical perspective:

- the process selected would have to be capable of handling a moderate level of information specificity

- because of the expected dynamic complexity and the long term impact of the issue, systems dynamics modeling was identified as one of the processes to be used

- there was considerable information available, but not necessarily in the form required

- initially only a minimal number of components were envisaged but those increased once feedback became available from those managers engaged in the process (of particular importance was the initial finding that indicated the impact of short-term leases in providing nearly new, used-cars to the superstores which in turn provided new car customers a less expensive alternative to a new car)

- given the time constraint, approximations of the component values would be used rather than detailed forecast estimates – based on this assessment, a combination of approaches were applied.

The Decision Analysis process (called the Dialogue Decision Process at GM) was applied to ensure that GM had framed the problem correctly from the ultimate decision-maker's perspective and that alternative approaches to be evaluated covered the many issues related to the problem. System dynamics modeling was chosen to ensure that the interaction of the critical elements could be evaluated and that the interaction could be understood and visualized over time.

Ensure that a full range of tools is available to meet the 3 dimensions: dialogue/collaboration, imagination/creativity and logical/analytical

To indicate the range of tools that should be available, twelve decision support tools are presented here. Depending on the structure of the enterprise and its containing environment, each enterprise should consider its own range of tools. What follows is only an example to demonstrate the need to assess whether there is a full range available to the enterprise. In this example we will simply use the three dimensions discussed at the beginning of this activity: (1) dialogue/collaboration, (2) imagination/creativity, and (3) logical/analytical. The scoring for each decision support tool was derived from discussions with colleagues who had familiarity with each of the processes displayed. With this format as an example, each enterprise should determine the criteria best suited to ensure its requirements are addressed. Readers are also encouraged to 'move the sliders' based on their own assessment.

Appreciative Inquiry

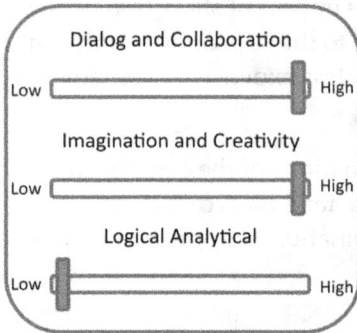

This positively focused method shifts concern from fixing problems or inadequacies to identifying and supporting the core strengths of a business. The issue or problem to be solved loses focus as decision-makers reflect on the enterprise as a whole: a process which engages all individuals to offer insight into what works well. There are four steps to this decision model – sometimes referred to as 4D:[113]

- Discover the 'best of what is' – identify where the company's processes worked perfectly

- Dream 'what might be' – envision processes that would work perfectly all the time

---

113   Kinni, 2003

- Design 'what should be' – define and prioritize the elements of perfect processes

- Create a destiny based on 'what will be' – participate in the creation of the design.

Cash Flow Forecasting with Spreadsheets

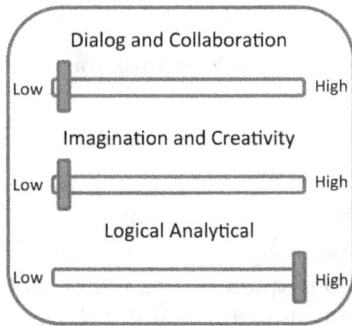

Cash flow forecasting enables firms to determine the profitability of a financial decision by outlining the potential outcomes. This method is helpful for considering different cash flow scenarios if variability is a possibility for factors like inputs or demand. To ensure that outcomes are determined correctly, a system-wide analysis of the organization's cash flows is necessary, potentially using a system diagram. After understanding all of the quantitative relationships, adjust costs and/or revenues according to the impact of the new financial decision. Finally, offer a prediction of sales or income to be gained and compare this to the initial estimates.

Critical Success Factors:

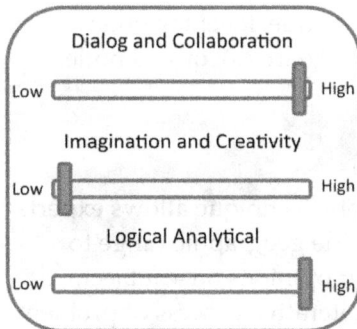

A critical success factor (CSF) is something that has a direct impact on the success of a company or a division/function. CSFs usually fall into one of four categories: industry, strategy, environmental, or temporal. Once identified, a CSF can offer a way of measuring the potential success of a new project or investment. To identify the CSFs:[114]

- establish your business's or project's mission and strategic goals

---

114   See Mind Tools in the Bibliography.

- for each strategic goal, ask yourself "what area of business or project activity is essential to achieve this goal?"

- evaluate the list of candidate CSFs to find the absolute essential elements for achieving success

- identify how you will monitor and measure each CSF

- communicate your CSFs along with the other important elements of your business or project's strategy

- keep monitoring and reevaluating your CSFs to ensure you keep moving toward your aims.

Decision Trees

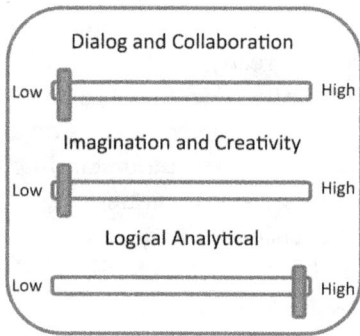

Dialog and Collaboration
Low —————————— High

Imagination and Creativity
Low —————————— High

Logical Analytical
Low —————————— High

A decision tree models a variety of decision pathways, show-casing the possible consequences and their costs and benefits. It is thus helpful when there is indecision and it is necessary to evaluate the multiple outcomes and consider the associated risks. To construct the tree, begin with the initial decision, map out the potential options, and continue iteratively with each potential subsequent decision until no further decisions are required. Offer utility measurements or other labels for these outcomes. Within the tree, label the nodes either decision nodes (squares), chance nodes (circles), or end nodes (triangles).

Delphi Technique

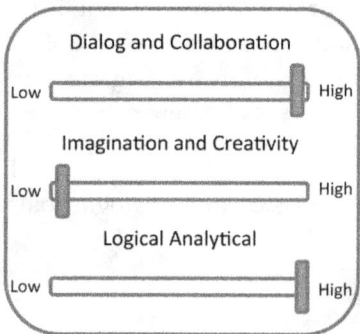

Dialog and Collaboration
Low —————————— High

Imagination and Creativity
Low —————————— High

Logical Analytical
Low —————————— High

The Delphi Technique allows experts from a wide geographic range to offer their opinions on a subject, using an iterative process of problem definition, discussion, feedback, and revisions. This tool prioritizes gathering opinions from a structured group of experts as opposed to an unstructured or uninformed group of individuals. To begin the Delphi process, first construct a questionnaire that asks questions surrounding the problem (as broadly as possible to extract all types of feedback) and determine the group of experts to consult. After mailing the questionnaire and receiving feedback, next summarize the responses and generate a second questionnaire that allows the experts to evaluate and rank all of the collected responses. The rank ordering is repeated until general consensus on a particular response or answer is clear.

Kepner Tregoe (rational process)

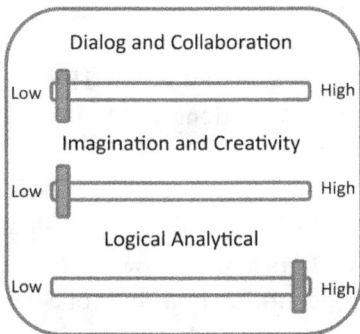

Kepner Tregoe offers a stepwise process for making decisions that attempt to assess and minimize risk. By focusing on the risk, this tool de-prioritizes the decision and mitigates bias for one option or another. It is useful when the solution is not clear and the options carry great risk. The goal thus becomes not to endlessly search for the optimal outcome "but rather the best possible choice, based on actually achieving the outcome with minimal negative consequences."[115] The four steps to complete the analysis are:

- Situation Appraisal: used to clarify the situation, outline concerns and choose a direction

- Problem Analysis: here the problem is defined and its root cause determined

- Decision Analysis: alternatives are identified and a risk analysis done for each

- Potential Problem Analysis: the best of the alternatives is further scrutinized against potential problems and negative consequences. Actions are proposed to minimize the risk.

---

115   McDermott, online.

Nominal Group Technique

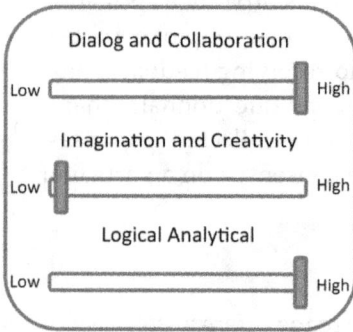

Nominal group technique enables groups to solve problems when group dynamics are not conducive to considering all potential decisions or outcomes (e.g. all new group, one or two vocal group leaders). Group members are first asked to consider the problem or decision at hand and generate individual responses without group consultation. These answers are then pooled, and discussion and questions begin around the generated solutions. The facilitator then has each person rank the available options and the lowest average is offered as the best response.

Porter's Five Forces

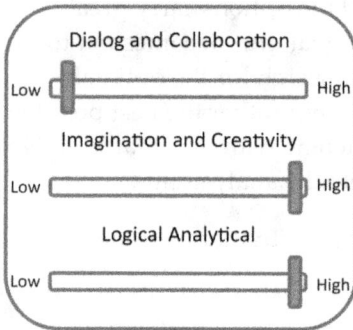

This tool offers a model for analyzing an industry as part of a business strategy to determine if new products, services, or businesses have the potential to be profitable. These forces help us to analyze everything from the intensity of competition to the profitability and attractiveness of an industry. The following five dimensions frame the assessment and the decision:

1. Supplier Power: How will suppliers be able to assert control over the business?

2. Buyer Power: How will buyers be able to assert control over the business?

3. Competitive Rivalry: How does the intensity of the competition affect returns?

4. Threat of Substitutes: Are there substitutes and what do the transaction costs look like for switching?

5. Threat of New Entrants: What are the barriers to entry and do they affect competition?

System Dynamics

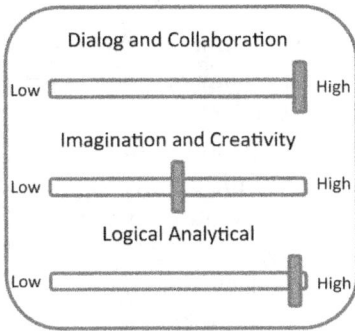

Dialog and Collaboration

Low [_____] High

Imagination and Creativity

Low [_____] High

Logical Analytical

Low [_____] High

System Dynamics is the art and science of observing and managing the interaction between structure and behavior for the purpose of modifying structure to improve behavior. Behavior refers to patterns of activity or outcomes over time (e.g. market share, unit sales, learning). Structure consists of non-linear interdependencies between variables that result in feedback loops. Variables are either stocks (e.g. inventories, populations, assets) or flows (e.g. rates of increase or decrease of stocks, shipments of products, or level of service).

Decision Analysis

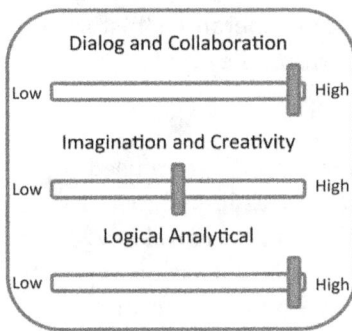

Dialog and Collaboration

Low [_____] High

Imagination and Creativity

Low [_____] High

Logical Analytical

Low [_____] High

Decision Analysis is a decision support tool that focuses on functional integration and involves a series of structured dialogues between the two groups responsible for reaching a decision and implementing the associated course of action.[116] It deals explicitly with the uncertainty and ambiguity that go hand-in-hand with decision-making. The first of the two groups is the set of decision-makers who typically represent different functions; what they have in common is their authority to allocate resources: people, capital, materials, time, and equipment. The second group is a team of cross-functional managers and specialists dedicated to the work at hand – those with a stake in the implementation. They represent design, engineering, manufacturing, marketing, and so forth. As a team drawn from the major functions, they embody the learning of the organization; in working together and sharing their learning, they create the knowledge upon which decisions will be based.

---

116   Howard *et al.* 1992

Agent-Based Models

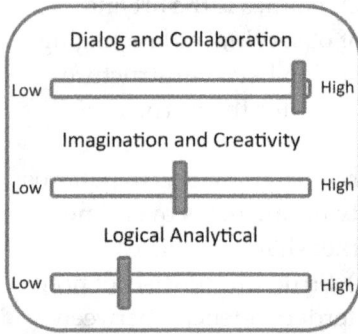

Agent-based models (ABM) computationally simulate the dynamic interactions of systems using agents to execute a series of activities. They are useful for measuring systemic interactions that are difficult to observe, measure linearly, or quantify. ABM typically has two properties; "first, the system is composed of interacting agents and second, the system exhibits emergent properties, that is, properties arising from the interactions of the agents that cannot be deduced simply by aggregating the properties of the agents."[117]

To begin an ABM, modelers need to study the system to create assumptions about agent interactions, define agent relationships and a method for their interaction. The program then generates a 'history' of how those assumptions manifest over time within the system.

Mind Maps

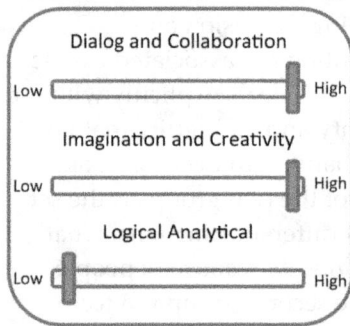

A mind map is a diagram used to represent ideas linked to and arranged around a central key word or idea. As a decision support tool, they use a non-linear method, anchored on associations (even if the idea seems irrelevant), to develop connections between elements of the decision-making process. Through these links, mind maps connect consequences of the various aspects of a decision to consider all of its dimensions .

The elements of a given mind map are arranged intuitively according to the importance of the concepts, and are classified into groupings, branches, or areas, with the goal of representing semantic or other connections between portions of information. By presenting ideas in a

---

117 Axelrod & Tesfatsion, 2011

radial, graphical, non-linear manner, mind maps encourage a highly creative brainstorming approach to decision-making.

After the enterprise has determined which of the decision approaches it believes will meet its needs, a quick summary of the choices should be conducted to determine the extent to which, in this case, the three dimensions have been met.

Decision Process	Collaborative	Creative	Logical
Appreciative Inquiry	HIGH	HIGH	LOW
Cash Flow Forecasting	LOW	LOW	HIGH
Critical Success Factors	HIGH	LOW	HIGH
Decision Trees	LOW	LOW	HIGH
Delphi Technique	HIGH	LOW	HIGH
Kepner Tregoe	LOW	LOW	HIGH
Nominal Group Technique	HIGH	LOW	HIGH
Porter's Five Forces	LOW	HIGH	HIGH
System Dynamics	HIGH	MEDIUM	HIGH
Decision Support & Risk Analysis	HIGH	MEDIUM	HIGH
Agent Models	HIGH	MEDIUM	LOW
Mind Maps	HIGH	HIGH	LOW
TOTAL HIGH SCORES	8	3	9
TOTAL MEDIUM SCORES		3	
TOTAL LOW SCORES	4	6	3

Table 3: Summary of decision support tools to ensure all three dimensions are covered throughout the enterprise.

In this example, the tools available appear to provide sufficient capabilities in the Collaborative and Logical dimensions, but are not as strong in providing the opportunity to develop Creative solutions.

A private sector example of improving the interaction between those who collect and those who use information

Around 1995 Harvey Bell and his colleagues at GM's Systems Engineering Centre engaged our market research group to help them design a (quality) process to improve communication between functions in the product development process. The modification provided a framework for effective direct interaction among market researchers, program managers, and engineers, minimizing the ambiguity or discrepancy that often existed between market information and product specifications. The purpose was to deliver market information to program teams so that it was clear, readily usable, more complete, and less filtered than it had been.

As an example, consider consumers' interest in 'years of durability,' which was translated into a product requirement of 'no visible rust in five years.' A part characteristic required to meet this requirement could be paint of a certain weight and crystal size. The manufacturing operation requirement might involve dip tanks and the application of three coats of paint. Finally, the production requirement would specify the required time, acidity, and temperature of the painting process.

Adapting a quality process known as Quality Function Deployment (QFD) led to the development of a matrix that provided a structure within which people could reconcile differences between the voice of the market and what GM was able – and willing – to provide. Initially, the approach was more linear than dynamic. However, given the principles driving QFD, the market research group gathered information with far more extensive participation by the product team than in the past. The product team, with assistance from the market research group and the jointly developed Market Dynamics Model (serving as a critical component of a Decision Loom), translated the information into product characteristics.

The increased collaboration proved critical. It helped GM provide products that more closely matched what customers wanted, as with the MS2000 program described in Episode 8.

The collaboration also gave us insight into how we could continuously improve our actions based on experience. Market Research learned more about the product managers and teams and their needs for extremely specific, timely and actionable information. Market Research came to understand that it is necessary to first satisfy the internal customer – the product program team – if the ultimate customer is to be eventually satisfied. The Product teams learned that by engaging the Market Research group in their early thinking, they were more likely to get timely and relevant information that they would value.

Inventing a more dynamic version of QFD

The trust that developed between research and the product teams also led to the creation of a whole that was greater than the sum of the parts. During one of our reviews, Harvey Bell commented that he was impressed with how collaboration was improving our vehicles, but he noted that the shelf life of the information his engineers were receiving wasn't very long. He wanted customers surveyed more frequently. Specifically, he wanted:

- Continuously up-to-date customer data

- Periodically updated product data

- More complete definitions of customer preferences

- Enterprise-wide availability

- Faster turn-around times

- Better accuracy

- Ease of use

Although Harvey's request was reasonable, the conjoint data collection and analysis process for the Market Dynamics Model cost several million dollars, so we conducted the survey to collect the basic information only every three years. Getting from Harvey's idealized design back to where we were, led us to consider further use of the *MyProductAdvisor* project described in Episode 9. The key idea was to take advantage of an auto advisor for automotive shoppers that would provide them with accurate, unbiased, comprehensive vehicle recommendations, and that would help them sort through the many vehicles currently on the market to find the best one for their individual needs. Each consumer visiting the advisor would leave behind an anonymous record of their preferences that would serve as a replacement for the conjoint data used in the Market Dynamics Model systems. This advisor data would have several key advantages over the traditional recruited consumer panel data used for the Market Dynamics Model:

- Respondents were actual shoppers

- Given their purpose for coming to the site, respondents had an intrinsic incentive to provide accurate data

- Respondents were entering their data 24/7, thereby creating large samples and a continuous record of customer preferences

- The data were relatively inexpensive to collect

- The data were always up-to-date, thereby decreasing turn-around times for analysis of results.

To provide easier access to the information, in 2003 an internally accessible worksite, the Automotive Market Insight System, was developed. After two years of use, the system evolved and had two modes of operation:

- The normal advisor mode that used customer data from the auto advisor on *MyProductAdvisor.com*

- A special survey mode that had an expanded set of vehicle attributes and which used a special customer data set collected annually by *MyProductAdvisor*.

The system grew into an established corporate-wide system used by many GM staff from many different internal functions. Some key metrics for the system were:

In the spirit of managing the interaction of the parts, today more than 200 staff have passwords to use the system, representing the following areas:

- Portfolio Planning

- Global Product and Consumer Research

- Long-Term Forecasting

- Revenue Management

- Advanced Vehicle Development

- Strategic Initiatives

- Research and Development

This led to a growing coherence among these internal functions with respect to customer needs and preferences. Given its extended use and relevance, the system was expanded to the China market and is in the process of establishing advisors in Europe and South America.

The existence of a 'Decision Loom' (at GM it is called Automotive Market Insight System) should not be misinterpreted as implying that this is the 'Center' of all enterprise knowledge. Rather, it is a distinct entity which recognizes that one of the enterprise's greatest assets is the capability of all its members to learn and generate knowledge about its markets and products. This requires the allocation of resources to 'knowledge use experts,' working within the system, to ensure this internal competency is developed and continually renewed. The information system is organizationally independent to ensure focus and objectivity on issues of knowledge use. What is more important, however, is that it is not independent from its enterprise colleagues – its customers. The degree of interdependence between the Market Insight System and those that use the capabilities it develops is a good measure of its success.

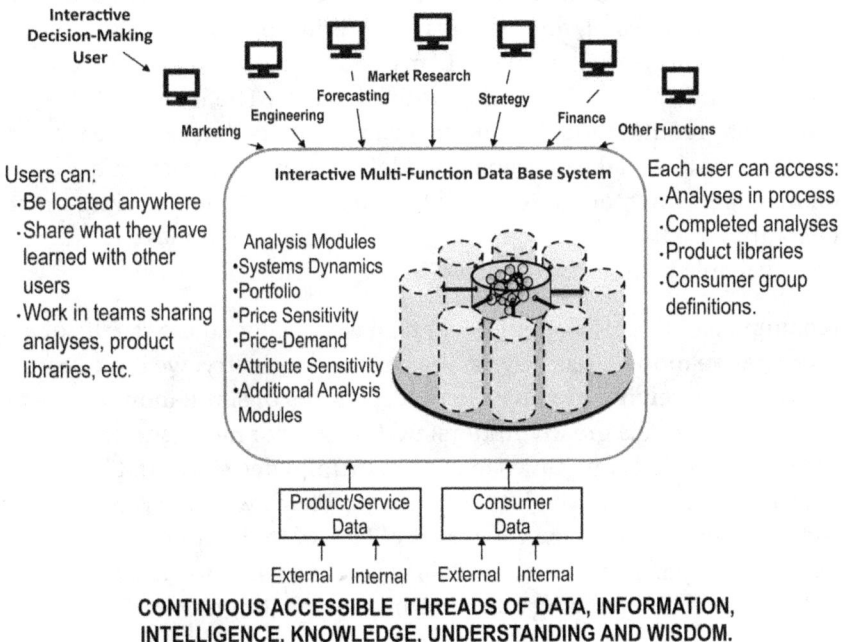

Figure 23: Example of an interactive Decision Loom

Thinking through the thinkable and the unthinkable – the role of Dynamic Modeling[118]

Dynamic Modeling is a technology for encouraging collaborative thinking to improve the enterprise's understanding of how the causal relationships in a complex system interact to generate the system's past or desired future behavior. Dynamic Modeling uses graphical techniques and quantitative simulation modeling to make mental models explicit and to rigorously understand their consequences. For example, in the automobile industry, managers make a continuous stream of decisions about vehicle attributes, price incentives, advertising and financial structure. Based on analysis and their best judgment, managers hope that the interaction of these choices with the causal relationships that govern the behavior of the system will generate profitable outcomes. Sometimes, gifted or lucky managers make choices that lead to long periods of above average growth and profitability. Unfortunately, for most companies, periods of above average performance are fleeting.

Dynamic Modeling tries to better the odds of superior performance by improving managers' mental models of complex business systems. As described in *Part 1*, after extensive experience with models at the Census Bureau, Xerox and Kodak, my colleagues and I formulated Barabba's Law: "Never say, 'the model says...'". The intent of the law was to remind modelers and decision-makers that *people* reach conclusions and make decisions. Models do not. All decisions are based on managers' mental models and the purpose of model building must be to upgrade the decision-maker's mental model and make it explicit and available to all those involved in the decision.

No important decision should ever be based solely on the results of a quantitative model. Recently, in the financial industry, we have seen the results of relying too literally on the results of simulation models. Simulation models greatly understated the risk of mortgage backed securities and led companies to make portfolio decisions that led to their bankruptcy. Although there were problems with the model's technical implementation, the real problem started with the model's purpose. In many cases, the models were used as a substitute for judgment instead of being a tool for improving judgment. Literally,

---

118   Mark Paich contributed to the content found in this section.

decision-makers were relying on what the model said. This point was clearly stated by Gregg Berman of RiskMetrics in an interview with *New York Times* reporter Joe Nocera discussing the role of risk models in the 2008 economic crisis:[119]

> *Obviously we are big proponents of risk models. But a computer does not do risk modeling. People do it. And people got overzealous and they stopped being careful. They took on too much leverage. And whether they had models that missed, or they weren't paying enough attention, I don't know. But I do think that this was much more a failure of management than of risk management. I think blaming models for this would be very unfortunate because you are placing blame on a mathematical equation.*

The car leasing case discussed in Episode 9 is a good example of the correct use of a dynamic simulation model. In the leasing case, senior management had little clarity around the impact of increased short-term leasing. Initially, management was concerned about the growth of vehicle superstores that were selling nearly new vehicles for low prices. In the process of formulating the simulation model, we were faced with the obvious fact that much of the superstores' product was coming from off-lease GM vehicles. We quickly reframed the problem to deal with the costs and benefits of short-term leasing instead of focusing on the superstores.

There was no consensus within the organization about the net benefit of short-term leasing. Some of the mental models were based on the belief that short-term leasing was good because some customers liked it, it brought people to the dealership more often and increased repurchase loyalty. They marshaled statistics that showed that people who leased vehicles were more loyal to GM vehicles. On the other side of the argument, some managers were concerned that vehicles coming off short-term leases would compete with new vehicles and reduce new vehicle sales. They were also concerned that cheap off-lease vehicles would erode brand equity and reduce the willingness to pay for new cars.

Which position was right and what policy changes concerning leasing should be made? In the process of coming to a decision like this, senior managers tend to debate the issues and reach a consensus based on their mental models. The process of discussion and debate can sharpen

---

119   Nocera, 2009

individual mental models but can also dull them through the effects of organizational power, the loudest voice in the room, and other well-known organizational pathologies. But, even worse, the correct decision on leasing depended on the structure of the market, including factors such as the elasticity of demand, relative profit margins, the magnitude of the flow of nearly new off-lease vehicles and many other factors. Who knows what assumptions about these linkages are included in the manager's mental models?

The simulation model we built to evaluate the leasing strategy included the best information GM had about these factors. We included in the model state-of-the-art consumer choice models from market research, a comprehensive representation of the stocks and flows of new and used product based on data from manufacturing, and the best financial data from the treasurer's office. The relevant factors were never left implicit and we acknowledged uncertainty when it was relevant.

We also included key feedback loops that were subtle and were not included in the managers' initial mental models. One feedback process made a big difference to the results and did not emerge until we started to build the model. We posited that an increase in the number of nearly new off-lease vehicles causes used-car prices to fall, with the effect of reducing the demand for new cars. After a delay, lower new-car sales cause vehicle producers to increase incentives. Because used-car prices track new-car prices closely, higher incentives immediately cause lower used-car prices which further reduce new-car demand. The result is a 'doom loop' that can cause large cumulative reductions in both new-car and used-car profitability. The 'doom loop' is not easy to see because it results from the interaction of two markets, for both new and used cars, with the decision-making process for incentives which itself crosses several organizational boundaries. To see the loop, one needs a perspective that looks at the system as a whole instead of individual pieces.

The 'doom loop' made a big difference in the results and tipped the balance of argument toward a significant reduction in short-term leasing. The decision to reduce leasing turned out to be very profitable – as described in Episode 9. Used-car prices collapsed over the next two years and other automakers took much larger losses on short-term leases than GM did.

In addition to presenting the results, we took one other step that was very successful in changing managers' mental models. The simulation model was turned into an interactive visualization which demonstrated the expected results of alternative decisions that could have been made by managers about the amount of leasing and lease rates. The game was played by the President of GM's North American operations and several of his direct reports. As the game play progressed, it became clear that short-term leasing was a losing strategy. One senior manager playing the game lost billions of "game" dollars with an aggressive short-term leasing strategy and took lots of lighthearted joking from his colleagues.

The Dynamic Model's ability to provide an instant visualization of results allowed managers to test their own ideas and get nearly instant answers. This capability made the management dialogue on the subject much more vivid and real. The competitive nature of each executive testing out ideas focused attention on the structure of the market and caused participants to engage in learning how the simulated market operated. Eventually the process of learning about the simulated market led to increased understanding about the real market.

Agent-Based Modeling – the difference

Underpinning Dynamic Models is the concept of a complex dynamic system that consists of multiple pieces that are connected by a dense network of interrelationships. Dynamic Models usually include all the following distinctions:[120]

1. Dense networks of interconnections between variables that play out over time

2. Feedback loops between variables instead of one way causation

3. The concept of accumulation points (stocks) and flows that add to and subtract from the stocks

4. Non-linear relationships: these create the possibility of tipping points.

There are several varieties of Dynamic Models. System Dynamics Models aggregate the entities in a system and focus on big picture

---

120   Sterman, 2000 has a more detailed description of Dynamic Modeling and examples of its application.

dynamics. For example, a System Dynamics Model of most markets would aggregate consumers into segments that have similar behavioral properties. The model would analyze the behavior of the aggregate segment over time.

Agent-Based Models represent the individual entities in a system. An Agent-Based Model of any market would model individual consumers as they move through time and make decisions relevant to that market. Agent-Based Models open up the possibility of dynamic behavior patterns that emerge from the decisions of individual interacting agents. The possibility of emergence is a strength of Agent-Based Models but also a weakness as they require a great deal of work to build, calibrate, and test.

No matter what its specific form, the value of a Dynamic Model comes from its potential to improve the quality of the decision-maker's mental model. The Dynamic Model can do this because it is explicit about the underlying relationships in the system, it is explicit about how the underlying relationships drive the dynamics, and it respects the four factors that distinguish Dynamic Models from spreadsheets.

However, for the potential of a Dynamic Model to be realized, it is essential to go beyond a presentation using static slides. Dynamic Modeling is most effective when senior management is engaged in the development and use of the model. As was pointed out in the leasing case, managers interacted with the model through a set of well-designed simulation gaming exercises. In other cases, the modeling process has been embedded in a decision process, like the Dialogue Decision Process (described in Episode 8) through which senior managers make real contributions to building and analyzing the Dynamic Model. In other situations, the model results were explained through the use of a board game. In every case, the productive use of a Dynamic Model required more than senior managers listening to another static slide presentation of the results. The 'create a deck' and 'listen to a slide presentation' modes of communication were much better suited to the linear decision processes of the last century.

Examples of the ideas presented

McDonald's: Puzzling competition

As the effectiveness of traditional channels like television commercials or physical media advertising wanes, advertisers are employing more creative means of reaching customers using social, interactive, or indirect marketing approaches. Marketers at McDonalds did just this when devising a dark marketing effort using an alternative reality game (ARG) 'The Lost Ring', to promote the 2008 Beijing Olympics and its sponsorship of the event.[121] ARGs blend "online and offline clues and rely on players collaborating to solve the puzzles."[122] Success for an ARG thus depends upon the design of the game to manage and inspire collaboration but ultimately relies on the player (consumer) to persist in the game.

In February 2008, 50 bloggers and known ARG gurus received packages with directions to the game's website, where videos of amnesiac athletes (actors) provided the background for a mystery about a lost ancient-Olympic sport. The characters provided clues "via YouTube videos, blogs, Flickr photos and Twitter updates," and actual physical clues were placed in cities around the world. Organic sites and networks developed around the game, with some players going so far as to recruit strangers in cities with the physical clues. Eventually, nearly 5 million people participated in more than 100 countries to solve the mystery that concluded with an actual lost sport competition in Beijing.

At no point was McDonalds or its products directly referenced apart from the terms of service identifying McDonalds' partnership with the IOC. This led some to question their intent but interviews with the company suggest they intended it as gift marketing, where "instead of merely getting people to talk about a product, with a clever advertisement or a viral video," sponsors can offer something for free and then take credit for it. This can work to change attitudes about a company or build relationships with consumers. Moreover, through this non-intrusive marketing, McDonalds gained insight into the interaction pathways both online and offline that propelled the game (and advertisement) forward. This perspective will be of use for future campaigns that will again rely on consumers participating.

---

121   Dark marketing hides the advertiser's identity (at least initially) and does not directly promote the product or service.

122   Clifford, 2008

The ability to gain understanding from experience requires the willingness to examine both successes and, particularly, failures. Yet, many organizational systems conceal mistakes and thereby reduce, if not preclude, experiential learning. Unable to learn from their mistakes, they may fail to adapt to customer needs and fail to improve their processes to meet increasing competition. Many eventually lose market share and drop out of the corporate sky.

The concept of the Decision Loom is intended to help organizations focus on information use in making decisions and to learn from those experiences.

Conclusion

My hope is that both The Journey described in *Part 1* and the sketch of a Decision Loom design for interactive decision-making in *Part 2* will have helped you to think about the way your enterprise makes decisions – and to think about improving it.

I imagine that some of you who see the potential value of implementing the design for interactive decision-making described in this book are also likely to be aware that implementing it in most enterprises will be difficult. In the spirit in which this 'sketch' has been presented, let me offer some advice on what I have learned to consider before starting something new in both public and private organizations. The advice comes in the form of six key questions. I am providing questions and not answers because relevant answers to these questions must reflect the conditions and characteristics of the enterprise in which you are attempting to cause a change.

If you cannot answer yes to the first question you probably will not have to answer the other five questions.

1. Is the senior leadership of the enterprise likely to agree that there is a need to change the process by which decisions are made?

   If YES, will they be willing to designate a 'champion' with the authority and responsibility to – at a minimum – get it started to demonstrate its potential value and possible pitfalls?

   If NO, stop wasting your time. Without a commitment from senior leadership the chances of success are very limited.

2. Who will participate in planning for the change – and who will not? Little will be gained if the parties that will be affected by the change do not believe their interests have been considered in the suggested solution.

3. What will the expected change modify or replace? How will personnel make the transition from the old process to the new process? Managers may find they need to rely less

on data analysts and get used to doing more of their own analyses. For the person leading the change, this will require providing guidance on how to discontinue old ways of thought and behavior and providing a bridge to new ways.

4. Who will benefit immediately from the change and who will benefit in the longer term? Understanding this will identify potential supporters who can encourage the change.

5. Conversely, who will suffer immediately and who will suffer in the longer run? Some may suffer initially but benefit over the longer term. For others it may be the reverse. As an example, when an innovative general tabulating programming language was introduced at the Census Bureau it was perceived by many of the mathematical software specialists as likely to diminish their job security eventually, even though their importance was enhanced initially because they were central in training users in the new system.

6. Finally, how will the change affect major relationships within the enterprise? These include individual job relationships as well as organizational, social, and other informal contacts. For example, how will efforts to increase cross-functional contact affect relationships with the highly specialized individuals within each of the functions?

So there it is… a sketch of a Decision Loom designed for interactive decision-making and the four capabilities required to make it happen. I have also presented a series of lessons learned that support the decision-making process when it is organized and operated as a system of interacting parts. Finally, you also have six key questions to consider should you want to make a difference in your enterprise.

This conclusion is written in the spirit of C. West Churchman's conclusion to *The Design of Inquiring Systems* where he said:

> *"Conclude" comes from the Latin concludere, meaning "to shut up together"; in one sense it means a Lockean community which agrees to shut up. This inquiring system dissents; in the words of one of my philosophical mentors, Henry Bradford Smith, the only conclusion of philosophical discussion is a question. What kind of a world must it be in which inquiry becomes possible?*[123]

---

123 Churchman, 1971, p. 277

In the same spirit this 'sketch' of a Decision Loom for interactive decision-making is not presented with a traditional conclusion. Instead, it has been presented as a series of questions which, if answered positively, will lead to the type of world in which this design becomes possible.

For some of you this will be the end – thank you for getting this far.

For some of you this is not the end – but a beginning.

For those interested in other perspectives on the approach to decision-making, or who want to share experiences with other people applying Systems Thinking and Design Thinking in their organizations, consider reaching out to the following communities:

Systems Wiki: http://bit.ly/loom_wikia and http://bit.ly/loom_wikib

Open University: http://bit.ly/loom_ou

Hull University Business School: http://bit.ly/loom_hubs

Ackoff Center: http://bit.ly/loom_ackoff

Institute of Design at Stanford: http://bit.ly/loom_stanford

The Rotman School: http://bit.ly/loom_rotman

Case Western Reserve University, Weatherhead School of Management: http://bit.ly/loom_case

Ideo: http://bit.ly/loom_ideo

Appendix A

The third chapter in *Part 2* – **The Decision Loom…an interactive decision-making process** – describes the elements of a typical decision-making process and the key steps for learning from that process. Figure 9 shows this basic decision-making process, complemented by the learning component of the Decision Loom. The diagram in this appendix elaborates on that process:

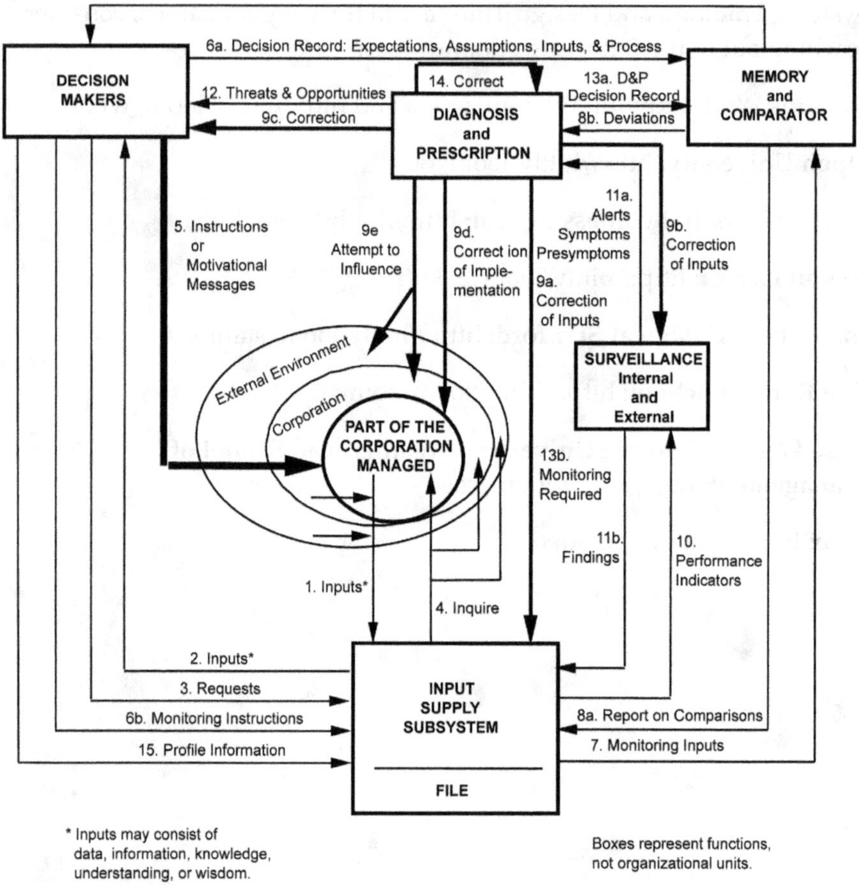

Figure 24: Learning and Adaptation Support System

What follows is a brief description of the above chart. The full description can be found in the article where the chart first appeared.[124] The apparent complexity of the chart derives from the not-so-apparent complexity of the processes of learning and adaptation. All the functions contained in the model are often carried out in the mind of one person who learns from experience, usually unconsciously.

We begin with the generation of Inputs (1) (Data, Information, Knowledge, Understanding, and Wisdom) about the behavior of the **Part of the Organization Managed** (which may be the whole organization) and its Environment. These inputs are received by the **Input Supply Subsystem**. Inputs (2) are then transmitted to the **Decision-Makers** in response to their Requests (3).

The receipt of Inputs (2) by Decision-Makers often leads them to additional Requests (3). Such requests require two additional capabilities of the **Input Supply Subsystem**. This subsystem must be able to generate new data – that is, Inquire (4) into the **Part of the Organization Managed** and its **Environment** so that the additional Inputs (2) required can be obtained. It must also have the ability to re-use data, information, knowledge, or understanding previously received or generated.

Once the new or old data have been processed to provide the information believed to be responsive to the request received from the **Decision-Makers**, it is transmitted back to them.

The expected value of information-to-wisdom (henceforth referred to as information+) should be estimated before any inputs are requested and used. A judgment should be made as to whether the maximum amount the decision-maker(s) is willing to pay for the input is justified by the value expected from using it.

The output of a decision to do something is a message that is either an Instruction or a Motivational Message (5) and is addressed to those in the **Part of the Organization Managed** whose responsibility it is to carry out the instructions or whose motivation is the target. When a decision to do nothing is made, no instructions may be required but a Decision Record (6a) is.

Every decision has only one of two possible purposes: to make something happen that otherwise wouldn't, or to keep something from

---

124 Figure 24 originally appeared as Figure 20.1 in Barabba, Pourdehnad, and Ackoff, 2002.

happening that otherwise would. In addition, there is always a time by which the effect of the decision is expected. Therefore, to control a decision, its expected effects and expected times of their realizations should be made explicit and recorded.

All this should be recorded in the Decision Record (6a) that should be placed and stored in an inactive **Memory and Comparator**. Because human memories are inclined to modify their content, especially forecasts and expectations, over time, it is important that the memory employed be completely inactive.

A Decision Record (6a) and Monitoring Instructions (6b) should be sent to the **Input Supply Subsystem** which has responsibility for checking the validity of the expectations, assumptions, and information+ used in making the decision and its implementation. When obtained, information about the validity of the expected effects, the relevant assumptions, and the information+ used should be sent to the **Memory and Comparator** as Monitoring Inputs (7). Then, using the information on the Decision Record (6a) stored in the **Memory**, and the Monitoring Inputs (7) a comparison should be made of the actual and expected effects, and the assumptions and relevant occurrences.

When the **Comparator** finds no significant difference between expectations/assumptions and the performance actually observed and reported in the Monitoring Inputs (7), nothing need be done other than enter a Report on Comparisons (8a) in the **Memory** for future reference and copy it to the **Decision-Makers** (8c). This record preserves what is known or believed. Therefore, it should be stored in an easily retrievable form; for example, by the use of key words. However, if significant differences are found, they are reported as Deviations (8b) to the **Diagnosis and Prescription** function.

Such deviations indicate that something has gone wrong. A diagnosis is required to determine what has, and what should be done about it. The purpose of the diagnosis is to find what is responsible for the deviations and to prescribe corrective action. In other words, the diagnostic function consists of *explaining* the mistake, and therefore, producing *understanding* of it.

There are only a few possible sources of error, each of which requires a different type of corrective action.

1. The Inputs (2) used in making the original decision were in error, and therefore the **Input Supply Subsystem** requires

Correction of Inputs (9a) so that it will not, or is less likely to, repeat that type of error. The information used in decision making can also come from the **Surveillance** function, described below. Therefore, it too may require Correction of Inputs (9b).

2. The decision-making process may have been faulty. In such a case, a Correction (9c) of this process should be made. It can be wrong in several different ways: it made incorrect assumptions; it drew incorrect conclusions from the information+ available to it – hence formulated unrealizable expectations; it did not have sufficient information+ available to make a correct decision; and incorrectly formulated the objective(s) to be pursued or problem(s) to be solved – that is, it either did the wrong thing or committed a so-called *type 3 error*.

3. The decision may have been correct but it was not implemented properly. In such a case a Correction of Implementation (9c) is required for the behavior of those in the **Part of the Organization Managed** that was responsible for the implementation.

4. The **Environment** may have changed in a way that was not anticipated. In such cases what is needed is a better way of either anticipating such changes, decreasing sensitivity to them, or reducing their likelihood. This may require Corrections of any of the types (9a-d).

Through these types of corrective actions, the **Diagnosis and Prescription** function assures both learning and adaptation.

If a diagonal is drawn in Figure 1 from the upper left-hand corner to the lower right-hand corner, the system is divided into the part below the diagonal that already exists to some extent in most companies, and the part above the diagonal that is missing in most companies. The usefulness of the part that exists (usually called a Management Information System, MIS) is very limited until it is embedded in the more comprehensive system that incorporates the functions shown above the diagonal. An MIS alone has relatively little effect on individual and organizational learning because it does not deal with one's own mistakes and their correction. Infrequently, and at best, an MIS informs one only about mistakes made by others. Vicarious experience is not a good substitute for one's own.

Appendix B

In *Capability 2* in *Part 2*, I use the term holistic to avoid the current discussions around the differences between Systems and Design Thinking, which too often try to convince us to choose one or the other.

Here I compare the approach of Roger Martin when discussing Design/Integrative Thinking and the approach of Russell Ackoff when discussing Systems Thinking:

Roger Martin: Design/Integrative Thinking	Russell Ackoff: Systems Thinking
Reliability: Reliability is the result of a process that produces a consistent and predictable result over and over. To enhance the reliability of any process, one has to reduce the number of variables considered and use quantitative, bias-free measurement. IQ testing is an example of a highly reliable process with these characteristics… The test achieves reliability by defining intelligence very narrowly, as the ability to solve simple analytical problems. It measures intelligence via a multiple-choice test that can be evaluated with no possibility of bias in measurement or judgment.	**Analysis:** In analysis we reduce a problem to its subsystem elements in order to develop insight and knowledge about them. Analysis tends to help us see how we can improve what we are currently doing… and usually leads to evolutionary improvement. It's all about breaking a system down into its component parts and analyzing those components… *in other words simplifying the problem so that we believe we can better understand it* (emphasis added).

Validity: The problem is that IQ doesn't serve as a particularly good predictor of anything… Daniel Goleman argues that EQ (Emotional Intelligence) makes for a much better predictor of success in life than IQ. To increase the validity of any process, one must consider a wide array of relevant variables. Goleman's EQ, for instance, builds on more qualitative considerations and judgment to produce what he argues has greater validity.	**Synthesis:** Synthesis is about expanding the focus to incorporate the complexity of the environment in which we operate and attempts to explain how both systems and their parts interact. Synthesis offers a deeper understanding of how we interact with our environment, and tends to lead to more revolutionary change. Synthesis is becoming a more and more important part of what information users do as they strive to create knowledge.
Need for Integrative Thinking: [Referring to his time at Monitor] Companies were hiring us for **messy problems** that didn't fit into one discipline or another. They wanted people who could design solutions to complicated business problems.	**Defining the Mess:** Problems… are related to experience as atoms are to tables. Tables are experienced, not atoms. Managers are not confronted with separate problems, but with situations that consist of complex systems of strongly interacting problems. I call such situations **messes**.
Role of Management: The CEO must take responsibility for safeguarding validity. If the CEO doesn't, the corporation's natural inclination toward reliability will win out.	**Role of Management:** Management should be directed at the interactions of the parts and not the actions of the parts taken separately.

Bibliography

Ackoff, R. (1978) *The Art of Problem Solving*, New York: John Wiley & Sons

Ackoff, R., Magidson, J., and Addison, H.J. (2006) *Idealized Design*, New Jersey: Wharton School Publishing

Argyris, C. (1991) "Teaching Smart People How to Learn," *Harvard Business Review*, May-June, pp. 99-109

Argyris, C. (1994) "Good Communication That Blocks Learning," *Harvard Business Review*, July- August, pp. 77-85

Axelrod, R and Tesfatsion, L. (2011) "On-Line Guide for Newcomers to Agent-Based Modeling in the Social Sciences" http://bit.ly/loom_ABM

Barabba, V. (1968) "Political Campaign Management: Myth and Reality" *The Ethics of Controversy: Politics and Protest*. Proceedings of the First Annual Symposium on Issues in Public Communication, held at the University of Kansas June 27-28

Barabba, V., Mason, R.O., and Mitroff, I.I., (1983) "Federal Statistics in a Complex Environment: The Case of the 1980 Federal Census," *The American Statistician*, Volume 37, No. 3, Washington, DC: The American Statistical Association

Barabba, V. (1985). "Steel Axes for Stone Age Men" in: Buzzell, R., *Marketing in an Electronic Age*, 75th Anniversary Harvard Business School Research Colloquium, Boston: Harvard Business School Press

Barabba, V. and Zaltman, G. (1991*) Hearing the Voice of the Market: Competitive Advantage through Creative Use of Market Information*, Boston: Harvard Business School Press

Barabba, V. (1994) "Never Say the Model Says. The Role of Models in Managerial Decision Making" in Wallace, W. *Ethics in Modeling*, New York: Pergamon Press

Barabba, V. (1998) "Revisiting Plato's Cave: Business Design in an Age of Uncertainty," in Tapscott, D. *et al.*, eds., *Blue Print for the Digital Economy*, New York: McGraw-Hill

Barabba, V., Huber, C., Cooke, F., Pudar, N., Smith, J., and Paich, M. (2002) "A Multi-Method Approach for Creating New Business Models: The General Motors OnStar Project", *Interfaces*, 32 (1), pp. 20-34

Barabba, V., Pourdehnad J. and Ackoff, R. (2002) "Above and Beyond Knowledge Management" in Chun, W. C. and Bontis, N. (eds) *The Strategic Management of Intellectual Capital and Organization Knowledge*, Oxford: Oxford University Press, pp. 359-369

Barabba, V. (2004), *Surviving Transformation*, New York: Oxford University Press. pp. 170-171

Bauer, R. A. (1958), "The Limits of Persuasion – The Hidden Persuaders are Made of Straw", *Harvard Business Review*, September-October

Blitzer, H. (1987) "Commentary", *Marketing Science* Vol. 6, No. 2, Spring

Bronowski, J. (1973) *The Ascent of Man*, Boston: Little Brown and Co.

Brown, T. (2009) *Change by Design*, New York: Harper Collins

Capra, F. (2002) *The Hidden Connections*, New York: Doubleday,

Carroll, P.B. and Mui, C. (2008) *Billion Dollar Lessons* , New York: Penguin Group

Casey, S. (2007) "Blueprint for Green Business," *Fortune*, 29 May, available at http://cnnmon.ie/loom_casey

Christensen, C. (1997) *The Innovator's Dilemma*, Boston: Harvard Business School Press

Christensen, C. and Roth, E. (2001) "OnStar: Not Your Father's General Motors" (A) N9-602-081 and (B) N9-682-082, Harvard Business School Case Study

Churchman, C. W. and Ackoff, R. L. (1950) *Methods of Inquiry*, Saint Louis, MO: Educational Publishers Inc.

Churchman, C. W. (1971) *The Design of Inquiring Systems*, New York: Basic Books

Churchman, C. W. (1979) *The Systems Approach and its Enemies*, New York: Basic Books

Cisco Corporation (2010) "Cisco Simplifies Mobile Collaboration with First-of-its-kind HD Video-Capable Business Tablet," 29 June; Internet; available at http://bit.ly/loom_cisco

Clifford, S. (2008) "An Online Game so Mysterious Its Famous Sponsor is Hidden," *New York Times*, 1 April; Internet; available at http://nyti.ms/loom_game

Deutschman, A. (2004) "The Fabric of Creativity," *Fast Company*, 1 December; Internet; available at http://bit.ly/loom_fabric

Downes, L. and Mui, C. (1998) *Unleashing the Killer App*, Boston: Harvard Business School Press

Drucker, P. F. (1954) *The Practice of Management*, New York: Harper and Row

Drucker, P. F. (1972) *The Concept of the Corporation*, Revised Edition, New York: The John Day Company

Englebart, D. C. (1962) SRI Summary Report AFOSR-3223 – Prepared for: Director of Information Sciences, Air Force Office of Scientific Research, Washington 25, DC, Contract AF 49(638)-1024-SRI Project No. 3578 (AUGMENT, 3906)

Federal Register (1980) Vol. 45, No 244, December 17, p.83110

Festinger, L. (1957) A theory of cognitive dissonance. Evanston, IL: Row, Peterson

Fortt, J. (2010) "Cisco's Online Video Gamble," *Fortune*, 27 October; Internet; available at http://bit.ly/loom_cisco2

Fritz, B. (2010) "Once-hot Nintendo Wii now struggling for sales", *Los Angeles Times*, November 30; Internet; available at http://lat.ms/loom_wii

Gaudiosi, J. (2007) "How the Wii is Creaming the Competition," *Business 2.0*, 25 April; Internet; available at http://cnnmon.ie/loom_wii2

Gladwell, M. (2010) "OVERDRIVE: Who really rescued General Motors?" *The New Yorker*, November 1

Grant, R.R. (2005) *Contemporary Strategy Analysis*, Oxford: Blackwell Publishing

Greene, J. (2010) "How LEGO Revived Its Brand," *Bloomberg Businessweek*, 23 July 2010; Internet; available at http://buswk.co/loom_lego

Hamel, G. (2010) "W.L. Gore: Lessons from a Management Revolutionary," *The Wall Street Journal*, 18 March; Internet; available at http://on.wsj.com/loom_gore

Harrington, A. (2003) "Who's Afraid of New Product," *Fortune*, 10 November; Internet; available at http://cnnmon.ie/loom_new

Henley, J. (2009) "Toy story," *The Guardian*, 26 March; Internet; available at http://bit.ly/loom_toys

Holmes, R. (2009) "Walmart wants to be more like us," *The Guardian*, 2 March; Internet; available at http://bit.ly/loom_cotton

Howard, R. A. (1968) "The Foundations of Decision Analysis," *IEEE Transactions on Systems Science and Cybernetics*, SCC-4, no. 3: pp. 211-219.

Jackson, M. C. (2003) *Systems Thinking: Creative Holism for Managers*, Chichester: John Wiley & Sons

Kinni, T. (2003) "The Art of Appreciative Inquiry", *Harvard Management Update*; Internet; available at http://bit.ly/loom_inquiry

Kleiner, A, (2005) "Our 10 Most Enduring Ideas," *Strategy + Business*, Winter 2005/Issue 41

Kohler, C. (2007) "Triumph of the Wii: How Fun Won Out in the Console Wars," *WIRED*, 11 June; Internet; available at http://bit.ly/loom_wired

Kotler, P., Jain, D., and Maesincee, S. (2002) *Marketing Moves*, Boston: Harvard Business School Press

Kusnic, M.W. and Owen, D. (1992) "The Unifying Vision Process: Value beyond Traditional Decision Analysis in Multiple-Decision-Maker Environments," *Interfaces* 22, no. 6 Nov-Dec: pp. 150-166

Lichtenstein, N. (2004) "Wal-Mart's Bargain with America," *San Jose Mercury News*, September 12

Marshall, A. (1920) *Principles of Economics*. London: Macmillan and Company

Maslow, A. (1962) *The Psychology of Science*, Chapel Hill, NC: Bassett Publishing

Maslow, A. (1965) "Memorandum on Syndrome Dynamics and Holistic, Organismic Thinking," *Eupsychian Management: A Journal*, Homewood, Ill.: Richard D. Irwin and the Dorsey Press

Mason, R. and Mitroff, I. (1981) *Challenging Strategic Planning Assumptions*, New York: John Wiley & Sons

McDermott, D (online) Kepner Tregoe Decision Making; Internet; available at http://bit.ly/loom_tregoe

McKenzie, A. (2011) "2011 Motor Trend Car of the Year," *Motor Trend Magazine*, January

Mind Tools; Internet; available at http://bit.ly/loom_tools

Mitroff, I and Silvers, A. (2010) *Dirty Rotten Strategies*, Stanford, CA.: Stanford Business School Press

Mitroff, I.I., Mason, R.O. and Barabba, V. (1982) *The 1980 Census: Policy Making Amid Turbulence*, Lexington, MA: Lexington Press

Mitroff, I.I., Mason, R.O. and Barabba, V., (1982) "Policy as Argument – a Logic for Ill-Structured Decision Problems" *Management Science*, Vol. 28, No. 12 December, pp. 1391-1403

Mitroff, I.I. (1983) *The Subjective Side of Science, A Philosophical Inquiry into the Psychology of the Apollo Moon Scientists*, Seaside, CA: Intersystems Publications

Negroponte, N. (1996) *Being Digital*, New York: Alfred A. Knopf

Nocera, J. (2009) "Risk Management," *New York Times*, January 2

Plato, (1952) *Protagoras, The Dialogues of Plato – The Great Books of the Western World*, Robert Maynard Hutchins (ed), Chicago: Encyclopaedia Britannica

Porter, M. (1985), *Competitive Strategy: Techniques for Analyzing Industries and Competitors*, New York: Free Press

Porter, M. and Siggelkow, N. (2008) "Contextuality Within Activity Systems and Sustainability of Competitive Advantage" *Academy of Management Perspectives*, 22 (2): 34-56

Pourdehnad, J. (2000) "Building Corporate 'Black Boxes': A Different Perspective on Organizational Learning" in *Proceedings, International Conference on Systems Thinking in Management*, Deakin University, Australia

Prahalad, C. K. and Ramaswamy, V. (2004) *The Future of Competition, Co-Creating Unique Value with Customers*, Boston: Harvard Business School Press

Rice, R. and Rogers. E. (1980) "Reinvention in the Innovation Process" *Knowledge: Creation, Diffusion, Utilization* Vol. 1 No. 4., Thousand Oaks, CA: Sage Publications

Riesman, D. (1961) *The Lonely Crowd*, New Haven: Yale University Press

Rogers, E, (1962) *The Diffusion of Innovations*, New York: The Free Press of Glencoe

Rowley, J, (2007) "The wisdom hierarchy: representation of the DIKW hierarchy", *Journal of Information Science*, February, pp. 163-180

Sculley, J. (2010) "John Sculley on Steve Jobs, The Full Interview Transcript," *Cult of Mac*; Internet; available at http://bit.ly/loom_sculley

Senge, P.M. (1990)*The Fifth Discipline: The Art and Practice of the Learning Organization*, New York: Doubleday

Slywotzky, A. J. (1996) *Value Migration*, Boston: Harvard Business School Press

Slywotzky, A. J. (1999) Foreword, in Haeckel, S. *The Adaptive Enterprise*, Boston: Harvard Business School Press

Slywotzky, A.J. and Morrison, D. (2000) How *Digital is your Business?* , New York: Crown Business

Smith R. G. and Farquhar, A. (2000) "The Road Ahead for Knowledge Management," *AI Magazine*

Sterling, R.W. and Scott, W.C. (1985) *The Republic/Plato: A New Translation*, New York: Norton

Sterman, J. D. (2000) "Automobile Leasing Strategy: Gone Today, Here Tomorrow", *Business Dynamics*, Boston: Irwin McGraw-Hill

Time Magazine, (1938) Vol. XXXII, Number 20; Internet; available at http://ti.me/loom_time

Urban, G. and Hauser, J. (2003) "Listening In to Find and Explore New Combinations of Customer Needs," *Journal of Marketing*, Vol. 68, April, pp. 72-87

Viereck, G. S. (1929). "What Life Means to Einstein" *The Saturday Evening Post*, October 26, pp. 110-117

Waller, R. J. (1983) "Knowledge for Producing Useful Knowledge and the Importance of Synthesis," in Kilmann, R.H. et al., (eds.) *Producing Knowledge for Organizations*, New York: Praeger

Wang, J. (2010) "Patagonia, From the Ground Up," *Entrepreneur*, June; Internet; available at http://bit.ly/loom_Pata

Wasser, S (1993) "Simply Z-Best," *Pennsylvania Times Leader*, April 26

Warren, K. (2008) *Strategic Management Dynamics*, Chichester: John Wiley and Sons

Weaver, H. G. (1931) *The Philosophy of Consumer Research*, Detroit, MI: General Motors Corporation

Harold Wilensky, (1967) *Organizational Intelligence: Knowledge and Policy in Government and Industry*, New York: Basic Books

Windelband, W. (1901) *History of Ancient Philosophy*, (Cushman, H.E. trans.), 2nd ed., New York: Charles Scribner's Sons,) p. 110

Woodall, B and Krolicki, K. (2011) "How Ford became Detroit's last man standing" *Reuters*, Jan 7.

About the Author

Vince Barabba is co-founder and chairman of Market Insight Corporation, a Commissioner of the California Citizen Redistricting Commission, and chairman of The State of the USA, a nonprofit corporation providing quality information to the public on changing societal, economic, and environmental conditions. He retired in 2003 as General Manager of Corporate Strategy and Knowledge Development at General Motors. He is a Past President and a Fellow of the American Statistical Association.

He twice served as director of the US Census Bureau and is the only person to have been appointed to that position by presidents of different political parties. Between his government service and GM assignments, he was manager of market research for Xerox and director of market intelligence for Eastman Kodak. He has been awarded:

- Induction into the Market Research Council's Hall of Fame
- The American Marketing Association's Parlin Award for leadership in the application of science to marketing research
- The MIT/GM Buck Weaver Award for individuals who have contributed significantly to the advancement of theory and practice in marketing science
- The System Dynamics Society's Applications Award for the best "real world" application of system dynamics
- The Distinguished Alumni Award from the California State University at Northridge
- The American Marketing Association's Explor Award (through the Market Insight Corporation) granted to organizations who have demonstrated the most innovative uses of technology in applications that advance research, online or otherwise
- The Certificate of Distinguished Service for Contribution to the Federal Statistical System from the US Office of Management and Budget

He is also the author of several books and articles (see Bibliography).

On the personal side, Vince lives in Capitola, California with his wife, the artist Sheryl Barabba. They have two children and two grandchildren.

About the Publisher

Triarchy Press is a small, independent publisher of good and clever books in the field of organizational and social praxis. Praxis is the cyclical process by which we apply theories and skills in practice, reflect on our experience, refine those theories and skills, and then apply them again in practice.

We look for the best new thinking on the organisations and social structures we work and live in. And we explore the most promising new practices in these areas. We look, in particular, for writers who can provide a bridge between academic research/theory and practical experience.

Our books cover innovative approaches to designing and steering organisations, the public sector, teams, society ... and the creative life of individuals.

To find out more, buy a book, write for us or contact us, please visit:

www.triarchypress.com

Triarchy Press

Related Titles and Authors from Triarchy Press

Russ Ackoff...............

Vince Barabba frequently talks about one of the founding fathers of Systems Thinking, Russ Ackoff, who died in 2009. An acknowledged genius, who often found himself in those lists of the most influential business thinkers and 'gurus', he was a pre-eminent consultant, practitioner, researcher and academic in this field.

Triarchy Press has had the good fortune to publish four of his books:

Management f-Laws: How organisations really work

Russell Ackoff ~ with Herbert Addison. Responses by Sally Bibb

We've all heard of Sod's (or Murphy's) Law - if anything can go wrong, it will. Most of us know Parkinson's Law – work expands to fill the time available for its completion. Now Management f-LAWS brings together a collection of 81 of Professor Russell Ackoff's wittiest and most subversive insights into the world of business.

"This book offers profound thoughts in digestible bites. It is easy to read and entertaining, yet full of wisdom. How much better our organizations would be if managers could really learn these lessons!"
Michael C Jackson ~ Professor of Management Systems, Hull University Business School.

2007, 180pp., paperback, 978-0-9550081-2-2, £18.00

Systems Thinking for Curious Managers - With 40 new Management f-LAWS

Russell Ackoff ~ with Herbert Addison and Andrew Carey

This more recent title added 40 new f-LAWS to those previously published as Management f-Laws. The book also includes an insightful, extended introduction to Systems Thinking as developed by Russ Ackoff.

2010, 96pp., paperback, 978-0-9562631-5-5, £18.00

Memories

Russell Ackoff ~ Foreword by Peter Senge

You might think Memories would be the fond autobiography of a grumpy old guru. Not a bit of it! There are stories of his chats with the Queen of Iran, his introduction of theme parks to the US, appearing naked in front of his commanding officer in World War II… but they're all there to do a serious job. Ackoff knew his students remembered stories better than teachings, so he uses them to deliver a succession of principles and aphorisms relating to management, organisations and work that he had developed during his life.

"Russ was an incisive, lifelong critic of the modern organizational form. He saw its limitations and argued for radical redesign. He was an advocate for major re-visioning and processes of change that started with helping people see what they truly valued and where they truly wanted to get - and then working backwards to see what it would take to get there."

Peter Senge, from his Foreword to *Memories*

2010, 120pp., paperback, 978-0-9565379-7-3, £16.00; hardback, 978-0-9565379-9-7, £25.00

Differences that make a Difference: An annotated glossary of distinctions important in management

Russell Ackoff ~ Foreword by Charles Handy

Towards the end of his life, Russ Ackoff determined to explain how some of the apparently insignificant misinterpretations of language and meaning he observed during his long years of research can, in practice, have far-reaching consequences. His aim was to dissolve (not solve or resolve) some of the many disputes in professional and private life that revolve around such misunderstandings. In this last manuscript that he was to complete before his death he does exactly that.

2010, 144pp., paperback, 978-1-908009-01-2, £14.00

Systems Thinking for public services.......................

Systems Thinking in the Public Sector

John Seddon

The best-selling analysis of why public services in the UK and around the world so often don't work – and how to fix the mess. This is the book that made a laughing stock of the UK Audit Commission (now abolished), famously ridiculed the culture of targets and 'deliverology' that for years has characterised public services in England and set in train the conversion of the public sector to systems thinking.

"This book provides the public sector with the means to deliver higher levels of public value and the opportunity to be seen to be doing so in a robust way with measurable results, high customer satisfaction and high morale."
   Jim Mather, Scottish Govt. Minister for Enterprise, Energy & Tourism

"Few books... come to define a new era. I can only hope that this passionate, yet informed, critique on the limitations of public sector management becomes one of them." Duncan Kerr, Chief Executive, South Kesteven District Council.

2008, 224pp., paperback, 978-0-9550081-8-4, £20.00

Delivering Public Services That Work: Systems Thinking in the Public Sector: Case Studies

Peter Middleton ~ Foreword by John Seddon

Six detailed and specific Case Studies which convincingly demonstrate that John Seddon's recipe (above) actually works and delivers the results he promised.

2010, 132pp., paperback, 978-0-9562631-6-2, £15.00

Managers as Designers in The Public Services: Beyond Technomagic

David Wastell

Professor Wastell's revealing explanation of why the public sector keeps turning to large-scale IT 'solutions' - and keeps being disappointed. He uses detailed case studies to present a workable way for public sector managers to design their way out of problems rather than imposing monolithic solutions. This is a book about Systems Thinking and Design Thinking in practice.

Applying Systems Thinking to your organisation...........

The Search for Leadership: An Organisational Perspective

William Tate

This Systems Thinking approach to leadership asks us to look beyond individuals, managers, leaders and management training programmes. Using the analogy of an aquarium (where water quality determines the health of the fish), Bill Tate reviews a range of issues like:

Distributing authority ~ management vs. organisation development ~ the structural gaps that account for waste, rework, poor communication and failure ~ transferring learning ~ organisational competence ~ accountability ~ the organisation's culture and shadow-side.

"Full of practical tips and insights... a 'must read' book for any leadership or organisational development practitioner who wants to make a difference to business success."

Linda Holbeche, CIPD

"...a book to challenge both orthodox thinking on leadership, and shift the focus to the organisation. He cleverly mixes generic concepts with case studies and real experience, in a blend of the commercial and public sectors. There is also a neat diagnostic tool to ensure engagement with the approach articulated."

Robin Field-Smith, Her Majesty's Inspector of Constabulary, London

2009, 324pp., paperback, 978-0-9557681-7-0, £28.00

Hardback, 978-0-9557681-8-7, £40.00; e-book, £40.00

Systemic Leadership Toolkit

William Tate

Designed for use in conjunction with The Search for Leadership (above) this toolkit presents nine self-assessment questionnaires in nine separate modules – designed to give any organisation a complete picture of itself: Management Development ~ Organisation Development ~ Learning ~ Competence ~ Culture ~ Decline ~ Systems ~ The Shadow ~ Accountability

2009, 152pp., paperback, 978-0-9562631-2-4, £55.00; e-toolkit, £95.00

Applying Systems Thinking at work and in daily life...

Growing Wings on the Way: Systems Thinking for Messy Situations

Rosalind Armson

This book is about dealing with messes. Sometimes known as 'wicked problems', messes (or messy situations) are fairly easy to spot, hard to pin down and impossible to 'solve'.

Systems Thinking offers many good ways to approach these situations and unravel them. Rosalind Armson is one of the world's foremost teachers and practitioners of Systems Thinking, and her remarkable book explains how these messes happen and what to do about them. Specifically, she sets out a series of sophisticated and challenging - but practical and easily learned - skills and techniques for thinking better when you're 'in a mess'.

The skills and techniques that she covers (with rules, advice and practical guidance on each one) in this book include:

- Escaping Mental Traps (History, Habit and Action Traps, Double Binds and Value Rigidity)
- Working with System Definitions
- Diagnosing with Multiple-Cause Diagrams
- Drawing Rich Pictures
- Drawing and using Influence Diagrams
- Understanding messes with Systems Maps
- Building Human-Activity System Diagrams
- Using the 5Es of Efficacy, Efficiency, Effectiveness, Elegance and Ethicality
- Viewing messes through an Understandascope

Whether you're new to Systems Thinking or have long experience, the book invites you to develop your skills through working with your own messy situations. It's written for managers, project managers, team leaders, 'change leaders', strategists, policy makers and concerned citizens as well as university students from a broad set of disciplines.

2011, 338pp., paperback, 978-1-908009-36-4, £35.00

Index

www.ingramcontent.com/pod-product-compliance
Lightning Source LLC
Chambersburg PA
CBHW052108230326
41599CB00054B/4317